French

A Self-Teaching Guide

Wiley Self-Teaching Guides teach practical skills from accounting to astronomy, management to mathematics. Look for them at your local bookstore.

Languages

German: A Self-Teaching Guide, by Heimy Taylor and Werner Haas

Italian: A Self-Teaching Guide, by Edoardo A. Lèbano

Practical Spanish Grammar: A Self-Teaching Guide, by Marcial Prado

Advanced Spanish Grammar: A Self-Teaching Guide, by Marcial Prado

Business Skills

Making Successful Presentations: A Self-Teaching Guide, by Terry C. Smith

Managing Assertively: A Self-Teaching Guide, by Madelyn Burley-Allen

Managing Behavior on the Job: A Self-Teaching Guide, by Paul L. Brown

Teleselling: A Self-Teaching Guide, by James Porterfield

Successful Time Management: A Self-Teaching Guide, by Jack D. Ferner

Science

Astronomy: A Self-Teaching Guide, by Dinah Moche

Basic Physics: A Self-Teaching Guide, by Karl F. Kuhn

Chemistry: A Self-Teaching Guide, by Clifford C. Houk and Richard Post

Biology: A Self-Teaching Guide, by Steven D. Garber

Other Skills

How Grammar Works: A Self-Teaching Guide, by Patricia Osborn

Listening: The Forgotten Skill, A Self-Teaching Guide, by Madelyn Burley-Allen

Quick Vocabulary Power: A Self-Teaching Guide, by Jack S. Romine and Henry Ehrlich

Study Skills: A Student's Guide for Survival, A Self-Teaching Guide, by Robert A. Carman

French
A Self-Teaching Guide
Second Edition

Suzanne A. Hershfield-Haims

John Wiley & Sons, Inc.
New York • Chichester • Weinheim • Brisbane • Singapore • Toronto

Published by John Wiley & Sons, Inc.
Published simultaneously in Canada

Library of Congress Cataloging-in-Publication Data:

Hershfield-Haims, Suzanne A.
    French, a self-teaching guide / Suzanne A. Hershfield-Haims.
        p. cm.
    ISBN 0-471-36958-6 (pbk.)
        1. French language—Textbooks for foreign speakers—English. 2. French language—Self-instruction. 3. French language—Grammar. I. Title: French.
    II. Title.

PC2129.E5 H47 2000
448.2′421—dc21   99-087283

Printed in the United States of America

10 9 8 7 6 5 4 3

To My Mother's Memory, S. D. A.

Contents

Preface

French: A Self-Teaching Guide is a simplified and practical beginner's course for anyone who would like to learn French. It is aimed in particular at self-learners, students in adult education courses, and those in a classroom setting of first-year college French.

The book is organized to teach the essentials of the French language in fifteen lessons. Each lesson introduces you to a useful list of words that are transformed into practical expressions, repeated in a French dialogue that is then translated into English, and finally practiced in a series of exercises. Material is presented in a clear and interesting manner, inviting you to teach and test yourself every step of the way. Your interest is further reinforced with cultural notes and current information on French trends.

French: A Self-Teaching Guide aims to teach reading, writing, and speaking with an equal emphasis on all three skills. Each of the book's fifteen lessons contains several "grammar boxes" designed to instruct you in the basics of French grammar and usage. The exercises within each lesson provide an opportunity for you to practice and test yourself on the concepts you have learned. There are answers for each exercise on the designated pages of the book. In addition to the lesson exercises, you can evaluate your newly acquired skills by taking the three review tests in this book, one for every five lessons. Check yourself against the answers that are provided immediately following the review questions.

To make the best use of this book, you should follow these steps:

1. At the beginning of each lesson, review the rules on pronunciation and then read each word aloud from the vocabulary list for that particular lesson.

2. Take your time in learning every part of a lesson before moving on to the next. Be sure to test yourself with each exercise; your results are a way of measuring your success in acquiring all the skills you need to learn French.

3. When testing yourself, allow yourself no more than two errors per exercise. If there are more, stay with the lesson until it's mastered.

4. Do your exercises with the vocabulary provided in the book. Do not rush to a French-English dictionary; this will not be helpful until you cover the fourteenth or fifteenth lesson.

5. The review tests are a way of making sure you have mastered each group of five lessons before tackling the next. Be sure to review thoroughly before you take each test.

6. Listen to French records, French movies, or, if you have a short-wave radio, French radio programs. This will accustom your ear to French sounds and inflections. It is not necessary for you to understand all that is said; merely concentrate on the French intonations and try to get a general sense of what is being discussed. You will soon learn how to pronounce a word on sight and to understand sentences as you hear them.

French: A Self-Teaching Guide also includes two unique features found in no other French textbook: a lesson on computers, introducing you to the newest French vocabulary on the subject, and another lesson on cognates, which shows you how to enrich your French vocabulary by some 2,000 words, without monotonous memorization.

The methodology and content of this book are based on a course I developed for doctoral students at Indiana University who were majoring in disciplines other than French. These students did not know a word of the language before they started but became fluent after nine weeks of intensive study, 80 percent of which was self-guided. The same teaching method was then used successfully in subsequent years with undergraduate students enrolled in a first-year course.

French: A Self-Teaching Guide will not turn you into a polished speaker of French overnight. It will not enable you to comprehend immediately every French text. But it will provide you with the basic tools to understand, to speak, read, and write simple French. It will open the door to a very gratifying experience: understanding and appreciating the language and culture of the French-speaking people.

Acknowledgments

I feel fortunate to have Chris Jackson of John Wiley & Sons as my editor. His guidance, kindness, and encouragement made my work a pleasant endeavor. Thank you, Chris!

I am grateful for the love and support of my family, including David, Debra, and Elizabeth.

Special thanks go to my Parisian niece, Joelle Abitbol, college professor of English in Paris, for information about the ongoing cultural and educational projects throughout France.

I also wish to thank my agents, Elizabeth Pomada and Mike Larsen, for their consistent encouragement.

Changes in the Second Edition

Although this second edition of *French: A Self-Teaching Guide* includes several changes in vocabulary lists and dialogue situations about home and family, two important changes make it truly stand out. First, the computer lesson required complete revisions in dialogue situations and in vocabulary expressions to showcase the rapid changes in the electronic age. Second, the cultural notes in this second edition reflect the intent of the French government to make France the international jewel for the new millennium. This is definitely a different France from the France of the 1980s. Mindful of the importance of the Internet and its global impact, France has undergone renewal and renovation in all areas and at all levels: commercial, cultural, educational, and social. Whether you are a student, a teacher, a perennial learner, a business executive, or a tourist, this updated edition will enlighten you.

Pronunciation Guide

The secret of proper French pronunciation lies in the distinct articulation of each syllable, word, and word group. In French, all words must be well articulated in a flowing, linking way, with only a slight stress on the last syllable in words of two syllables or more. Examples are: ca*fé*, gara*ge*, monu*ment*, évolu*tion*.

English and French have many similar sounds. There are, however, certain English sounds that do not exist in French, while some French sounds, involving vowels and consonants, are different from English sounds with the same vowels or consonants. For example, there is no *h* sound in French, and the letter combination *th* in French has the same sound the English *t*. Following are other differences in vowels and consonant sounds.

A. *Vowels.* The vowels *a, e, i, o,* and *u* acquire a nasal sound in French when they are followed by *m* or *n*. There are no exact English equivalents for French nasal sounds, but there are approximations that could be termed "neighbor sounds." There are four French nasal sounds:

	English Neighbor Sounds	French Words
1. an, em, en	*alm* in balm	ch*an*ter (to sing)
2. om, on	*on* in don't	*on*cle (uncle)
3. in, im, eim, ein	*en* in represent	c*ein*ture (belt)
4. un, um	*am* in amber	*un* (one)

The fourth nasal sound is not as frequently encountered as the other three. You can practice all four nasal sounds in this phrase: *un bon vin blanc* (a good white wine).

B. *Consonants*

1. English and French consonants basically have the same sounds, except for the *th* and *h,* in English, and the *r* and *ch* in French:

   - *th* in French has the *t* sound; *théâtre* is pronounced *téâtre*
   - there is no *h* sound in French, as previously stated
   - *r* in French is guttural and is made in the back of the mouth to resemble a gargling sound
   - *ch* in French has the *sh* sound

2. In French, consonants at the ends of words are not pronounced, with the exception of *c, f, l, r,* and *q* (however, the *r* in *-er* verbs is not pronounced). Examples are: *arc, neuf, naturel, fleur, coq.*

3. $c + e, i, y = s$, as in *cela, ceci, Cyrano*

4. $ç + o, a, u = s$, as in *garçon, ça*

5. $c + a, o, u = k$, as in *café, coq*

6. $g + e, i = j$, as in ga*r*a*ge*

7. $g + a, o, u = g$, as in *garage*

8. *gn* is pronounced *ni,* as in o*n*ion

9. *ph* is pronounced *f,* as in *phil*o*sphie*

10. *ll* preceded by *i* is pronounced *y,* as in *yet*—travai*ller*

11. *qu* is pronounced *k,* as in musi*qu*e

12. x + a consonant is pronounced *ks,* as in e*x*tase (ekstase)

    x + a vowel is pronounced *gz,* as in e*x*aminer (egzaminer)

13. *s* + any vowel is pronounced *z*

C. *The liaison (linking of words).* In French pronunciation, a consonant at the end of a word is generally linked to the vowel at the beginning of the following word. This is called *la liaison* (linking). There are instances where the liaison is imperative, and others where it is absolutely not allowed.

1. The liaison is imperative in the following:
   - personal pronouns + verbs. Example: *ils aiment* (il*za*iment)
   - verbs + personal pronouns. Example: *aiment-ils* (aimen*t*ils)
   - adjectives + nouns. Example: *vieux arbres* (vieu*z*arbres)
   - short adverbs + adjectives. Example: *très intelligent* (trè*z*intelligent)
   - after *sans.* Example: *sans avis* (san*z*avis)
   - after *est.* Example: *c'est intérressant* (c'es*t*intéressant)

2. The liaison is absolutely not allowed in the following cases:
   - after *et.* Example: *il est gentil et intelligent*
   - before an aspirate *h,* as in *Hollande, haricot.* Example: *les haricots* (beans); *les Hollandais* (the Dutch)

3. The following sound changes occur in the liaison:
   - the *s* at the end of a word becomes *z.* Example: *ils aiment*
   - the *x* becomes *z.* Example: *vieux arbres*
   - the *d* becomes *t.* Example: *un grand ami* (gran*t*ami)
   - the *f* becomes *v.* Example: *neuf ans* (neu*v*ans)

1 Basic Expressions

Bonjour, madame.	Good morning, ma'am.
Comment allez-vous, monsieur?	How are you, sir?
Assez bien, merci.	Fairly well, thank you.
Comment vous appelez-vous?	What's your name?
Je m'appelle Jacques.	My name is Jack.
Où habitez-vous?	Where do you live?
J'habite à San Francisco.	I live in San Francisco.
Puis-je vous aider?	May I help you?
Oui, s'il vous plaît.	Yes, please.
Où sont les toilettes?	Where are the restrooms?
Là-bas à gauche.	Over there to the left.
En face du cinéma.	In front of the movie theater.
Comment dit-on *on the right* en français?	How do you say *on the right* in French?
On dit *à droite*.	We say *à droite*.
À bientôt.	See you soon.
À demain.	See you tomorrow.
Au revoir.	Goodbye.

PRACTICE THE FOLLOWING EXPRESSIONS

Answers for Lesson 1, pp. 52–53

1. How do you say *Good morning* in French? _____.
2. How do you say *My name is?* _____.
3. How do you say *Where do you live?* _____.
4. How do you reply to *Comment allez-vous?* _____.
5. How do you reply to *Où sont les toilettes?* _____.
6. How do you say *to the left?* _____.

7. What is the opposite of *à droite?*_____.

8. How do you say *please?*_____.

9. *À bientôt* is translated into English as _____.

10. How do you say *in front of?*_____.

11. Two ways of answering to *au revoir* are _____ and _____.

12. *À demain* is translated into English as_____.

MOTS NOUVEAUX (New Words)

Try to memorize these words. They will be repeated in exercises and future lessons. Pronounce each word aloud.

après	after	l'homme (masc.)	man
l'arbre (masc.)	(the) tree	le jour	day
l'arc-en-ciel (masc.)	rainbow	la leçon	lesson
		le livre	book
aujourd'hui	today	la lumière	light
avant	before	le lundi	Monday
la bougie	candle	la maison	house
la chaise	chair	le matin	morning
le chat	cat	la mer	sea
le chien	dog	la mère	mother
la couleur	color	le mot	word
le crayon	pencil	la nuit	night
demain	tomorrow	l'oiseau (masc.)	bird
l'enfant	child	le papier	paper
la famille	family	le parapluie	umbrella
la femme	woman	le père	father
la fille	girl	le soleil	sun
le frère	brother	le stylo	pen
le garçon	boy	le temps	time; weather
le goût	taste	la tête	head
hier	yesterday	la vérité	truth

PRACTICE THE VOCABULARY

Match the two columns by writing the appropriate letters in the spaces provided.

Example: 1. *F*

1. _____arbre   A. pen

2. _____chaise   B. head

3. _____papier   C. chair

4. _____stylo	D. woman
5. _____parapluie	E. paper
6. _____femme	F. tree
7. _____tête	G. umbrella
8. _____demain	H. taste
9. _____mot	I. tomorrow
10. _____matin	J. house
11. _____goût	K. word
12. _____maison	L. morning
13. _____soleil	M. light
14. _____lumière	N. rainbow
15. _____arc-en-ciel	O. sun
16. _____nuit	P. mother
17. _____vérité	Q. night
18. _____mère	R. book
19. _____hier	S. truth
20. _____livre	T. yesterday
21. _____père	U. cat
22. _____bougie	V. father
23. _____homme	W. man
24. _____chat	X. candle
25. _____crayon	Y. time
26. _____oiseau	Z. bird
27. _____temps	a. dog
28. _____garçon	b. pencil
29. _____fille	c. girl
30. _____chien	d. boy

GRAMMAR I   Definite Articles • Gender of Nouns

A. The definite article *the* is translated into French by *le, la, les,* and *l'*. We use *le* before masculine singular nouns, *la* with feminine singular nouns, and *les* with plural nouns, both masculine and feminine. *L'* is the contraction of *le* and *la* when followed by a noun starting with a vowel or a mute *h* as in: *l'homme, l'avion,* and *l'hôtel.*

B. In French, *nouns* are either masculine or feminine. There is no neuter gender of nouns as in English. Articles in French must agree with the nouns they precede, as in: *la table, le garçon, la chaise, la maison, le matin, le stylo, le père,* and *la mère.*

C. Although there is no way to know the gender of a noun without memorizing it, there are patterns that will help you distinguish the feminine nouns from the masculine nouns. Be aware, however, that these are patterns only, with numerous exceptions; there are no hard and fast rules. The only sure way to know the gender of each noun is to memorize.

1. Females are always feminine, and males are always masculine.

    EXAMPLE: *l'homme* (the man) masc.

    la femme (the woman) fem.

    le garçon (the boy) masc.

    la fille (the girl) fem.

2. Most nouns ending in *on, in, o, ier, al,* and *ot* are masculine, as in: *le bouillon, le matin, le métro, le papier, le cheval* (the horse), and *le gigot* (the leg of lamb).

3. Most nouns ending in *ion, eur, ance, ence, te, ie,* and *ude* are feminine, as in: *l'aviation, la passion, la grandeur, la chance, la présence, la bonté, la biologie,* and *la latitude.*

NOTE:

About 2 percent of the nouns contained in this book do not belong to the preceding categories. The following is a small sample of those nouns: *le livre* (the book), *le soleil* (the sun), *le parapluie* (the umbrella), *l'ordinateur* (masc., the computer), *le chat* (male cat), *la chatte* (female cat), *le chien* (male dog), *la chienne* (female dog).

PRACTICE THE ARTICLES

1. List four translations of *the* _____.
2. Things in French are either _____ or _____.
3. List two masculine definite articles_____.
4. What does *l'* stand for?_____ and when?_____.
5. What is the definite article for _____ *splendeur* (the splendor)? _____ *santé* (the health)?
6. What are two feminine definite articles?_____.
7. Write the definite articles of _____ *arbre* (the tree) _____, *homme* (the man), _____ *papier* (the paper).
8. Write the definite articles of _____ *location* (the rent, the rental), _____ *patience* (the patience), _____ *zoologie* (the zoology), _____ *attitude* (the attitude), _____ *longueur* (the length).

EXERCISE

Fill in the correct article *le, la,* or *l'*. Then say each word aloud.

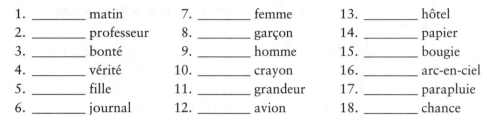

1. _____ matin
2. _____ professeur
3. _____ bonté
4. _____ vérité
5. _____ fille
6. _____ journal

7. _____ femme
8. _____ garçon
9. _____ homme
10. _____ crayon
11. _____ grandeur
12. _____ avion

13. _____ hôtel
14. _____ papier
15. _____ bougie
16. _____ arc-en-ciel
17. _____ parapluie
18. _____ chance

GRAMMAR II   Indefinite Articles

A. The indefinite articles in French are *un* for masculine singular nouns and *une* for feminine singular nouns—for example, *un garçon* (a boy) and *une fille* (a girl). Both indefinite and definite articles must agree in gender with the nouns they precede. All nouns are either masculine or feminine, even when they are objects or things.

B. The neuter gender *it*, used with things and objects in English, does not exist in French.

C. In French, every effort is made to avoid the "hiatus" or the juxtaposition of two consecutive vowels, one at the end of a word followed by another at the beginning of the next word. (A silent *h* is considered a vowel in such a case.) One of the largest exceptions to this rule occurs with *une*, the indefinite feminine article. Thus, there is no problem with saying *une addition, une abréviation, une histoire, une altitude*, etc.

PRACTICE THE INDEFINITE ARTICLES

1. What are the indefinite articles in French?_____.
2. What is the gender of *un?*_____.
3. What is the gender of *une?* _____.
4. What is the gender of *un garçon?*_____.
5. Which nouns are always masculine?_____.
6. Which nouns are always feminine?_____.
7. What is the meaning of "hiatus"?_____.
8. Are there neuter nouns in French?_____.
9. Objects in French are either_____ or _____.
10. What is a major exception to the hiatus?_____.

EXERCISE

Write the appropriate indefinite article (*un* or *une*) before each noun. Then say each combination aloud.

1. _____ action
2. _____ jour
3. _____ livre
4. _____ garçon
5. _____ papier
6. _____ chien

7. _____ chat
8. _____ crayon
9. _____ couleur
10. _____ matin
11. _____ soleil
12. _____ nuit

13. _____ tête
14. _____ oiseau
15. _____ chaise
16. _____ goût
17. _____ mot
18. _____ parapluie

GRAMMAR III   Subject Pronouns and the Verbs *être* and *avoir* • The Interrogative

A. Memorize the verbs *être* (to be) and *avoir* (to have).

Subject	*Être*	Subject	To Be
je	**suis**	I	am
tu (sing. familiar)	**es**	you	are
il (masc.), elle (fem.), on	**est**	he, she, it, one	is
nous	**sommes**	we	are
vous	**êtes**	you	are
ils (masc. pl.), elles (fem. pl.)	**sont**	they	are

Subject	*Avoir*	Subject	To Have
je = j'	**ai**	I	have, am having, do have
tu (familiar)	**as**	you	have
il (masc.), elle (fem.), on	**a**	he, she, it, one	has
nous	**avons**	we	have
vous	**avez**	you	have
ils (masc. pl.), elles (fem. pl.)	**ont**	they	have

B. The interrogative form, or question, in French is expressed in two ways. The first is by beginning the question with the phrase *est-ce-que*.

> EXAMPLE: *Est-ce que* tu es un garçon?   (Are you a boy?)
> *Est-ce que* vous avez des stylos? (Do you have pens?)

The second way is by inverting the pronoun subject and verb as in English, except that French adds a hyphen between the words.

EXAMPLE: *Es-tu* un garçon?   (Are you a boy?)
             Avez-vous des stylos?   (Do you have pens?)

Note that French adds the letter *-t-* between two vowels in the interrogative form in order to avoid the "hiatus."

EXAMPLE: *A-t-il?*   Has he?
           A-t-elle?   Has she?
           Mange-t-on?   Are we eating? (Does one eat?)
           Aide-t-elle?   Is she helping?
           Commande-t-il?   Is he ordering?

NOTES:

1. In French, *je* is not capitalized as is the English *I*; *tu* (*you*, singular) is used with friends and relatives and in informal situations.

2. *Vous* (you) is used in formal situations when speaking with one person and in formal and informal situations when speaking with more than one person.

   EXAMPLE: Monsieur, *vous* mangez bien.
               Mesdames et messieurs, *vous* mangez bien.

3. *Il* is the masculine singular (*he*), and *elle* is the feminine singular (*she*).

4. *Ils* is used for *they* (plural masculine) and *elles* for *they* (plural feminine). *Ils* and *elles* have the same sound as *il* and *elle*: the last consonant (*s*) is mute.

   EXAMPLE: *Ils* (les garçons) sont ici.
               Elles (les filles) sont ici.

5. *Ils* refers also to a mixed group of people, people in general, as in *ils* (les garçons et les filles) *sont ici. Il* is also used in what is called "impersonal expressions" such as *il fait chaud* (it is warm) and *il fait froid* (it is cold). This is the only time we encounter the impersonal equivalent of the English *it*. French also has another third-person singular construction, which is *on*. This *on* translates as the English *one*, as in *on dit* (one says, we say, people say), *on fait* (one does, we do, people do).

6. *Il, elle, ils,* and *elles* also refer to animals and to things that are either masculine or feminine, singular or plural. *Le chat est blanc* (the cat is white), *il est blanc* (he is white); *la table est grande* (the table is big), *elle est grande* (it is big).

7. Note that *j'ai* can convey the equivalent of the English expressions "I have," "I'm having," or "I do have."

PRACTICE THE SUBJECT PRONOUNS

1. Which pronoun is always capitalized in English and not in French?_____.

2. The pronoun *you* has two equivalents in French. What are they?_____.

3. The pronoun *tu* is used in_____.

4. What is the singular formal equivalent of *you?* _____.
5. What is the plural formal equivalent of *you?*_____.
6. What are two ways in which *il* is used?_____.
7. What is the feminine form of *il?*_____.
8. What is the plural of *elle?*_____.
9. What are two uses of *ils* (they)?_____.
10. How do you say *it is cold* in French?_____.
11. When is the impersonal *it* used in French?_____.
12. Write the English for *il fait chaud.*_____.

EXERCISES

A. Write the French pronouns with the correct form of *être* (to be).

    Example: you are—*vous êtes*

1. you (formal) are _____
2. you (familiar sing.) are _____
3. I am _____
4. we are _____
5. you (pl.) are _____
6. they (masc. pl.) are _____
7. they (fem. pl.) are _____
8. he is _____
9. she is _____
10. they (all females) are _____
11. they (mixed male and female) are_____
12. they (things in general) are _____
13. they (people in general) are _____
14. they (animals in general) are _____

B. Write the correct form of the verb for each pronoun.

    Example: 1. Je *suis* (to be) une fille. 2. Nous *avons* (to have) le temps
                                 aujourd'hui.

1. J (e) _____ (to have) une maison.
2. Ils _____ (to have) deux frères.
3. Je _____ (to be) une fille.
4. Elles _____ (to have) des crayons.
5. Vous _____ (to be) une mère.
6. Ils _____ (to have) le temps aujourd'hui.
7. Tu _____ (to be) le père.
8. Vous _____ (to have) des bougies.
9. Elles _____ (to be) des chattes.
10. Tu _____ (to have) des stylos.

C. Change the following to the interrogative (question) form, as in *avez-vous?*
Remember to add the *-t-* when necessary to avoid the hiatus.

1. vous avez _____
2. il a_____
3. il est_____
4. nous avons _____
5. nous sommes _____
6. vous êtes _____
7. ils sont _____
8. vous étudiez_____
9. elles ont _____
10. nous parlons _____

2 Au restaurant
(At the Restaurant)

l'addition (fem.)	(the) bill, check	la glace	ice cream
l'agneau (masc.)	lamb	le homard	lobster
l'assiette (fem.)	plate, dish	le jardin	garden
la caissière	cashier	la laitue	lettuce
les côtelettes (fem.)	chops	la langouste	crayfish
le couteau	knife	les légumes (masc.)	vegetables
les crevettes (fem.)	shrimp	le plat	dish
le déjeuner	lunch	le poisson	fish
le flan	custard	le poulet	chicken
la fourchette	fork	le repas	meal
les frites	fries	la serviette	napkin
les fruits de mer (masc.)	seafood	le veau	veal
		le verre	glass
le garçon	waiter	la viande	meat
acheter	to buy	partir	to leave
avoir	to have	préférer	to prefer
boire	to drink	prendre	to take
chercher	to look for	revenir	to come back
commander	to order	savoir	to know
commencer	to start	travailler	to work
demander	to ask	trouver	to find
entendre	to hear	vendre	to sell
être	to be	vouloir	to want
manger	to eat		
après-midi	afternoon	moi aussi	me too
avec	with	parce que	because

bien sûr	of course	peut-être	maybe
déjà	already	quelquefois	sometimes
depuis	since, as of	souvent	often
en retard	late	superbe	superb
excellent	excellent	tard	late
maintenant	now	vraiment	truly

CULTURAL NOTE:

Since November 1, 1992, French law has restricted smoking in all enclosed areas, including the métro, métro stations, theaters, and all public places. Hotels and restaurants have posted *"Espace non-fumeur"* (No Smoking) and *"Espace fumeur"* (Smoking) signs in their establishments.

PRACTICE THE VOCABULARY

Answers for Lesson 2, pp. 54–55

A. Write the correct article *(le, la,* or *l')* in front of each word.

1. _____ couteau
2. _____ assiette
3. _____ repas
4. _____ plat
5. _____ fourchette
6. _____ viande

7. _____ veau
8. _____ salade
9. _____ glace
10. _____ crème
11. _____ langouste
12. _____ homard

13. _____ poisson
14. _____ poulet
15. _____ addition
16. _____ caissière
17. _____ assiette
18. _____ flan

B. Match the two columns below.

1. _____ repas
2. _____ maintenant
3. _____ assiette
4. _____ déjà
5. _____ frites
6. _____ côtelettes
7. _____ langouste
8. _____ fruits de mer
9. _____ caissière
10. _____ poisson
11. _____ viande
12. _____ flan
13. _____ plat
14. _____ crevettes

A. plate
B. custard
C. seafood
D. dish
E. meat
F. fish
G. shrimp
H. crayfish
I. already
J. chops
K. cashier
L. fries
M. meal
N. now

DIALOGUE Au restaurant Chez Jeannine

LE GARÇON:	Bonjour, mesdames. Puis-je vous aider?
MME RAYMOND:	Nous voulons une table pour deux personnes, espace non-fumeur, s'il vous plaît.
LE GARÇON:	Bien, mesdames. Suivez-moi.
MME SIMON:	Voilà, c'est parfait en face du jardin. Merci.
LE GARÇON:	Voici la carte, mesdames.
MME RAYMOND:	Ils ont mon plat préféré.
LE GARÇON:	Vous voulez commander maintenant?
MME RAYMOND:	Oui, pour moi la salade de laitue, le plat de fruits de mer, des frites, et du café. Merci.
MME SIMON:	Moi, je préfère les côtelettes d'agneau et les légumes. Merci.
LE GARÇON:	Quelque chose à boire pour commencer?
MME RAYMOND:	Oui. Une bouteille de Perrier avec le repas, s'il vous plaît.
MME SIMON:	C'est vraiment délicieux. Ce restaurant est excellent.
MME RAYMOND:	Je suis d'accord. La cuisine est superbe ici.
MME SIMON:	Garçon, l'addition s'il vous plaît. Nous sommes pressées—nous travaillons cet après-midi.
LE GARÇON:	Payez la caissière là-bas s'il vous plaît. Au revoir et à bientôt.

DIALOGUE At Jeannine's Restaurant

WAITER:	Hello, ladies. May I help you?
MRS. RAYMOND:	We want a table for two people, non-smoking, please.
WAITER:	Very well, ladies. Follow me.
MRS. SIMON:	In front of the garden; that's perfect. Thank you.
WAITER:	Here's the menu, ladies.
MRS. RAYMOND:	They have my favorite dish.
WAITER:	Do you want to order now?
MRS. RAYMOND:	Yes, I'll have the salad, the seafood dish, fries, and coffee. Thank you.
MRS. SIMON:	I prefer the lamb chops and the vegetables. Thank you.
WAITER:	Something to drink to start?
MRS. RAYMOND:	Yes, a bottle of Perrier with the meal, please.
MRS. SIMON:	It's really delicious. This restaurant is excellent.
MRS. RAYMOND:	I agree. The food is superb here.
MRS. SIMON:	Waiter, the bill please. We're in a hurry—we are working this afternoon.
WAITER:	Pay the cashier over there, please. Goodbye; see you soon.

DIALOGUE EXERCISES

A. Complete the sentences, based on the dialogue.

1. Madame Raymond et Madame Simon sont chez _____.
2. Le restaurant est _____ et la cuisine est _____.
3. Madame Raymond veut boire du _____.
4. Madame Simon commande les côtelettes _____.
5. Madame Raymond préfère la salade de _____.
6. Le garçon dit au revoir et _____.
7. Madame Raymond boit du Perrier avec _____.
8. Madame Simon aime les _____ et la viande.
9. Madame Raymond préfère les fruits de mer et les _____.
10. Madame Simon et Madame Raymond sont _____.
11. Elles travaillent cet _____.
12. Madame Simon et Madame Raymond paient la _____.

B. Select the appropriate word and fill in the blank.

1. La cuisine dans le restaurant est _____ (table, fourchette, délicieuse).
2. Madame Simon veut boire _____ (du flan, du homard, du café).
3. Madame Simon préfère _____ (les légumes, le couteau, l'assiette).
4. Madame Raymond paie _____ (le garçon, la caissière, la table).
5. La table de Madame Simon est en face du _____ (poisson, plat, jardin).
6. Madame Simon et Madame Raymond sont _____ (à la maison, à l'hôtel, au restaurant).
7. Madame Simon et Madame Raymond partent du restaurant parce qu'elles _____ (mangent, commandent, travaillent, sont pressées).
8. Les côtelettes d'agneau sont _____ (du poisson, des crevettes, de la viande).
9. Le homard est _____ (un agneau, un veau, un fruit de mer).
10. Les frites sont _____ (des légumes, du flan, de la viande).

GRAMMAR I   Regular Verbs in the Present Indicative Tense

A. There are three groups of regular French verbs:

1. Verbs ending in -ER are of the first group: *parler* (to speak).
2. Verbs ending in -IR are of the second group: *choisir* (to choose).
3. Verbs ending in -RE are of the third group: *attendre* (to wait for).

All the verbs in the above groups have two parts, a *stem* and an *ending*.

EXAMPLE: *parler:* stem—*parl-;* ending *-er*

NOTE:

Payer (to pay for) and other verbs with *-yer,* such as *employer* (to use), *envoyer* (to send), and *ennuyer* (to bore, to bother) change the *y* into *i* with all pronouns except *nous* and *vous.*

je paie	nous payons
tu paies	vous payez
il, elle paie	ils, elles paient

B. Present indicative of *parler*:

Subject	*Parler*	Subject	To Speak
je	**parl** e	I	speak, am speaking, do speak
tu	**parl** es	you (sing. fam.)	speak, are speaking, do speak
il, elle (on)	**parl** e	he, she, it, one	speaks, is speaking, does speak
nous	**parl** ons	we	speak, are speaking, do speak
vous	**parl** ez	you (plural)	speak, are speaking, do speak
ils, elles	**parl** ent	they	speak, are speaking, do speak

NOTES:

1. In French, the present indicative has three different equivalents in English.

    EXAMPLE: *Je parle:* I speak, I am speaking, I do speak

2. The French word *on* is used the same way that *one* is used in English, with the third-person singular form of the verb.

3. The third-person plural is pronounced the same as the third-person singular, even though the ending is different.

PRACTICE THE REGULAR FRENCH VERBS

A. Answer the following questions.

1. How many groups of regular verbs are there in French? _____.
2. What are the infinitive endings of each group? _____.
3. Why are these verbs called regular? _____.
4. Write the stem of the verb *parler* (to speak) _____.
5. Write the stem of the verb *danser* (to dance) _____.
6. What is the French equivalent of *we are speaking*? _____.

B. Complete the following sentences with the correct verb forms.

1. Vous _____ (parler) beaucoup.
2. Charles et Antoinette _____ (commander) le repas.
3. Le garçon _____ (travailler) au Restaurant Parisien.
4. Elles _____ (chercher) le cinéma Voltaire.

5. Ils _____ (voyager) toujours.

6. Nous _____ (regarder) la télévision.

7. J(e) _____ (aimer) la glace au chocolat.

8. J(e) _____ (étudier) la leçon.

9. Charles et Antoinette _____ (penser) beaucoup.

10. Nous _____ (rentrer) tard.

GRAMMAR II   Present Indicative of Regular Verbs Ending in *-ir* and *-re*

A. The present indicative of regular *-ir* verbs, such as *choisir* (to choose).

Verbs in these groups are also divided into stems and endings. As with the *-er* verbs, the stems remain the same and the endings change according to tense and subject.

Subject	*Choisir*	Subject	To Choose
je	**chois is**	I	choose, am choosing, do choose
tu	**chois is**	you	choose, are choosing, do choose
il, elle (on)	**chois it**	he, she, it, one	chooses, is choosing, does choose
nous	**chois issons**	we	choose, are choosing, do choose
vous	**chois issez**	you	choose, are choosing, do choose
ils, elles	**chois issent**	they	choose, are choosing, do choose

NOTE:
The addition of *-iss* in the plural forms is to be observed in all the *-ir* regular verbs. This group includes *finir* (to finish), *agir* (to act), *réussir* (to succeed), and *réfléchir* (to reflect, to consider).

B. Present indicative of regular verbs ending in *-re*, such as *attendre* (to wait for).

As with the regular verbs ending in *-er* and *-ir,* the stems remain the same and the endings change according to tense and subject.

Subject	*Attendre*	Subject	To Wait For
j'	**attend s**	I	wait for, do wait for, am waiting for
tu	**attend s**	you	wait for, do wait for, are waiting for
il, elle (on)	**attend**	he, she, it, one	waits for, does wait for, is waiting for
nous	**attend ons**	we	wait for, do wait for, are waiting for
vous	**attend ez**	you	wait for, do wait for, are waiting for
ils, elles	**attend ent**	they	wait for, do wait for, are waiting for

NOTE:

Other -re verbs include *vendre* (to sell), *entendre* (to hear), *rendre* (to give back), *perdre* (to lose), and *répondre* (to answer).

C. Recapitulation of endings to be attached to the stems of the regular verbs in -er, -ir, and -re:

Parler	Choisir	Attendre
je -e	je -is	j'(e) -s
tu -es	tu -is	tu -s
il, elle -e	il, elle -it	il, elle
nous -ons	nous -issons	nous -ons
vous -ez	vous -issez	vous -ez
ils, elles -ent	ils, elles -issent	ils, elles -ent

EXERCISES

A. Complete the sentences with the appropriate verb forms.

1. Charles _____ (répondre) à Antoinette.
2. Le monsieur _____ (attendre) la dame.
3. Monsieur et Madame _____ (finir) la conversation.
4. Antoinette _____ (réussir) à l'examen.
5. Le garçon _____ (réfléchir) à l'addition.
6. Nous _____ (rendre) les livres.
7. Vous _____ (choisir) le restaurant.
8. Elles _____ (agir) rapidement.
9. Charles et Antoinette _____ (répondre) à Juliette.
10. Ils _____ (vendre) des maisons.

B. Write the French equivalent of the following sentences, then read them aloud.

1. I am finishing the book. _____.
2. We do speak French. _____.
3. We are looking for the restaurant. _____.
4. She is waiting for Charles. _____.
5. They do like the cake. _____.

GRAMMAR III   The Negative Form of *être* and *avoir*

The simplest way to change an affirmative verb into the negative form is to follow this formula:

Subject +	Ne +	Verb +	Pas
Je	ne	suis	pas.
Je	ne	parle	pas.

NOTE: When *ne* precedes a verb beginning with a vowel, it is written *n'*.

A. Study the formation of the negative with the verb *être* (to be).

Subject +	Ne +	Verb +	Pas
je	ne	suis	pas
tu	n'	es	pas
il, elle	n'	est	pas
nous	ne	sommes	pas
vous	n'	êtes	pas
ils, elles	ne	sont	pas

B. Study the formation of the negative with the verb *avoir* (to have).

Subject +	Ne +	Verb +	Pas
je	n'	ai	pas
tu	n'	as	pas
il, elle	n'	a	pas
nous	n'	avons	pas
vous	n'	avez	pas
ils, elles	n'	ont	pas

PRACTICE THE NEGATIVE FORM

Write the negative form of the following.

1. Je _____ suis _____ une fille.
2. Elle _____ a _____ le stylo.
3. Nous _____ avons _____ le menu.
4. Ils _____ sont _____ au restaurant.
5. Vous _____ êtes _____ Américain.
6. Vous _____ avez _____ quelque chose à boire.

7. Ils _____ commandent _____ le poulet.

8. Charles _____ finit _____ tard.

9. Antoinette _____ travaille _____ beaucoup.

10. Ils _____ attendent _____ l'autobus.

11. Nous _____ payons _____ l'addition.

12. Ils _____ finissent _____ le repas.

13. Nous _____ cherchons _____ le restaurant.

14. Vous _____ trouvez _____ le parapluie.

3 Au grand magasin
(At the Department Store)

l'achat (masc.)	(the) purchase	les meubles (masc.)	furniture
l'argent (masc.)	money	le prix	cost
la boîte	box	le rayon	aisle
le camion	truck	la robe	dress
la caisse	cashier's desk	la valeur	value
le cendrier	ashtray	le vendeur	salesman
la chambre	room	la vendeuse	saleswoman
la chose	thing	le voisinage	neighborhood
le fauteuil	armchair	la volonté	will
le lit	bed		

accompagner	to accompany	fêter	to celebrate
admirer	to admire	gaspiller	to waste
aider	to help	hésiter	to hesitate
apporter	to bring	marcher	to walk; to work (a machine, a motor)
bricoler	to putter around		
compter	to count		
coûter	to cost	montrer	to show
dépenser	to spend	porter	to carry
descendre	to get off	ramener	to bring back
désirer	to wish, to desire	rentrer	to return home, to come back
discuter	to discuss		
durer	to last	suivre	to follow
espérer	to hope		

c'est	it is	avec plaisir	with pleasure
déjà	already	zut! (familiar)	darn!
depuis	since		

cher, chère	dear, expensive	petit(e)	small
étroit(e)	big	prêt(e)	ready
grand(e)	narrow	que	which, whom
il n'y a pas de quoi	you're welcome	satisfait, satisfaite	satisfied
large	wide	surtout	mostly, especially
mais	but	tout de suite	immediately
(avec) moi	(with) me	utile	useful
par ici	over here	vrai, vraie	true
partout	everywhere		

NOTES:

1. *L'achat* means "a purchase." It is derived from *acheter*, to buy.

2. The word *(les) meubles* is always used in the plural form when referring to the contents of a room or a house and used to mean *furniture*. It is used in the singular only to denote a single piece of furniture, as in: *"J'ai un meuble Louis XV."* ("I have a piece of Louis XV furniture.")

3. *L'argent* is *money*, and *la monnaie* is *change*, as in *"Avez-vous de la monnaie?"* ("Do you have any change?")

4. *Cher* (masc.), *chère* (fem.) means *dear*, as in "Dear Charles" at the beginning of a letter. It also means *expensive*, as in *"Le meuble Louis XV est cher."* (The piece of Louis XV furniture is expensive.) Other examples are: *c'est cher* (it's expensive) and *ce n'est pas cher* (it's not expensive).

PRACTICE THE VOCABULARY

A. Write the correct definite article *(le, la, les, l')* before each noun.

1. _____ chose
2. _____ argent
3. _____ rayon
4. _____ meubles
5. _____ employé
6. _____ lampes
7. _____ cendrier
8. _____ trottoir
9. _____ achats

B. Complete the sentences with the appropriate words.

1. Charles admire _____ (les meubles, surtout, depuis).
2. Le camion est _____ (descendre, petit, la rue).
3. Les fauteuils ne sont pas _____ (satisfait, grands, déjà).
4. Le magasin n'accepte pas le _____ (rue, chaise, crédit).
5. Charles compare les _____ (chambres, miroirs, prix).
6. Antoinette ne compte pas _____ (la chose, le voisinage, l'argent).
7. La rue est _____ (chère, étroite, prête).
8. Charles et Antoinette ne marchent pas dans _____ (le magasin, la robe, la rue).

DIALOGUE   Au grand magasin

LE VENDEUR: Bonjour, mademoiselle!

ANTOINETTE: Je cherche une grande lampe et un fauteuil pour ma chambre.

LE VENDEUR: Très bien, mademoiselle. Suivez-moi.

ANTOINETTE: Ah! Voici les lampes! Mais je n'aime pas les couleurs.
Avez-vous quelque chose en blanc?

LE VENDEUR: Oui, mademoiselle. Suivez-moi; nous avons des lampes blanches mais elles sont en haut.

ANTOINETTE: Montrez-moi cette lampe à côté du grand lit là-bas.

LE VENDEUR: La voici.

ANTOINETTE: C'est combien?

LE VENDEUR: Cent francs, mademoiselle.

ANTOINETTE: C'est parfait. Maintenant, j'ai besoin d'un fauteuil; montrez-moi le rayon des meubles, s'il vous plaît.

LE VENDEUR: Le voilà en face de vous.

ANTOINETTE: C'est combien, le fauteuil rouge?

LE VENDEUR: Cinq cent francs.

ANTOINETTE: Oh là là! Comme c'est cher! Mais j'aime le style.

LE VENDEUR: La qualité a de la valeur, mademoiselle.

ANTOINETTE: Vous avez raison. Voici ma carte de crédit; je prends la lampe et le fauteuil.

LE VENDEUR: Allons à la caisse, par ici, mademoiselle.

ANTOINETTE: Je vous remercie, monsieur.

LE VENDEUR: Il n'y a pas de quoi, mademoiselle. A bientôt.

DIALOGUE   At the Department Store

THE SALESMAN: Good morning!

ANTOINETTE: I'm looking for a big lamp and an armchair for my room.

THE SALESMAN: Very well, follow me.

ANTOINETTE: Ah! Here are the lamps! But I don't like the colors. Do you have something in white?

THE SALESMAN: Yes, follow me; we do have white lamps, but they are upstairs.

ANTOINETTE: Show me the lamp next to the big bed over there.

THE SALESMAN: Here it is.

ANTOINETTE: How much is it?

THE SALESMAN: One hundred francs.

ANTOINETTE: It's perfect. Now I need an armchair; show me the furniture department, please.

THE SALESMAN: It's there, across from you.

ANTOINETTE:	How much is the red armchair?
THE SALESMAN:	Five hundred francs.
ANTOINETTE:	Ooh la la! How expensive! But I like the style.
THE SALESMAN:	Quality does have value.
ANTOINETTE:	You're right. Here's my credit card; I'll take the lamp and the armchair.
THE SALESMAN:	Let's go to the cashier's over here.
ANTOINETTE:	Thank you, sir.
THE SALESMAN:	You're welcome. See you soon.

DIALOGUE EXERCISES

A. Based on the dialogue, fill in the missing words.

1. Antoinette a besoin d'une _____ et d'un _____ pour sa (her) chambre.

2. Antoinette et le vendeur vont _____ (upstairs).

3. La lampe est _____ (expensive).

4. Le fauteuil est dans le _____ (furniture department).

5. Antoinette n'aime pas les _____ (colors) des lampes.

6. Antoinette donne _____ (the credit card) au vendeur.

7. Le vendeur pense que _____ a de la _____.

8. Antoinette prend la _____ et le _____.

9. Le fauteuil coûte _____ et la lampe coûte _____.

10. Antoinette achète une lampe _____ (white) et un fauteuil _____ (red).

B. Match the two columns by writing the appropriate letters in the spaces provided.

1. _____ Elle dépense beaucoup.		A.	She organizes the room.
2. _____ Il aide le vendeur.		B.	He looks for the ashtray.
3. _____ Le miroir est petit.		C.	She spends a lot.
4. _____ Êtes-vous prêt?		D.	He helps the salesman.
5. _____ Aimes-tu marcher?		E.	Are you ready?
6. _____ Il va partout.		F.	I need money.
7. _____ Il cherche le cendrier.		G.	The mirror is small.
8. _____ J'ai besoin d'argent.		H.	Do you like to walk?
9. _____ Elle organise la chambre.		I.	He goes everywhere.
10. _____ Il vend les meubles.		J.	He sells furniture.

GRAMMAR I   Adjective-Noun Agreement • Descriptive Adjectives

A. An adjective modifies a noun, conveying shape, color, quality, size, nationality, etc. The adjective must agree in number and gender with the noun it modifies.

> EXAMPLE: *un homme intelligent* (masc. sing.)
> *des hommes intelligents* (masc. pl.)
> *une femme intelligente* (fem. sing.)
> *des femmes intelligentes* (fem. pl.)

The feminine singular form is obtained by adding *e* to the masculine form.

> EXAMPLE: *intéressant* is the masculine form (interesting)
> *intéressante* is the feminine form

B. To form the plural, both nouns and adjectives add *s* to the singular form.

> EXAMPLE: *un homme intelligent*
> *des hommes intelligents*
> *une femme intelligente*
> *des femmes intelligentes*

NOTES:

1. Observe that both nouns and adjectives require *s* in the plural.

2. If the masculine form of an adjective ends with a silent *e,* the ending does not change in the feminine form.

> EXAMPLE: un homme sociab*le*
> une femme sociab*le*

3. In French, the final consonants: *t, d, s,* are usually silent, as in *intelligent, anglais,* and *grand.*

4. If the masculine singular form of a noun or an adjective ends with *s, x,* or *z,* the ending does not change in the plural:

> EXAMPLE: *Adjectives*
>
> Le garçon est *français.*
> Le garçons sont *français.*
> Le garçon est *sérieux.*
> Les garçons sont *sérieux.*
>
> *Nouns*
>
> le *cours* (course) les *cours*
> le *nez* (nose) les *nez*
> le *choix* (choice) les *choix*

C. Adjectives with irregular forms:

1. Adjectives ending in *-eux* and *-eur* in the masculine form require *-euse* in the feminine form.

> EXAMPLE: un garçon *sérieux*
> une fille *sérieuse*
> un garçon *travailleur*
> une fille *travailleuse*

2. Adjectives ending in *er* require *-ère* in the feminine form:

> EXAMPLE: un fauteuil *cher*
> une lampe *chère*

The *r* in *cher* is pronounced in the singular form, even though there is no vowel after it. The feminine form of *chère,* is pronounced exactly like the masculine form. Notice that an accent grave (`) is required on the *e* before the *r* in the feminine form.

3. Adjectives ending with *-if* require *-ive* in the feminine form:

> EXAMPLE: un garçon *actif*
> une fille *active*

4. Adjectives ending with *il* and *el* in the masculine require *ille* and *elle* in the feminine form:

> EXAMPLE: un garçon *gentil*
> une fille *gentille*
> un homme *intellectuel*
> une femme *intellectuelle*

5. Adjectives ending with *-ien* in the masculine require *-ienne* in the feminine form:

> EXAMPLE: Jacques est *canadien*
> Juliette est *canadienne*

6. Other adjectives that follow the above rules include: *paresseux* (lazy), *courageux* (courageous), *naif* (naïve), *fier* (proud), *ancien* (old, antique). Please note that adjectives of nationality and place are not capitalized:

> EXAMPLE: *Jacques est français* (Jacques is French)
> *un restaurant parisien* (a Parisian restaurant)

D. A certain number of adjectives precede the nouns they modify. They often describe physical attributes:

> EXAMPLE: *une jolie fille* (a pretty girl)
> *un grand garçon* (a big boy)

Adjectives denoting color generally follow the nouns they modify:

> EXAMPLE: *une robe verte* (a green dress)

NOTES:

1. Nouns ending in *-eau* in the singular require the ending *x* in the plural form.

> EXAMPLE: *le tableau* (the board)
> *les tableaux* (the boards)

2. Nouns ending in -al or -ail require *aux* in the plural form.

> EXAMPLE: *un cheval* (a horse), *des chevaux* (horses)
> *le travail* (the work), *les travaux* (the works)

3. When describing a group that includes one or more males, French uses the masculine form.

> EXAMPLE: *un Français et neuf Françaises = dix* (ten) *Français.*

4. When *t,s,d,* and *n* end a masculine word, they are not pronounced. When they are followed by *e,* they are pronounced.

5. Nouns ending in -te have the same ending in the masculine and feminine forms.

> EXAMPLE: | *le touriste* | the tourist (masc.) |
> | *la touriste* | the tourist (fem.) |
> | *le scientiste* | the scientist (masc.) |
> | *la scientiste* | the scientist (fem.) |

6. In words ending in *r, f, rs,* and *fs* the *r* or the *f* is pronounced, but the *s* is not.

> EXAMPLE: *voir* (to see)
> *cher* (dear, expensive)
> *neuf* (new) (masc.)

Other exceptions that require pronunciation of a consonant ending are: *cinq (q = k), six (x = ss), dix (x = ss), sept (pt = t), huit (t = t).* Note that *neuf* means *nine,* but is also used as an adjective meaning *new.* The feminine of *neuf* meaning new is *neuve.*

EXERCISES

ANSWERS p. 56

A. Practice the grammar.

1. An adjective describes a _____, conveying _____ and _____.

2. What do you add to a masculine adjective to change it to the feminine form? _____.

3. What is the feminine of *arménien*? _____.
4. What is the masculine of *française*? _____.
5. What is the feminine of *gentil*? _____.
6. What is the feminine of *vif* (alert, alive)? _____.
7. What is the feminine of *joyeux* (joyful, happy)? _____.
8. What is the feminine plural of *sérieux*? _____.
9. What is the masculine plural of *joyeux*? _____.
10. What is the masculine plural of *anglais*? _____.
11. What is the feminine plural of *complet* (complete)? _____.
12. What is the masculine of *lumineuse* (luminous)? _____.

13. What is the masculine plural of *heureuses* (happy)? _____.
14. What is the feminine plural of *chanteur* (singer)? _____.
15. What is the feminine singular of *fier* (proud)? _____.

ANSWERS p. 56 **B. Write the plural forms of the following, then say them aloud.**

> *Example:* le grand chien   *les grands chiens.*

1. le petit chalet _____.
2. la grande chambre _____.
3. l'arbre vert _____.
4. l'homme sportif (athletic) _____.
5. le chien noir (black) _____.
6. le meuble anglais _____.
7. l'étudiant sérieux _____.

GRAMMAR II   The Partitive Constructions: *du, de la, des,* and *de l'* • Numbers

A. The *partitive* means part of a whole, conveying the idea of *some,* or *any.* Sometimes *some* and *any* are only implied in English, while in French they must be expressed. For example, "There is wine in the bottle" implies there is *some* wine in the bottle. In French, the partitive is expressed by *de* + the definite article.

> EXAMPLE: *Il a de la bière.* (He has [some] beer.)
> *J'ai du vin.* (I have [some] wine.)
> *Ils ont des fleurs.* (They have [some] flowers.)

B. The definite articles *le* and *les* are contracted in the following manner: *de* + *le* becomes *du,*

> EXAMPLE: *Il a du vin.*

and *de* + *les* becomes *des.*

> EXAMPLE: *Il a des stylos.*

Note that *la* and *l'* do not change.

> EXAMPLE: *J'ai de l'argent.* (I have [some] money.)
> *Il a de la bière.* (He has [some] beer.)

C. In general, the partitive is expressed by *de* or *d'* alone in a negative sentence.

> EXAMPLE: *Je n'ai pas d'argent.* (I don't have [any] money.)
> *Il ne commande pas de vin.* (He is not ordering [any] wine.)
> *Nous ne cherchons pas de restaurant.* (We are not looking for [any] restaurant.)
> *Il n'a pas de courage.* (He does not have [any] courage.)

D. Memorize the following numbers in French

1. *un*	5. *cinq*	9. *neuf*	13. *treize*	17. *dix-sept*
2. *deux*	6. *six*	10. *dix*	14. *quatorze*	18. *dix-huit*
3. *trois*	7. *sept*	11. *onze*	15. *quinze*	19. *dix-neuf*
4. *quatre*	8. *huit*	12. *douze*	16. *seize*	20. *vingt*

EXERCISES

**ANSWERS
p. 56**

A. Complete the sentences with *du, de la, des,* or *de l'.*

1. Avez-vous _____ bière?

2. Nous avons besoin _____ argent.

3. Nous n'avons pas _____ poulet.

4. Vous avez _____ vin blanc.

5. Ils n'ont pas _____ patience (fem.).

6. Charles a _____ courage (masc.).

7. Voulez-vous _____ viande?

8. Les roses ont _____ pétales.

9. Antoinette a _____ talent (masc.).

10. Charles a _____ chance (fem.).

Note: avoir de la chance = to be lucky, to have (some) luck

B. Practice the numbers 1–12 by memorizing this short nursery rhyme.

Un, deux, trois = One, two, three

nous allons au bois = we go to the woods

quatre, cinq, six = four, five, six

ramasser des cerises = to gather cherries

sept, huit, neuf = seven, eight, nine

dans mon panier neuf = in my new basket

dix, onze, douze = ten, eleven, twelve

elles sont toutes rouges. = they are all red.

**ANSWERS
p. 57**

C. Practice the partitives *de, du, de la, des, de l'.*

1. What is a partitive?

2. How is the idea of *some* and *any* rendered in French?_____.

3. Are *some* and *any* ever implied, but not expressed, in French? _____.

4. How is the partitive always expressed in a negative sentence? _____.

5. What is the partitive equivalent of *de + les*? _____.

6. What is the partitive equivalent of *de + le*? _____.

7. Which two definite articles do not change in a partitive construction?
_____.

D. Match the French partitives with their English equivalents.

1. ___ J'ai de jolies robes (dresses).

2. ___ Avez-vous du vin blanc?

3. ___ Nous avons des cendriers.

4. ___ Ont-ils des fauteuils anciens?

5. ___ Elle ne mange pas de viande.

6. ___ Nous ne commandons pas de dessert.

7. ___ Ils n'ont pas de livres français.

8. ___ Tu n'as pas d'argent.

A. We're not ordering any dessert.

B. They don't have any French books.

C. You don't have any money.

D. Do they have any antique armchairs?

E. We have (some) ashtrays.

F. She does not eat (any) meat.

G. I have some pretty dresses.

H. Do you have any white wine?

GRAMMAR III   Present Indicative of *aller* • Question Words

A. The verb *aller* (to go) is an irregular verb, as are *être* (to be) and *avoir* (to have). These three verbs are very important and should be memorized because all three are used to form other tenses and verb constructions.

Subject	*Aller*	Subject	To Go
je	**vais**	I	go, am going, do go
tu	**vas**	you	go, are going, do go
il, elle, on	**va**	he, she, it	goes, is going, does go
nous	**allons**	we	go, are going, do go
vous	**allez**	you	go, are going, do go
ils, elles	**vont**	they	go, are going, do go

NOTE:
To go to is *aller à*. The contraction of *à* and *la* or *le* is handled as follows: *à + la = à la; à + le = au,* as in *Je vais au cinéma.*

B. When spoken, questions always end with a rise in pitch, as in English. The verb usually precedes the noun or pronoun.

EXAMPLE: *Comment allez-vous?* (How are you?)

The verb precedes the subject. Other question words are:

> *quand,* as in *Quand étudiez-vous?* When do you study?
> *où,* as in *Où étudiez-vous?* Where do you study?
>
> *comment,* as in *Comment étudiez-vous?* How do you study?
> *pourquoi,* as in *Pourquoi étudiez-vous?* Why do you study?
> *combien,* as in *Combien étudiez-vous?* How much do you study?

NOTES:

1. *Combien c'est?* How much is it?

2. *Combien de?* How many? as in *Combien de garçons?* (How many boys?)

C. The other question words are the English equivalents of *who, whom,* and *what.* They are: *qui* (who), *quoi* (what), and *que* (which, whom). *To whom, of whom,* and *about what* translate into the following French question expressions:

> *à qui?* to whom, as in *À qui parlez-vous?* To whom are you speaking?
> *de qui?* of whom, as in *De qui parlez-vous?* Of whom are you speaking?
> *à quoi?* about what, as in *À quoi pensez-vous?* What are you thinking about?
> *de quoi?* about what, as in *De quoi parlez-vous?* What are you talking about?

EXERCISES

ANSWERS p. 57

A. Fill in the blank with the correct form of the verb *aller* (to go).

1. Charles _____ (goes) au cinéma avec Antoinette.
2. Charles et Antoinette _____ (are going) à la maison.
3. Les étudiants (students) _____ (do go) au théâtre.
4. Charles et moi _____ (are going) au restaurant.
5. Tu _____ (are going) à la maison.
6. Vous _____ (go) au rayon des meubles.
7. _____ (When are you going) au restaurant?
8. Je ne _____ (go) pas au magasin.
9. Nous n' _____ (go) pas au cinéma.
10. Ils ne _____ (are not going) à la mer avec nous.

ANSWERS
p. 57

B. Match the questions with the appropriate English translations.

1. Où cherchez-vous les lampes? ___
2. Quand travaillez-vous? ___
3. Est-ce que vous aimez l'argent? ___
4. À qui téléphonez-vous aujourd'hui? ___
5. De quoi discutez-vous? ___
6. Comment voulez-vous le biftek? ___
7. Combien de fauteuils avez-vous? ___
8. À quoi penses-tu? ___
9. De qui parlent-elles? ___
10. Pourquoi fumez-vous? ___

A. Whom are they talking about?
B. How do you want the steak?
C. Where do you look for lamps?
D. How many armchairs do you have?
E. What are you thinking about?
F. Do you like money?
G. Why do you smoke?
H. What are you discussing?
I. Whom are you calling today?
J. When do you work?

4 À l'aéroport
(At the Airport)

l'aéroport (masc.)	(the) airport	la douane	customs
aller et retour	round-trip	le douanier	customs officer
annoncer	to announce	le fenêtre	window
l'arrivée (fem.)	arrival	le haut-parleur	loudspeaker
l'atterrissage (masc.)	landing	l'hôtesse (fem.)	hostess
l'avion (masc.)	airplane	la lumière	light
les bagages (masc.)	baggage	le passager	passenger
le billet	ticket	le pilote	pilot
la carte d'embarquement	boarding pass	la piste de décollage	runway
la ceinture	belt	la porte	door
le choix	choice	le siège	seat
les commandes (fem.)	controls	la sortie	exit
le départ	departure	les vacances (fem.)	vacation
		la valise	suitcase
		le vol	flight
		le voyage	trip
		le voyageur	traveler
aider	to help	faire escale	to stop over
allumer	to light	faire la queue	to stand in line
arrêter	to stop	faire vite	to hurry
arriver	to arrive, to happen	fumer	to smoke
attacher	to fasten	monter	to go up
atterrir	to land	partir	to leave
décoller	to take off	pouvoir	to be able to
descendre	to go down	recevoir	to receive
détacher	to unfasten	sortir	to go out
devoir	to have to	voler	to fly, to steal
embarquer	to board	vouloir	to want

à l'heure	on time	fabuleux (-se)	fabulous
aussi	also	heureusement	happily
car	for, therefore	loin de	far from
court(e)	short	lourd(e)	heavy
devant	before, in front of	poli(e)	polite
		tout à fait	quite

PRACTICE THE VOCABULARY

A. Complete the sentences with the appropriate words.

1. Les passagers arrivent à la _____ (bagages, douane, parachute).
2. L'hôtesse de l'air _____ (arrête, fume, aide).
3. Nous ne _____ (achetons, partons, fumons) pas dans la cabine.
4. Nous achetons les _____ (billets, bagages, pilote) à l'aéroport.
5. L'avion _____ (dépense, décolle, la queue) à temps.
6. Nous _____ (partons, dépensons, attachons) les ceintures de sécurité.
7. Le douanier inspecte _____ (les commandes, les bagages, les cigarettes).
8. L'hôtesse de l'air est _____ (le pilote, passager, polie).
9. Le voyage de New York à Paris n'est pas _____ (lourd, court, poli).
10. "Attention, attention!" annonce _____ (la sécurité, la douane, le haut-parleur).

B. Write the appropriate words and read the sentences aloud.

1. Les bagages sont _____ (gentils, lourds, polis).
2. L'hôtesse est _____ (à l'heure, aussi, polie).
3. Les passagers attachent _____ (les bagages, les valises, les ceintures).
4. L'avion décolle _____ (lourd, fenêtre, à l'heure).
5. Le douanier inspecte _____ (l'avion, le voyageur, les bagages).
6. L'avion atterrit _____ (à l'hôtel, à la fenêtre, à l'aéroport).

DIALOGUE   À l'aéroport

Charles arrive à l'aéroport pour acheter deux billets, aller et retour New York-Paris. Antoinette attend au café.

L'EMPLOYÉ: Bonjour, Monsieur, puis-je vous aider?

CHARLES: Oui, j'ai besoin de deux billets aller et retour New York-Paris.

L'EMPLOYÉ: Nous avons deux vols, le vol 620 décolle à deux heures de l'après-midi et le vol 412 décolle à six heures trente du soir.

CHARLES: Je voudrais deux billets pour le vol 620.

L'EMPLOYÉ:	Très bien, Monsieur. Voilà vos billets. Pour le choix des sièges, allez à la porte douze pour obtenir la carte d'embarquement.
ANTOINETTE:	Dans une heure, l'avion décolle et dans quelques heures nous allons atterrir à Paris, quelle chance!
CHARLES:	Faites vite, il faut aller à la porte douze pour les cartes d'embarquement.
LE HAUT-PARLEUR:	Attention, attention! Vol 620, embarquement immédiat.
ANTOINETTE:	C'est ici, Charles. Il faut faire la queue.
CHARLES:	Deux sièges, s'il vous plaît, section non-fumeur.
L'EMPLOYÉ:	Voilà, monsieur, deux sièges dans la section non-fumeur, près de la fenêtre. Bon voyage!
CHARLES ET ANTOINETTE:	Merci beaucoup, monsieur.

DIALOGUE   At the Airport

Charles arrives at the airport to buy two New York–Paris round-trip tickets. Antoinette is waiting at the coffee shop.

EMPLOYEE:	Good morning, sir, may I help you?
CHARLES:	Yes, I need two round-trip tickets, New York-Paris.
EMPLOYEE:	We have two flights, flight 620 departing at 2:00 P.M. and flight 412 at 6:30 P.M.
CHARLES:	I would like two tickets for flight 620.
EMPLOYEE:	Very well, sir. Here are your tickets. To select your seats, go to gate 12 to get the boarding pass.
ANTOINETTE:	In one hour the plane takes off, and in a few hours we will land in Paris. What luck!
CHARLES:	Hurry up, we have to go to gate 12 for the boarding passes.
THE LOUDSPEAKER:	Attention, attention! Flight 620, boarding immediately.
ANTOINETTE:	It's here, Charles. We have to stand in line.
CHARLES:	Two seats, please, in the nonsmoking section.
EMPLOYEE:	Here, sir, two seats in the nonsmoking section, near the window. Bon voyage!
CHARLES AND ANTOINETTE:	Thank you very much, sir.

DIALOGUE EXERCISES

ANSWERS
p. 58

A. Match the two columns based on the dialogue.

1. L'avion _____ dans une heure.   A. aide
2. Charles achète _____.   B. au café
3. Antoinette attend _____.   C. à Paris
4. L'hôtesse _____ Antoinette.   D. les billets
5. Antoinette est _____.   E. ne fument pas
6. Il faut faire la queue _____.   F. décolle
7. Ils ont deux sièges _____.   G. heureuse
8. Charles et Antoinette _____.   H. pour la carte d'embarquement
9. L'avion atterrit _____.   I. de la chance
10. Antoinette et Charles ont _____.   J. près de la fenêtre

ANSWERS
p. 58

B. Complete the sentences based on the dialogue.

1. Charles arrive à _____ pour _____ deux billets _____ New York–Paris.
2. Où Antoinette attend-elle? _____.
3. De quoi Charles a-t-il besoin? _____.
4. Charles choisit le vol _____.
5. Où va Charles après? _____.
6. Qu'est-ce que Charles veut (wants) à la porte douze? _____.
7. Pourquoi Charles et Antoinette font la queue? _____.
8. Pourquoi ont-ils de la chance? _____.
9. Où Charles et Antoinette vont-ils atterrir? _____.
10. Les sièges de Charles et Antoinette sont dans la section _____.
11. Le haut-parleur annonce _____.

GRAMMAR I   Present Indicative of *faire*

A. Memorize the following chart.

Subject	Verb	Subject	Verb
je	fais	I	do, make
tu	fais	you	do, make
il, elle (on)	fait	he, she, it, one	does, makes
nous	faisons	we	do, make
vous	faites	you	do, make
ils, elles	font	they	do, make

B. *Il fait,* the third-person singular, is used in describing the weather. In French, as in English, *il* (it) replaces *le temps* (the weather). Thus we have the following expressions, which should be memorized:

il fait beau (temps)	it is beautiful (weather)
il fait mauvais (temps)	it is bad (weather)
il fait chaud	it is warm
il fait froid	it is cold
il fait du vent (wind)	it is windy
il fait du soleil	it is sunny

C. Other useful expressions with *faire* are:

faire des courses	to go shopping, to run errands
faire une promenade	to take a walk
faire la cuisine	to cook
faire le ménage	to do housework
faire un voyage	to take a trip
faire partie de	to belong to
faire la vaisselle	to do the dishes
faire le marché	to do the (grocery) shopping
faire du français	to study French

EXERCISES

**ANSWERS
p. 58**

A. Answer the following questions in French, then read the answers aloud.

> *Example:* Est-ce qu'il joue au football?
>
> *Oui, il joue au football.*

1. Est-ce qu'il fait chaud? _____.
2. Est-ce qu'elles font du ski? _____.
3. Est-ce que vous faites des courses? _____.
4. Est-ce qu'il fait du soleil? _____.
5. Est-ce qu'il fait beau? _____.
6. Est-ce qu'il fait mauvais? _____.
7. Est-ce qu'il fait froid? _____.
8. Est-ce qu'il fait du vent? _____.
9. Est-ce que vous faites la vaisselle? _____.
10. Est-ce qu'elles font du sport? _____.
11. Est-ce que vous faites une promenade? _____.
12. Est-ce qu'elle fait le ménage? _____.

ANSWERS
p. 58

B. Write the following sentences in French, using the verb *faire.*

1. _____. I'm (studying) skiing; I'm a skier.
2. _____. She's going shopping.
3. _____. He plays music.
4. _____. They do housework.
5. _____. The weather is beautiful.
6. _____. I'm going skiing.
7. _____. We're taking a walk.
8. _____. She does the cooking.
9. _____. They study French.
10. _____. We're doing the dishes.

GRAMMAR II   *Quelle heure est-il?* (What time is it?) More numbers

A. Memorize the following chart and related expressions. The response to *Quelle heure est-il?* is *Il est,* followed by the hour and minutes. The chart below shows how to tell time in French.

1.	Exact hour:	**Il est une heure.**	It's one o'clock.
	(l'heure exacte)	**Il est quatre heures.**	It's four o'clock.
		Il est six heures.	It's six o'clock.
2.	After the hour:	**Il est une heure dix.**	It's 1:10.
	(aprés l'heure)	**Il est quatre heures vingt.**	It's 4:20.
		Il est six heures quinze.	It's 6:15.
3.	Before the hour:	**Il est une heure moins dix.**	It's 12:50.
	(avant l'heure)	**Il est quatre heures moins vingt.**	It's 3:40.
		Il est six heures moins quinze.	It's 5:45.

NOTES:

1. To express time with the half hour and the quarter hour, we say for half past: *il est six heures et demie,* or *il est six heures trente;* for quarter past we say: *il est six heures et quart,* or *il est six heures quinze.*

2. We express time before the hour by *moins* (minus), as in *il est six heures moins quinze.* Note that we add the article *le* when we use *moins* with *quart,* as in *moins le quart.*

     EXAMPLE: *Il est une heure moins le quart.*   (It's a quarter to one.)

     Il est sept heures moins le quart. (It's a quarter to seven.)

   This is the only time we use *le* to tell time.

3. French expresses the difference between P.M. and A.M. by adding *du matin* for the A.M. hours and *de l'après-midi* for the P.M. hours. Also used is the expression *du soir* for the evening hours.

EXAMPLE: *Je prends mon café au lait à huit heures du matin.*
(I take my coffee with milk at eight A.M.)

Je fais des courses à deux heures de l'après-midi.
(I go shopping at two P.M.)

Je dîne au restaurant à sept heures du soir.
(I have dinner at the restaurant at seven P.M.)

4. To translate the English *sharp,* as in "it is twelve noon sharp," French uses the word *pile,* as in *il est midi pile.* To translate *about,* as in "it's about noon," French uses *vers* or *environ,* as in *il est environ midi,* or *je rentre vers midi* (I return home around noon).

B. Memorize the numbers 20–1,000.

vingt, vingt et un, vingt-deux, etc.	20, 21, 22, etc.
trente, trente et un, trente-deux, etc.	30, 31, 32, etc.
quarante, quarante et un, quarante-deux, etc.	40, 41, 42, etc.
cinquante, cinquante et un, cinquante-deux, etc.	50, 51, 52, etc.
soixante, soixante et un, soixante-deux, etc.	60, 61, 62, etc.
soixante-dix, soixante et onze, soixante-douze, etc.	70, 71, 72, etc.
quatre-vingts, quatre-vingt-un, quatre-vingt-deux, etc.	80, 81, 82, etc.
quatre-vingt-dix, quatre-vingt-onze, quatre-vingt-douze, etc.	90, 91, 92, etc.
cent, cent un, cent deux, etc.	100, 101, 102, etc.
deux cents, deux cent un, deux cent deux, etc.	200, 201, 202, etc.
mille, deux milles, trois milles, etc.	1,000, 2,000, 3,000, etc.

NOTES:

1. From 21 to 61, French adds *et un.* To say 71 and 91 French uses *onze* with 60 and with 80: *soixante et onze, quatre-vingt-onze.*

2. The numbers between 2 and 9 are added immediately following 21, 31, 41, etc., up to 69: *soixante-neuf.* Then the structure changes to *soixante-dix* and continues counting after ten, as in *soixante-douze, soixante-treize, soixante-quatorze,* etc. This pattern continues up to 99: *quatre-vingt-dix-neuf.* Then comes *cent* (100). After *cent,* counting in French follows the English pattern, as in *cent* (100), *deux cents* (200), *trois cents* (300), and so on up to *neuf cents* (900).

EXERCISES

A. Answer the following questions.

1. Write the answer to : Quelle heure est-il? _____.

2. What are the two ways to express fifteen minutes past the hour, as in, *il est une heure* _____ and _____.

3. In telling time, "half past" is expressed in two ways: *il est une heure* _____ and _____.

4. To indicate the minutes before the hour, we use the word _____.

5. What does French use to indicate A.M.? _____.

6. What are the two ways of specifying P.M. in French? _____ and _____.

7. Write the two French words that translate *about:* _____.

8. How do you say "It is one o'clock sharp"? *Il est une heure* _____.

9. Write the French for "What time is it?" _____.

10. Translate into French "a quarter to". _____.

B. Translate the following time expressions into French.

1. It's 4:20 P.M. _____.

2. It's 10:10 A.M. _____.

3. It's 9:15 P.M. _____.

4. It's 2:05 A.M. _____.

5. It's 6:30 P.M. _____.

6. It's 8:15 A.M. _____.

7. It's 7:08 P.M. _____.

8. It's 3:05 P.M. _____.

9. It's 1:10 A.M. _____.

10. It's 2:00 P.M. sharp _____.

C. Practice the numbers.

1. French uses *et* before *un* in _____, _____, _____, _____, and _____.

2. What happens after *soixante-dix* and *quatre-vingt-dix?*

3. With what number between *20* and *90* do the French not use *et* with *un?* _____.

4. Write out the following numbers in French:

81 _____.

91 _____.

97 _____.

75 _____.

61 _____.

71 _____.

GRAMMAR III Present Indicative of Irregular Verbs: *pouvoir* and *vouloir*

A. Memorize the verbs *pouvoir* (to be able to) and *vouloir* (to want).

Subject	Pouvoir	Vouloir
je	**peux**	**veux**
tu	**peux**	**veux**
il, elle, on	**peut**	**veut**
nous	**pouvons**	**voulons**
vous	**pouvez**	**voulez**
ils, elles	**peuvent**	**veulent**

B. Observe the changes in the above verbs: the stem vowels in *pouvoir* and *vouloir* alternate between *eu* and *ou*. We have the *eu* vowel in all the forms of the verbs except with *nous* and *vous*.

C. *Vouloir* (to want) and *pouvoir* (to be able to) are used with direct objects.

> EXAMPLE: *Je veux de la salade.* (I want some salad.)
>
> *Nous voulons du vin.* (We want some wine.)
>
> *Je peux comprendre le menu.* (I can understand the menu.)

However, *vouloir* is also used with the infinitive, and as such *vouloir* translates as "to wish to" + infinitive.

> EXAMPLE: *Je veux écrire une lettre.* (I wish to write a letter.)
>
> *Nous voulons regarder le film.* (We wish to see the movie.)
>
> *Il veut comprendre la leçon.* (He wants to understand the lesson.)

NOTE:
The general rule in French is that when one verb follows another, the second verb is always an infinitive.

> EXAMPLE: *J'aime danser.* (I like to dance.)

They are also called direct independent infinitives, as in *je veux manger, je peux manger.* French uses no prepositions to denote an infinitive, except with verbs that require *à* or *de,* which we will discuss in chapter 6.

EXERCISES

ANSWERS
p. 59

A. Fill in the blank with the correct form of the verb *vouloir* (to want).

1. They want the books. _____.

2. He does want to eat. _____.

3. We wish to understand. _____.

4. Do you want to travel? _____.

5. You do wish to help. _____.

6. The customs officer wants the luggage. _____.

7. She wishes to smoke. _____.

8. You do want to finish the lesson. _____.

9. We wish to speak French. _____.

10. They want to stop over in Paris. _____.

ANSWERS p. 59

B. **Fill in the blank with the correct form of the verb *pouvoir* (to be able to).**

1. L'avion _____ faire escale à Paris.

2. Charles et Antoinette _____ aider le douanier.

3. Le capitaine _____ comprendre les voyageurs.

4. Est-ce que Charles _____ fumer dans l'avion?

5. L'hôtesse et le capitaine _____ parler.

6. Les passagers ne _____ pas toucher les commandes.

7. L'avion _____ décoller à l'heure.

8. Vous ne _____ pas aider le capitaine.

9. Nous _____ acheter les billets.

10. Les passagers _____ montrer les cartes d'embarquement.

5 La famille
(The Family)

l'ami (masc.)	friend	la machine (à laver)	washing machine
le bain	bath	la maison	house
le balcon	balcony	la salle d'attente	waiting room
les bijoux (masc.)	jewels	la salle de bains	bathroom
le camion	truck	la salle à manger	dining room
le couloir	hallway	le salon	living room
la cour	yard	la vaisselle	dishes
la douche	shower	le voisin (masc.)	neighbor
le jardin	garden	la voisine (fem.)	neighbor
le beau-fils	son-in-law	le fils	son
le beau-frère	brother-in-law	le frère	brother
les beaux-parents	parents-in-law	la grand-mère	grandmother
le beau-père	father-in-law	les grands-parents	grandparents
la belle-fille	daughter-in-law	le grand-père	grandfather
la belle-mère	mother-in-law	maman	mom
la belle-soeur	sister-in-law	le mari	husband
le cousin (masc.)	cousin	la mère	mother
la cousine (fem.)	cousin	le neveu	nephew
l'enfant	child	la nièce	niece
l'épouse (fem.)	spouse (wife)	l'oncle (masc.)	uncle
l'époux (masc.)	spouse (husband)	le père	father
les époux	spouses	la petite-fille	granddaughter
la femme	wife, woman	le petit-fils	grandson
le fiancé (masc.)	fiancé	la soeur	sister
la fiancée (fem.)	fiancée	la tante	aunt

appeler	to call	entendre	to hear
apporter	to bring	envoyer	to send
baigner (se)	to bathe (oneself)	essayer	to try
bricoler	to tinker	faire la table	to set the table
conduire	to drive	habiter	to live in, inhabit
connaître	to know	laver (se laver)	to wash (oneself)
croire	to believe	rester	to stay, to remain
devoir	to have to	savoir	to know
dormir	to sleep	venir	to come
écouter	to listen		

aujourd'hui	today	jeune	young
aussi	also	jolie (fem.)	pretty
célibataire	single	maintenant	now
chez moi	at my home	mon, ma, mes	my
demain	tomorrow	plein (masc.)	full
dès que	as soon as	plus ou moins	more or less
enchanté	pleased (enchanted)	souvent	often
gentil	kind	tôt	early
heureux	happy, glad	vraiment	truly
hier	yesterday		

NOTES:

1. The adjectives *beau* (beautiful), *nouveau* (new), and *vieux* (old) always precede the nouns they modify. They also are irregular. Please note the following examples:

   beau   *un beau garçon,* but *un bel homme* (a handsome man)

   nouveau *un nouveau livre,* but *un nouvel ami* (a new friend, masc.)

   vieux   *un vieux livre,* but *un vieil homme* (an old man)

   These irregular forms occur only in the masculine and only when the nouns start with a vowel or a mute *h*.

2. The feminine forms of the above adjectives are:

   belle   *une belle femme, des belles femmes*

   nouvelle *une nouvelle maison, des nouvelles maisons*

   vieille *une vieille table, des vieilles tables*

3. Note also that *beau* and *belle* used with a hyphen and with members of a family always translate as *in-law,* as in *belle-soeur* (sister-in-law).

4. *Laver* (to wash) + direct object, as in *laver la vaisselle* (to wash the dishes), and *baigner* (to bathe), as in *baigner l'enfant* (to bathe the child). These verbs are also used with *se,* the reflexive pronoun. Thus, *se laver* translates as "to wash oneself," and *se baigner* is "to bathe oneself." We will study these constructions in Chapter 9.

5. *Mon, ma,* and *mes* are possessive adjectives meaning *my. Mon* is used with masculine singular nouns and feminine singular nouns beginning with a vowel, *ma* with feminine singular nouns, and *mes* is used with plural nouns of either gender. We will study these adjectives in chapter 6.

PRACTICE THE VOCABULARY

ANSWERS
p. 60

A. Write *un* or *une* in front of the following nouns, as appropriate.

1. _____ couloir
2. _____ cousine
3. _____ fils
4. _____ père
5. _____ salon
6. _____ douche
7. _____ oncle
8. _____ mère
9. _____ tante
10. _____ balcon
11. _____ machine
12. _____ voisine

ANSWERS
p. 60

B. Complete the following sentences.

1. Le frère de ma mère est mon _____.
2. La sœur de mon père est ma _____.
3. Le mari de ma mère est mon _____.
4. La femme de mon père est ma _____.
5. Les enfants de ma tante sont mes _____.
6. Mes grands-parents sont les _____ de mon _____.
7. Le père de mon mari est mon _____.
8. Le frère de ma femme est mon _____.
9. La fille de ma mère est ma _____.
10. Le fils de mon père est mon _____.
11. Les parents de mon mari sont mes _____.
12. La sœur de ma femme est ma _____.

ANSWERS
p. 60

C. Underline the appropriate words to complete each sentence.

1. La cuisine est dans (le jardin, la salle de bains, la maison).
2. La douche est dans (la chambre, le balcon, la salle de bains).
3. Se baigner est aussi (dormir, appeler, se laver).
4. Les parents aident (l'avion, la cour, les enfants).
5. Ma belle-mère est (la nièce, l'oncle, gentille).
6. Nous apportons (la télévision, le jardin, les fleurs).
7. Nous bricolons dans (le camion, la chambre, la cuisine).
8. Les fauteuils sont (heureux, calmes, chers).
9. Nous passons le weekend (avec des fleurs, avec des amis, avec la lampe).
10. J'admire et j'aime les (couloirs, bijoux, balcons) de ma mère.

11. Le fauteuil et la lampe sont dans (la cuisine, le salon, le bain).

12. Mes beaux-parents sont les parents de (mon oncle, mon frère, mon mari).

D. Translate the following phrases into French and write them in the spaces provided.

1. A handsome man _____.

2. A beautiful woman _____.

3. A new tree _____.

4. An old hotel _____.

5. An old boyfriend _____.

6. My sister-in-law is beautiful _____.

7. My lamp is old _____.

8. My garden is new _____.

9. My parents are kind _____.

10. My husband does the dishes _____.

DIALOGUE La fiancée de Charles

CHARLES:	Demain ma fiancée arrive de Boston.
ANTOINE:	C'est vrai? À quelle heure?
CHARLES:	L'avion atterrit à quatre heures de l'après-midi, plus ou moins.
ANTOINE:	As-tu besoin de ma voiture?
CHARLES:	Non, merci, mes parents vont conduire à l'aéroport. Ma sœur et ma tante vont venir avec nous.
ANTOINE:	Tu m'invites pour faire la connaissance de la jeune fille!
CHARLES:	Bien sûr, cher ami!
	(arrivée à la maison)
CHARLES:	Chérie, voici ta chambre. Elle est à côté de la petite salle de bains.
JULIETTE:	Oh! C'est charmant. Elle donne sur le jardin. Je suis vraiment heureuse d'être ici!
CHARLES:	Et moi aussi, je suis très heureux de t'avoir avec nous.
JULIETTE:	Nous sortons demain?
CHARLES:	Oui, si tu veux. Aussi, mon ami Antoine veut faire ta connaissance.
JULIETTE:	Ah, c'est vrai, tu parles toujours d'Antoine dans tes lettres.
CHARLES:	Tu sais, ma sœur et ma tante veulent aller faire des courses demain. Peut-être que nous pouvons aller ensemble dans la voiture d'Antoine.
MAMAN:	Faites vite, les enfants, Papa rentre tôt aujourd'hui.
CHARLES:	Papa rentre tôt sûrement pour célébrer ta visite.
JULIETTE:	Comme c'est gentil! Maintenant je dois ranger mes affaires et aller à la cuisine pour aider ma future belle-mère à préparer le dîner.
CHARLES:	Ah! Une fiancée parfaite et une belle-fille idéale!

DIALOGUE   Charles's Fiancée

CHARLES: Tomorrow my fiancée arrives from Boston.

ANTOINE: At what time?

CHARLES: The plane lands at four P.M., more or less.

ANTOINE: Do you need my car?

CHARLES: No, thanks, my parents are going to drive to the airport. My sister and my aunt are going to come with us.

ANTOINE: Will you invite me to (make the acquaintance of) meet the young lady?

CHARLES: Of course, dear friend!

(arrival at home)

CHARLES: Darling, here's your room. It's next to the small bathroom.

JULIETTE: Oh! It's charming. It overlooks the garden. I'm truly happy to be here!

CHARLES: And me too, I'm very happy to have you with us.

JULIETTE: Are we going out tomorrow?

CHARLES: Yes, if you like. Also, my friend Antoine wants to meet you.

JULIETTE: Ah! It's true, you're always talking about Antoine in your letters.

CHARLES: You know, my sister and my aunt want to go shopping tomorrow. Maybe we'll all go together in Antoine's car.

MOM: Hurry up, children. Dad is coming home early today.

CHARLES: Dad is surely coming home early to celebrate your visit.

JULIETTE: How nice! Now I have to put away my things and go to the kitchen to help my future mother-in-law prepare dinner.

CHARLES: Ah! A perfect fiancée and an ideal daughter-in-law!

DIALOGUE EXERCISE

**ANSWERS
p. 60**

Match the English with the French.

1. _____ Ma future belle-sœur s'appelle Juliette.

A. I know my future in-laws well.

2. _____ Mes parents aiment ma future femme.

B. My friend is always willing to help.

3. _____ Mon ami veut toujours m'aider.

C. My future sister-in-law's name is Juliette.

4. _____ Je connais bien mes futurs beaux-parents.

D. My parents like my future wife.

5. _____ Ma sœur apprécie mes amis.

E. My girlfriend likes being single.

6. _____ Mémé reste à la maison.

F. My fiancée is happy at my home.

7. _____ Mon ami veut m'accompagner à l'aéroport.

G. My sister appreciates my friends.

8. ____ Ma fiancée est heureuse chez moi.
9. ____ Mon amie aime être célibataire.
10. ____ Je préfère être marié(e).

H. Grandma stays at home.
I. I prefer being married.
J. My friend wants to accompany me to the airport.

GRAMMAR I Present Indicative of Stem-Changing Verbs: *manger, commencer, acheter,* and *payer*

A. Memorize the stem-changing verbs *manger* (to eat), *commencer* (to start), *acheter* (to buy), and *payer* (to pay for).

Subject	*Manger*	*Commencer*	*Acheter*	*Payer*
je	mange	commence	j'achète	paie
tu	manges	commences	achètes	paies
il, elle, on	mange	commence	achète	paie
nous	mangeons	commençons	achetons	payons
vous	mangez	commencez	achetez	payez
ils, elles	mangent	commencent	achètent	paient

B. Please note the following rules:

1. In French, *g* and *c* have the hard sounds of *g* and *k* before *a, o, oi,* and *ou;* and soft sounds of *j(g)* and *s(c)* before *e* and *i*. The consonant *c* has a soft sound when a cedilla is added under the *c,* as in *garçon*.

2. With the verbs *manger, changer,* and others ending in *-ger,* an *e* is added to the *-ons* ending to keep the soft sound throughout the conjugation, as in nous mangeons, nous changeons. The remaining forms follow the regular endings of the *-ER* verbs.

3. With the verbs ending in *-cer,* such as *commencer,* the soft sound is kept throughout the conjugation by adding a cedilla to the *c* of the *-ons* ending, as in *nous commençons*.

4. With a few verbs like *acheter,* the *e* of the stem (*ach*) is not pronounced in the infinitive nor in the *nous achetons* and *vous achetez* forms; but the *e* in all other forms is pronounced, thanks to the *accent grave,* as in *j'achète,* etc.

5. With *payer* and other verbs ending in *-yer,* the *y* of the stem (*pay*) becomes *i* in all forms except with *nous* and *vous,* as in *nous payons, vous payez,* but *je paie, tu paies,* etc.

C. Below is a chart containing some of the verbs that follow the same patterns as these four stem-changing verbs.

Manger	Commencer	Acheter	Payer
changer (de) (to change)	dénoncer (to denounce)	achever (to complete)	employer (to hire, to employ)
engager (to engage; to engage in)	menacer (to threaten)	amener (to bring)	essayer (de) (to try)
juger (to judge)	prononcer (to pronounce)	(se) lever (to rise)	
nager (to swim)	remplacer (to replace)	(se) promener (to take a walk)	
partager (to share)	tracer (to outline)		
voyager (to travel)			

PRACTICE THE STEM-CHANGING VERBS

ANSWERS
pp. 60–61

1. The consonants *g* and *c* are hard-sounding before _____, _____, _____, and _____.

2. The consonants *g* and *c* become soft with _____ and _____.

3. What is added to *c* to change it to an *s* sound before the vowels *o* and *u?* _____

4. The verbs ending in -*ger* remain soft throughout the conjugation thanks to _____.

5. The correct form of the verb *tracer* (to trace) with the pronoun *nous* is _____; name two more verbs requiring the same forms: _____ and _____.

6. The verb *achever* (to complete) is among a small number of verbs that require an *accent grave*. Give all the forms where this occurs: _____, _____, _____, _____.

7. *Essayer* (to try) is among the few verbs that change *y* to *i* (except in the first- and second-person plural). Name two other verbs: _____ and _____.

8. Name the two forms of *employer* (to employ) in which the *y* remains: _____ and _____.

9. Say and write in French: *We pronounce well.* _____.

10. Say and write in French: *We travel a lot.* _____.

EXERCISE

ANSWERS
p. 61

Fill in the blank with the correct form of the following verbs.

1. Nous _____ (to replace) le vieux fauteuil.
2. Tu _____ (to buy) les beaux meubles.
3. Pourquoi _____ -vous (to change) d'hôtel?
4. Vous ne _____ (to pay) pas bien les employés.
5. Nous _____ (to try) d'acheter une maison.
6. Comment _____ -tu (to buy) un avion?
7. Il _____ (to bring) sa sœur.
8. Nous ne _____ (to travel) pas assez.
9. Nous _____ (to pronounce) bien.
10. Nous ne _____ (to judge) pas nos voisins.

GRAMMAR II Present Indicative of *connaître* and *savoir* • The Difference between *connaître* and *savoir*

Memorize the conjugation below.

Subject	*Connaître*	*Savoir*
je	**connais**	**sais**
tu	**connais**	**sais**
il, elle, on	**connaît**	**sait**
nous	**connaissons**	**savons**
vous	**connaissez**	**savez**
ils, elles	**connaissent**	**savent**

NOTES:

1. The verb *connaître* translates as the English "to be familiar with" or "to be acquainted with." *Connaître* is always used with persons, animals, and places:

    EXAMPLE: *Je connais Antoinette.*   I know Antoinette.

    Je connais cette maison. I know this house.

    Elle connaît mon chien. She knows my dog.

    Note that in *connaître*, the *accent circonflexe* (^) on the *i* always appears before a *t* (connaître, connaît).

2. The verb *savoir*, on the other hand, is used to indicate something we know for certain. It never involves human beings, animals, or places:

> EXAMPLE: *Je sais très bien la leçon.*   I know the lesson very well.
>
> *Elle sait mon âge.*   She knows my age.
>
> *Nous savons notre problème.*   We know our problem.

3. *Savoir* followed by an infinitive translates as the English "to know how to" (do something), although the English also uses *can* or *to be able to*.

> EXAMPLE: *Je sais danser.*   I know how to dance. I can dance.
>
> *Savez-vous nager?*   Do you know how to swim? Can you swim?

PRACTICE *CONNAÎTRE* AND *SAVOIR*

ANSWERS p. 61

1. *Connaître* is used with direct objects denoting _____, _____, and _____.
2. *Savoir* is never used with _____, _____, and _____.
3. *Connaître* is the French equivalent of _____ and _____.
4. *Savoir* followed by an infinitive is the French equivalent of _____, _____, and _____.

EXERCISE

ANSWERS p. 61

Complete the following sentences with the correct form of *connaître* or *savoir.*

1. Est-ce que Jacques _____ ses parents?
2. Je _____ que Jacques est gentil.
3. Nous _____ le théâtre Sarah Bernhardt.
4. Vous _____ la question et la réponse.
5. Ils _____ la Maison Blanche.
6. Elle _____ pourquoi le restaurant est plein.
7. Vous _____ mon petit chat.
8. Je _____ que le restaurant ferme *(closes)* à onze heures du soir.
9. Ils _____ ma tante et mon oncle.
10. Je _____ quand l'avion décolle.
11. Il ne _____ pas la réponse.
12. Nous ne _____ pas l'hôtesse.
13. Jeannine et Charles _____ parler français.
14. Je ne _____ pas les voisins.
15. Il ne _____ pas faire du ski.

GRAMMAR III   Negative Constructions

Memorize the negative constructions in the chart below.

ne + verb + jamais	never
ne + verb + plus	no more, no longer
ne + verb + personne	no one
ne + verb + ni . . . ni	neither, nor
ne + verb + que	only
ne + verb + rien	nothing
ne + verb + pas encore	not yet

NOTES:
Note the following facts about the above negations:

1. The most important part of the negation *ne + verb + pas* is the word *pas*. In negatives responses to questions it can stand on its own.

> EXAMPLE: *Voulez-vous du vin?* Do you want some wine?
> Negative answer: *Pas moi, merci.* Not me, thanks.
> Other examples:
> > *pas ici* not here
> > *pas encore* not yet
> > *pas nous* not us
> > *pas elle* not her

2. The negation *ne + verb + pas* is always kept in this order: *ne + verb + pas*. In using the other negative forms, *pas* is replaced by *plus* in *ne + verb + plus*, or *pas* is replaced by *jamais* in *ne + verb + jamais*. Study the following examples:

> EXAMPLE: *Je ne danse pas.*   I don't dance.
> *Je ne danse jamais.*   I never dance.
> *Je ne danse plus.*   I no longer dance.
> *Je ne mange rien à midi.*   I eat nothing at noon.
> *Il ne connaît personne.*   He knows no one.

3. In the negative forms, the indefinite article and the partitive article become *de* and *d'*, except with *ni . . . ni,* where the article and the partitive are not used at all.

> EXAMPLE: *Je n'ai pas d'argent.*   I don't have any money.
> *Je n'ai plus d'argent.*   I have no more money.
> *Je n'ai jamais d'argent.*   I never have any money.
> *Je n'ai ni argent, ni cigarettes.* I have neither money nor cigarettes.
> *Je n'achète ni vin, ni bière.*   I buy neither wine nor beer.

4. The negative interrogative expression *n'est-ce pas* is used as in English—at the end of a sentence, as a confirmation of a suggested fact or statement.

> EXAMPLE: *Vous fumez, n'est-ce pas?*   You smoke, don't you?
> *Il est gentil, n'est-ce pas?*   He's kind, isn't he?
> *Vous êtes français, n'est-ce pas?* You're French, aren't you?

5. *Jamais, rien, personne,* and *pas* may be used without *ne* in answering questions.

> EXAMPLE: *Que cherchez-vous?*   What are you looking for?
> *Rien.*   Nothing.
> *Qui est à la maison?* Who is in the house?
> *Personne.*   No one.

6. *Jamais,* on the other hand, when used in the affirmative without *ne,* translates as *ever,* as in:

> *Peut-il jamais danser.*   Can he ever dance!

7. *Rien* and *personne* can be used as subjects in a sentence, as in:

> Personne *ne* fume.   No one smokes.
> Rien *ne* change.   Nothing changes.

Note that in these constructions *ne* follows immediately after *rien* and *personne.*

PRACTICE THE NEGATIVE CONSTRUCTIONS

ANSWERS
p. 61

1. All the negative forms use a two-word negation. Name the most common one. _____.

2. Which of these two words is more important? _____.

3. Which part of the negation remains constant? _____

4. What happens to the indefinite and partitive articles in negative expressions? _____.

5. What is unusual about the negative construction *ne* + *verb* + *ni* . . . *ni* regarding all articles? _____.

6. What is the English equivalent of *jamais* when used alone in an affirmative sentence? _____.

7. When *rien* and *personne* are used as subjects of a sentence, what happens to *ne?* _____.

8. What is the usual place of *ne* in negative constructions? _____.

9. Name the four negative words that are used without *ne* in answers to questions. _____, _____, _____, _____.

10. Give the French equivalent of: *neither . . . nor* _____.

EXERCISES

ANSWERS
p. 62

A. Match the two columns.

1. ____ Il n'a plus de confiance.
2. ____ Nous ne savons jamais l'heure du départ.
3. ____ Elle ne cherche rien ici.
4. ____ Vous n'allez jamais au balcon.
5. ____ Ils ne connaissent personne ici.
6. ____ Rien n'est facile à faire.
7. ____ Personne n'admire les méchants.
8: ____ Est-il jamais à l'heure?

A. No one admires mean people.
B. He does not have any more confidence.

C. Is he ever on time?
D. She's not looking for anything here.
E. Nothing is easy to do.
F. They don't know anyone here.
G. You never go to the balcony.
H. We never know the time of departure.

ANSWERS
p. 62

Write in French, then say aloud:

1. Not yet _____
2. Not I _____
3. Not you _____
4. Not at the airport _____

5. Not with me _____
6. Not with us _____
7. Not now _____
8. Not tomorrow _____

ANSWERS   LESSONS 1–5

Lesson 1

Basic Expressions

1. Bonjour
2. Je m'appelle . . .
3. Où habitez-vous?
4. Je vais bien, merci
5. En face du cinéma *or* Là-bas à gauche.
6. À gauche
7. À gauche
8. S'il vous plaît
9. See you soon
10. En face de . . .
11. Au revoir and À bientôt
12. See you tomorrow

Vocabulary

1. F	6. D	11. H	16. Q	21. V	26. Z
2. C	7. B	12. J	17. S	22. X	27. Y
3. E	8. I	13. O	18. P	23. W	28. d
4. A	9. K	14. M	19. T	24. U	29. c
5. G	10. L	15. N	20. R	25. b	30. a

Grammar I

Practice

1. le, la, les, l'
2. masculine or feminine
3. le, les
4. le, la, with words starting with a vowel or silent *h*
5. la, la
6. la, les
7. l', l', le
8. la, la, la, l', la

Exercise

1. le	7. la	13. l'
2. le	8. le	14. le
3. la	9. l'	15. la
4. la	10. le	16. l'
5. la	11. la	17. le
6. le	12. l'	18. la

Grammar II

Practice

1. *un, une*
2. masculine
3. feminine
4. masculine
5. nouns referring to males
6. nouns referring to females
7. juxtaposition of two vowels in two consecutive words
8. no
9. masculine or feminine
10. *une*

Exercise

1. une	7. un	13. une
2. un	8. un	14. un
3. un	9. une	15. une
4. un	10. un	16. un
5. un	11. un	17. un
6. un	12. une	18. un

Grammar III

Practice

1. I
2. *tu* (familiar), *vous* (formal sing.), *vous* (pl.)
3. informal situations
4. *vous*
5. *vous*
6. personal (he), impersonal (it)
7. *elle*
8. *elles*
9. Masc. pl./mixed
10. *il fait froid*
11. in impersonal expressions
12. it's warm (hot)

Exercises

A.		
1. vous êtes	6. ils sont	11. ils sont
2. tu es	7. elles sont	12. ils sont
3. je suis	8. il est	13. ils sont
4. nous sommes	9. elle est	14. ils sont
5. vous êtes	10. elles sont	

B.	
1. j'ai	6. ils ont
2. ils ont	7. tu es
3. je suis	8. vous avez
4. elles ont	9. elles sont
5. vous êtes	10. tu as

C.	
1. avez-vous?	6. êtes-vous?
2. a-t-il?	7. sont-ils?
3. est-il?	8. étudiez-vous?
4. avons-nous?	9. ont-elles?
5. sommes-nous?	10. parlons-nous?

Lesson 2

Vocabulary

Practice

A. 1. le   7. le   13. le   B. 1. M   8. C
   2. l'   8. la   14. le   2. N   9. K
   3. le   9. la   15. l'   3. A   10. F
   4. le   10. la   16. la   4. I   11. E
   5. la   11. la   17. la   5. L   12. B
   6. la   12. le   18. le   6. J   13. D
                            7. H   14. G

Dialogue Exercises

A. 1. Jeannine   7. le repas
   2. excellent, délicieuse   8. légumes
   3. Perrier   9. frites
   4. d'agneau   10. pressées
   5. laitue   11. après-midi
   6. à bientôt   12. caissière

B. 1. délicieuse   6. au restaurant
   2. le café   7. travaillent
   3. les légumes   8. de la viande
   4. la caissière   9. un fruit de mer
   5. jardin   10. des légumes

Grammar I

Practice

A. 1. three
   2. *er, ir,* and *re*
   3. Because the stem remains the same throughout the conjugation.
   4. *parl-*
   5. *dans-*
   6. *nous parlons*

B. 1. parlez   6. regardons
   2. commandent   7. j'aime
   3. travaille   8. j'étudie
   4. cherchent   9. pensent
   5. voyagent   10. rentrons

Grammar II

Exercises

A. 1. répond
   2. attend
   3. finissent
   4. réussit
   5. réfléchit
   6. rendons
   7. choisissez
   8. agissent
   9. répondent
   10. vendent

B. 1. Je finis le livre.
   2. Nous parlons français.
   3. Nous cherchons le restaurant.
   4. Elle attend Charles.
   5. Ils, elles aiment le gâteau.

Grammar III

Practice

A. 1. Je ne suis pas . . .
   2. Elle n'a pas . . .
   3. Nous n'avons pas . . .
   4. Ils ne sont pas . . .
   5. Vous n'êtes pas . . .
   6. Vous n'avez pas . . .
   7. Ils ne commandent pas . . .
   8. Charles ne finit pas . . .
   9. Antoinette ne travaille pas . . .
   10. Ils n'attendent pas . . .
   11. Nous ne payons pas . . .
   12. Ils ne finissent pas . . .
   13. Nous ne cherchons pas . . .
   14. Vous ne trouvez pas . . .

Lesson 3

Vocabulary

Practice

A. 1. la
   2. l'
   3. le
   4. les
   5. l'
   6. les
   7. le
   8. le
   9. les

B. 1. les meubles
   2. petit
   3. grands
   4. crédit
   5. prix
   6. l'argent
   7. étroite
   8. la rue

Dialogue Exercises

A. 1. lampe, fauteuil
   2. en haut
   3. chère
   4. rayon des meubles
   5. couleurs
   6. . . . la carte de crédit
   7. . . . la qualité, valeur
   8. lampe, fauteuil
   9. cinq cents francs, cent francs
  10. blanche, rouge

B. 1. C
   2. D
   3. G
   4. E
   5. H
   6. I
   7. B
   8. F
   9. A
  10. J

Grammar I

Exercises

A. 1. noun, shape, quality
   2. *e*
   3. arménienne
   4. français
   5. gentille
   6. vive
   7. joyeuse
   8. sérieuses
   9. joyeux
  10. anglais
  11. complètes
  12. lumineux
  13. heureux
  14. chanteuses
  15. fière

B. 1. les petits chalets
   2. les grandes chambres
   3. les arbres verts
   4. les hommes sportifs
   5. les chiens noirs
   6. les meubles anglais
   7. les étudiants sérieux

Grammar II

Exercises

A. 1. de la
   2. d'
   3. de
   4. du
   5. de
   6. du
   7. de la
   8. des
   9. du
  10. de la

B. Nursery rhyme: Recite it without looking at the words.

C. 1. part of a whole, some, any   5. des
   2. de, du, de la, des, de l'   6. du
   3. no   7. la and l'
   4. pas de . . .

D. 1. G   5. F
   2. H   6. A
   3. E   7. B
   4. D   8. C

Grammar III

Exercises

A. 1. va   6. allez
   2. vont   7. Quand allez-vous? (or) Quand vas-tu?
   3. vont   8. vais
   4. allons   9. allons
   5. vas   10. vont pas

B. 1. C
   2. J
   3. F
   4. I
   5. H
   6. B
   7. D
   8. E
   9. A
   10. G

Lesson 4

Vocabulary

Practice

A. 1. douane   6. attachons
   2. aide   7. les bagages
   3. fumons   8. polie
   4. billets   9. court
   5. décolle   10. le haut-parleur

B. 1. lourds   4. à l'heure
   2. polie   5. les bagages
   3. les ceintures 6. à l'aéroport

Dialogue Exercises

A. 1. F   6. H
   2. D   7. J.
   3. B   8. E
   4. A   9. C
   5. G   10. I

B. 1. l'aéroport, acheter, aller et retour
   2. au café
   3. . . . de deux billets
   4. 620
   5. à la porte numéro douze (12)
   6. les cartes d'embarquement
   7. pour obtenir les cartes
   8. Parce que dans quelque heures ils vont atterrir.
   9. à Paris
  10. pour non-fumeurs
  11. Attention, attention! Vol 620, embarquement immédiat.

Grammar I

Exercises

A. 1. Oui, il fait chaud.
   2. Oui, elles font du ski.
   3. Oui, je fais des courses.
   4. Oui, il fait du soleil.
   5. Oui, il fait beau.
   6. Oui, il fait mauvais.
   7. Oui, il fait froid.
   8. Oui, il fait du vent.
   9. Oui, je fais la vaisselle.
  10. Oui, elles font du sport.
  11. Oui, je fais une promenade.
  12. Oui, elle fait le ménage.

B. 1. Je fais du ski.
   2. Elle fait des courses.
   3. Il fait de la musique.
   4. Ils, elles font le ménage.
   5. Il fait beau.
   6. Je vais faire du ski.
   7. Nous faisons une promenade.
   8. Elle fait la cuisine.
   9. Ils, elles font du français.
  10. Nous faisons la vaisselle.

Grammar II

Exercises

A. 1. Il est une heure trente. (or any time you wish)
   2. Il est une heure quinze (and) il est une heure et quart.
   3. Il est une heure trente (and) il est une heure et demie.
   4. moins
   5. du matin

6. de l'après-midi (and) du soir
7. environ, vers
8. pile
9. Quelle heure est-il?
10. moins le quart

B. 1. Il est quatre heures vingt de l'après-midi.
2. Il est dix heures dix du matin.
3. Il est neuf heures quinze du soir.
4. Il est deux heures cinq du matin.
5. Il est six heures et demie du soir.
6. Il est huit heures et quart du matin.
7. Il est sept heures huit du soir.
8. Il est trois heures cinq de l'après-midi.
9. Il est une heure dix du matin.
10. Il est deux heures de l'après-midi, pile.

C. 1. In 21, vingt et un, in 31, trente et un, in 41, quarante et un, in 51, cinquante et un, and in 61, soixante et un
2. After *soixante-dix* and *quatre-vingt-dix, onze, douze,* etc. are used.
3. quatre-vingt-un
4. quatre-vingt-un
   quatre-vingt-onze
   quatre-vingt-dix-sept
   soixante-quinze
   soixante et un
   soixante et onze

Grammar III

Exercises

A. 1. Ils veulent les livres.
2. Il veut manger.
3. Nous voulons comprendre.
4. Voulez-vous voyager?
5. Vous voulez aider.
6. Le douanier veut les bagages.
7. Elle veut fumer.
8. Vous voulez finir la leçon.
9. Nous voulons parler français.
10. Ils, elles veulent faire escale à Paris.

B. 1. peut
2. peuvent
3. peut
4. peut
5. peuvent
6. peuvent
7. peut
8. pouvez
9. pouvons
10. peuvent

Lesson 5

Vocabulary

Practice

A. 1. un
   2. une
   3. un
   4. un
   5. une
   6. une
   7. un
   8. une
   9. une
   10. un
   11. une
   12. une

B. 1. oncle
   2. tante
   3. père
   4. mère
   5. cousins
   6. parents, père
   7. beau-père
   8. beau-frère
   9. sœur
   10. frère
   11. beaux-parents
   12. belle-sœur

C. 1. la maison
   2. la salle de bains
   3. se laver
   4. les enfants
   5. gentille
   6. les fleurs
   7. la cuisine
   8. chers
   9. avec des amis
   10. bijoux
   11. le salon
   12. mon mari

D. 1. un bel homme
   2. une belle femme
   3. un nouvel arbre
   4. un vieil hôtel
   5. un vieil ami
   6. Ma belle-soeur est belle.
   7. Ma lampe est vieille.
   8. Mon jardin est nouveau.
   9. Mes parents sont gentils.
   10. Mon mari fait la vaisselle.

Dialogue Exercise

1. C
2. D
3. B
4. A
5. G
6. H
7. J
8. F
9. E
10. I

Grammar I

Practice

1. *a, o, oi,* and *ou*
2. *e* and *i*

3. a cedilla
4. the vowel *e*
5. nous traçons, nous plaçons, nous commençons
6. j'achève, tu achèves, il, elle achève, ils, elles achèvent
7. payer, employer
8. nous employons, vous employez
9. Nous prononçons bien.
10. Nous voyageons beaucoup.

Exercise

1. remplaçons
2. achètes
3. changez
4. payez
5. essayons
6. achètes
7. amène
8. voyageons
9. prononçons
10. jugeons

Grammar II

Practice

1. people, places, animals
2. people, places, animals
3. to be acquainted with, to be familiar with
4. to know how to do, to be able to, can

Exercise

1. connaît
2. sais
3. connaissons
4. savez
5. connaissent
6. sait
7. connaissez
8. sais
9. connaissent
10. sais
11. sait
12. connaissons
13. savent
14. connais
15. sait

Grammar III

Practice

1. ne . . . pas
2. pas
3. ne
4. they become *de* and *d'*
5. no articles and no partitives are used
6. ever
7. *ne* follows immediately after *rien* or *personne*
8. after the subject and before the verb
9. jamais, rien, personne, pas
10. ne . . . ni . . . ni . . .

Exercises

A. 1. B
   2. H
   3. D
   4. G

5. F
6. E
7. A
8. C

B. 1. Pas encore.
   2. Pas moi.
   3. Pas vous.
   4. Pas à l'aéroport.

5. Pas avec moi.
6. Pas avec nous.
7. Pas maintenant.
8. Pas demain.

REVIEW EXAM   LESSONS 1–5

COMPREHENSION: VOCABULARY

Read the following text aloud, once, to get a general idea, then a second time for detailed understanding.

Juliette et Charles sont de bons amis; ils sont aussi des voisins. Aujourd'hui ils décident d'aller faire des courses ensemble (together). Juliette a besoin d'acheter une robe pour le mariage de sa sœur, et Charles veut une lampe pour sa salle de séjour. Après les courses, Charles a faim et demande à Juliette de l'accompagner au restaurant. Juliette n'a pas faim mais elle accepte l'invitation de Charles. Au restaurant Charles commande une bière et un plat de fruits de mer; Juliette, une glace et un morceau (piece) de gâteau au chocolat. Les deux amis commencent à parler de leurs (their) familles. Charles pense que son père travaille beaucoup, mais n'a jamais le temps de partir en vacances. Juliette refuse de croire que sa sœur va devenir l'épouse du Docteur Godard, le grand médecin (doctor) de la ville. Charles et Juliette finissent le repas et retournent à la maison à quatre heures moins le quart, satisfaits de leurs achats et de leur après-midi ensemble.

ANSWERS p. 66

In French, answer the following questions based on the text. Answer in complete sentences.

1. Qui sont Juliette et Charles? _____.
2. Que décident-ils de faire? _____.
3. Quand vont-ils faire des achats? _____.
4. Est-ce que Juliette et Charles sont célibataires? _____.
5. Que veut acheter Juliette? _____.
6. Que pense Charles de son père? _____.
7. Le Docteur Godard est-il le futur beau-frère de Juliette? _____.
8. Qui est le Docteur Godard? _____.
9. Que commande Juliette au restaurant? _____.
10. Pourquoi Charles commande-t-il un repas? _____.
11. Que font Charles et Juliette après le repas? _____.
12. À quelle heure retournent-ils à la maison? _____.

NOTE:
Whenever a question begins with *pourquoi* (why?), the response begins with *parce que* (because).

EXAMPLE: Pourquoi Charles commande-t-il un repas?

Parce qu'il a faim.

GRAMMAR EXERCISES

**ANSWERS
p. 66**

A. Complete the sentences with the correct form of the present indicative

1. Pourquoi _____ (to have)-tu les billets?
2. Les enfants ne _____ (to be) pas à la maison.
3. Ils _____ (wish, want) acheter des fauteuils.
4. Mémé ne _____ (never + can, be able to) distinguer les couleurs.
5. Quand l'avion _____ (land)?
6. Nous ne _____ (to know) pas la ville.
7. Elles n' _____ (to buy) rien.
8. Vous n' _____ (to like) plus les cigarettes.
9. Le douanier ne _____ (to know) pas mon adresse.
10. Est-ce que le capitaine _____ (is looking for) l'hôtesse?
11. Nous _____ (to share) le repas avec nos voisins.
12. Après le repas nous _____ (to pay) la caissière.
13. Le vol de Paris à New York _____ (to start) bien.
14. À quelle heure _____ (to eat) -vous?
15. Pourquoi _____ (to finish) -ils tard?
16. Comment _____ (to go) les petites-filles?
17. Nous _____ (to buy) toujours du vin blanc.
18. Que _____ (to wish) -ils commander?
19. Aujourd'hui ma sœur _____ (to do) la vaisselle.
20. Mon frère n' _____ (to be) jamais en retard.

**ANSWERS
p. 66**

B. Write the appropriate indefinite article before each noun.

1. _____ avion
2. _____ maison
3. _____ billet
4. _____ valise
5. _____ langouste
6. _____ flan
7. _____ glace
8. _____ attitude
9. _____ ferveur
10. _____ gigot
11. _____ métro
12. _____ lampe
13. _____ valeur
14. _____ miroir
15. _____ robe
16. _____ meuble
17. _____ chose
18. _____ couloir
19. _____ choix
20. _____ époux

**ANSWERS
p. 66**

C. Complete the following sentences with the appropriate adjective.

1. Ma belle-sœur est _____ (beautiful).
2. Ma grand-mère est _____ (old).
3. Le restaurant est _____ (near, next to) de l'aéroport.

4. Ils sont toujours _____ (kind).
5. Le rayon des meubles est _____ (big).
6. L'hôtesse est _____ (ready) à aider les passagers.
7. Le douanier n'est pas _____ (polite).
8. Mémé est _____ (happy) d'habiter chez nous.
9. Ma sœur est _____ (sociable).
10. Les femmes sont toujours _____ (curious).
11. Les hommes sont souvent _____ (serious).

ANSWERS   REVIEW EXAM

Lessons 1–5

Comprehension

1. Ils sont de bons amis.
2. Ils décident d'aller faire des courses.
3. Ils vont faire des achats aujourd'hui.
4. Oui, ils sont célibataires.
5. Juliette veut acheter une robe.
6. Il pense que son père travaille beaucoup.
7. Le docteur Godard est le futur beau-frère de Juliette.
8. Le docteur Godard est le grand médecin de la ville.
9. Juliette commande une glace et un morceau de gâteau.
10. Parce qu'il a faim.
11. Ils parlent de leurs familles.
12. Ils retournent à quatre heures moins le quart.

Grammar

A.
1. as		11. partageons
2. sont		12. payons
3. veulent		13. commence
4. peut jamais		14. mangez
5. atterrit-il		15. finissent
6. connaissons		16. vont
7. achètent		17. achetons
8. aimez		18. veulent-ils
9. connaît		19. fait
10. cherche		20. est

B.
1. un	8. une	15. une
2. une	9. une	16. un
3. un	10. un	17. une
4. une	11. un	18. un
5. un	12. une	19. un
6. un	13. une	20. un
7. une	14. un	

C.
1. belle	7. poli
2. vieille	8. heureuse
3. à côté	9. sociable
4. gentils	10. curieuses
5. grand	11. sérieux
6. prête	

6 À l'hôtel
(At the Hotel)

l'armoire (fem.)	wardrobe (furniture)	le mer	sea
l'ascenseur (masc.)	elevator	la montagne	mountain
la bibliothèque	library	l'oreiller (masc.)	pillow
la chambre	room	le paysage	scenery
la clef	key	la plage	beach
la commode	dresser	le prix	price
la couverture	blanket	le propriétaire	owner
le drap (de lit)	sheet	la réception	front desk
l'eau (fem.)	water	le rez-de-	ground floor
l'évasion (fem.)	escape	chaussée	
la femme	maid	le savon	soap
de chambre		la serviette	towel
le lavabo	washbasin	le soleil	sun
le lit	bed	la taie d'oreiller	pillowcase
le lit à une place	single bed	le tapis	rug
les loisirs (masc.)	activities	le trésor	treasure
le loyer	rent	les vêtements (masc.)	clothing
le matelas	mattress		
avertir	to notify	dire	to say
s'amuser	to have fun	dormir	to sleep
composer	to compose, to dial	quitter	to leave, to quit
devenir	to become	taquiner	to tease
à part	separate	meublé(e)	furnished
autrement dit	in other words	nuageux (-se)	cloudy
bruyant(-e)	noisy	par hasard	by chance
disponible	available	prochain(e)	next
mauvais(e)	mean, bad		

67

PRACTICE THE VOCABULARY

A. Write in the appropriate word.

ANSWERS
p. 123

1. Le paysage est _____ (armoire, nuageux, beau).
2. Elle _____ (arrange, compose, choisit) le numéro de téléphone.
3. Nous aimons les _____ (montagnes, savons, loisirs).
4. La chambre n'est pas _____ (loisirs, loyer, disponible).
5. Le propriétaire est vraiment _____ (chambre, lavabo, aimable).
6. L'armoire est à côté de _____ (la chance, l'ascenseur, la commode).
7. Nous cherchons la _____ (lit, plage, clef).
8. Les voisins ne sont pas _____ (tapageurs, disponibles, meubles).

B. Match the two columns.

ANSWERS
p. 123

1. Nous désirons une chambre _____.   A. étroite
2. Mon époux veut _____ au tennis.   B. avertir
3. Nous aimons beaucoup les _____ de l'hôtel. C. quitte
4. Nous devons (have to) _____ le propriétaire aujourd'hui.   D. l'ascenseur
5. La chambre est _____ et petite.   E. quelle chance!
6. Nous voulons passer deux jours à _____.   F. mauvais
7. La femme de chambre _____ l'hôtel.   G. loisirs
8. Nous prenons _____ pour le sixième.   H. jouer
9. L'hôtel est près de la plage, _____ !   I. à part
10. Il ne fait jamais _____ temps ici.   J. la plage

DIALOGUE   À l'Hôtel Rivoli

Jacques et Odette sont devant la réception de l'Hôtel Rivoli à Nice.

JACQUES: Bonjour, Madame, ma fiancée et moi avons besoin d'une chambre à deux lits.

LA CONCIERGE: Très bien, Monsieur, j'ai une très belle chambre qui donne sur la plage.

ODETTE: Oh! C'est magnifique! J'adore la mer.

LA CONCIERGE: Laissez vos valises ici et suivez moi.

JACQUES: D'accord. Cet hôtel est vraiment beau. Combien de chambres a-t-il?

LA CONCIERGE: Dans ce quartier les hôtels n'ont pas plus de cinquante chambres. Le nôtre a trente-huit chambres.

JACQUES: Oh! la chambre a l'air d'être parfaite pour nous!

ODETTE: Oui, tu as raison, c'est une chambre magnifique. Regarde ce lit et cette commode-là, et ces grandes fenêtres!

JACQUES: Nous la prenons. Vous avez la clef?

LA CONCIERGE: Oui, voici deux clefs. Celle-ci est pour la chambre et celle-là est pour l'armoire. On ne sait jamais, surtout si vous avez des bijoux.

JACQUES: Nous avons quatre jours à Nice, et nous voulons tout visiter.

LA CONCIERGE: Pas de problème. Dans cette ville tout est près de tout; vous pouvez traverser toute la ville en quinze minutes.

JACQUES: C'est parfait. Je vais manger à tous les restaurants!

ODETTE: Et moi, je vais faire toutes les boutiques, et le marché aux puces! Autrement dit, pendant que toi, tu prends du poids, moi je vais faire de l'exercice.

JACQUES: Oui, c'est vrai. Mais à la fin de la journée, moi je vais être heureux et satisfait, alors que toi tu vas être fatiguée et affamée.

LA CONCIERGE: Bon, je vous laisse à vos amours, mes pigeons. Amusez-vous bien!

JACQUES: Merci, Madame. Au revoir!

DIALOGUE   At the Rivoli Hotel

Jacques and Odette are at the front desk of the Rivoli Hotel in Nice.

JACQUES: Good morning, ma'am. My fiancée and I need a room with two beds.

THE CONCIERGE: Very good, sir, I have a very beautiful room overlooking the beach.

ODETTE: Oh! That's wonderful (magnificent)! I adore the sea.

THE CONCIERGE: Leave your suitcases here and follow me.

JACQUES: All right. This hotel is truly beautiful. How many rooms does it have?

THE CONCIERGE: In this section (of town) the hotels don't have more than fifty rooms. Ours has thirty-eight rooms.

JACQUES: Oh! This room looks like it is perfect for us!

ODETTE: Yes, you are right, it's a magnificent room. Look at this bed and that dresser, and those big windows!

JACQUES: We are taking it. Do you have the key?

THE CONCIERGE: Yes, here are two keys. This one is for the room and that one is for the wardrobe. One never knows, especially if you have jewels.

JACQUES: We have four days in Nice, and we want to visit everything.

THE CARETAKER: No problem. In this town, everything is near everything else; you can cross the whole city in fifteen minutes.

JACQUES: That's perfect. I am going to eat at all the restaurants!

ODETTE: And I will do all the little shops, and the flea market! In other words, while you're gaining weight, I'll exercise!

JACQUES: That's true. But at the end of the day, I'm going to be happy and satisfied, while you are going to be tired and hungry.

THE CARETAKER: Well, I leave you with your sweet talk, my lovebirds. Have a good time!

JACQUES: Thank you, Madam. Good-bye!

DIALOGUE EXERCISES

ANSWERS p. 123

A. Answer the questions in complete sentences, based on the dialogue.

Example: Qui est Odette? *Odette est la fiancée de Jacques.*

1. Où sont Jacques et Odette? _____.
2. À qui parle Jacques à la réception? _____.
3. Dans quelle ville est l'Hôtel Rivoli? _____.
4. Que veulent Jacques et Odette? _____.
5. Qui est Odette? _____.
6. Comment Jacques trouve-t-il la chambre? _____.
7. Sur quoi donne la chambre? _____.

ANSWERS p. 123

B. Complete the sentences with the appropriate word or words.

1. Jacques aime la chambre parce qu'elle est _____ (grande, belle, parfaite).
2. La concierge taquine Jacques et Odette parce qu'ils sont_____ (américains, amis, sarcastiques).
3. L'Hôtel Rivoli est magnifique parce qu'il _____ (est petit, est beau, donne sur la plage).
4. Odette a besoin d'une clef pour protéger ses _____ (meubles, robes, bijoux).
5. Jacques va être _____ (méchant, gentil, heureux) et Odette va être _____ (heureuse, pressée, affamée).

GRAMMAR I   Idiomatic Expressions with *avoir*

A. Most of the ideas expressed in English by *to be* are translated by *avoir* in French. Below are some of the most commonly used expressions:

avoir besoin de	to be in need of (to need)
avoir chaud	to be hot
avoir de la chance	to be lucky
avoir envie de	to feel like
avoir faim	to be hungry
avoir froid	to be cold

avoir l'air de	to look like
avoir l'intention de	to intend to
avoir peur de	to be afraid of
avoir raison	to be right
avoir sommeil	to be sleepy
avoir tort	to be wrong

B. Some verbs in French are followed directly by an infinitive, as in *il aime manger* (he likes to eat), *il veut danser* (he wants to dance).

C. However, many other verbs require either *de* or *à* before the infinitive. In expressions like *avoir besoin de* and *avoir peur de*, *de* is always used before a noun or a verb.

> EXAMPLE: *J'ai besoin de mon stylo.* I need my pen.
>
> *J'ai besoin de travailler.* I need to work.

The same is true with the verbs that require the preposition *à* before the infinitive.

> EXAMPLE: *Je commence à comprendre.* I am beginning to understand.

Verbs that require *à* or *de* before infinitives are always designated with these prepositions in dictionaries. There are no set rules to determine which preposition is correct.

GRAMMAR II Verbs Used with *à* and *de*

The following chart lists the most commonly used verbs in the three verb categories:

1. Verbs using a direct infinitive.

2. Verbs using the preposition *de*.

3. Verbs using the preposition *à*.

Verbs + Infinitive		Verbs + *de* + Infinitive		Verbs + *à* + Infinitive	
aimer	to like, to love	**accepter de**	to accept	**aider à**	to help
aller	to go	**cesser de**	to stop	**apprendre à**	to learn
détester	to dislike	**conseiller de**	to advise	**commencer à**	to begin
devoir	to have to	**décider de**	to decide	**encourager à**	to encourage
espérer	to hope	**essayer de**	to try	**inviter à**	to invite
oser	to dare	**demander de**	to ask	**hésiter à**	to hesitate
pouvoir	to be able to	**oublier de**	to forget	**réussir à**	to succeed
préférer	to prefer	**regretter de**	to regret	**tenir à**	to be eager, to insist
vouloir	to wish, to want	**suggérer de**	to suggest		

Notes:

1. The verbs *conseiller de*, *demander de*, and *suggérer de* require *à* before a person and *de* before an infinitive.

> EXAMPLE: *Je conseille à Jacques de partir.* I advise Jacques to leave.

> So we have: verb + *à* + person + *de* + infinitive.

2. Other verbs following this pattern include: *dire* + *à* + person + *de* + infinitive.

> EXAMPLE: *Je dis à Odette de sortir.* I tell Odette to go out.

> *demander* + *à* + person + *de* + infinitive
> *défendre* + *à* + person + *de* + infinitive
> *ordonner* + *à* + person + *de* + infinitive

> EXAMPLE: *Il demande à Marie de danser.*   He asks Marie to dance.
> *Il défend à Marie de danser.*   He forbids Marie to dance.
> *Il ordonne à Marie de danser.*   He orders Marie to dance.

PRACTICE

ANSWERS
p. 123

A. Practice the expressions with *avoir* and the three verb categories.

1. The verb *avoir* translates as _____ in many English expressions.
2. Name two French verbs with a direct infinitive: _____ et _____.
3. *Avoir peur de* and *avoir envie de* always use *de* with _____ and _____.
4. What is the best way to be sure that a verb takes *à* or *de*? _____.
5. There are three categories of verbs using infinitives: _____, _____, and _____.
6. Some of the verbs requiring *de* also require *à*. Which verbs are these? _____, _____, _____, _____, and _____.
7. Are there any set rules for the use of prepositions in these verb categories? _____.

ANSWERS
p. 123

B. Write the following expressions in French, then say them aloud.

1. "We are hungry today." _____.
2. "Odette is afraid of Jacques." _____.
3. "I feel like dancing." _____.
4. "The concierge seems nice." _____.
5. "I am thirsty when I am here." _____.
6. "I need to go shopping." _____.
7. "I intend to succeed." _____.
8. "We are lucky to be here." _____.

GRAMMAR III   Demonstrative Adjectives and Pronouns

A. The demonstrative adjectives are *ce, cette, ces,* and *cet* (used with masculine nouns beginning with a vowel or mute *h*). Memorize the following chart of demonstrative adjectives.

Distance	Masculine	Feminine	Plural	English
Not indicated	ce garçon	cette fille	ces (garçons, filles)	this boy, this girl; these (boys, girls)
Near speaker	ce garçon-ci	cette fille-ci	ces garçons-ci, ces filles-ci	this boy, this girl; these boys, these girls
Far speaker	ce garçon-là	cette fille-là	ces garçons-là, ces filles-là	that boy, that girl, those boys, those girls

1. Demonstrative adjectives precede the nouns they modify and agree with them in number and gender. Demonstrative adjectives translate as the English *this, that, these,* and *those* and are used to designate a specific place, idea, object, or person.

    EXAMPLE: *J'aime ce livre parce qu'il est intéressant.*

    Il aime cette ville parce qu'elle est belle.

    Nous aimons cette solution parce qu'elle est parfaite.

    Vous aimez cette femme parce qu'elle est intelligente.

2. Remember how French avoids the "hiatus" by adding a *t* in *a-t-il?* With demonstrative adjectives, *ce* becomes *cet* before any masculine noun starting with a vowel or a silent *h.*

    EXAMPLE: *cet homme* this, that man

    cet arbre this, that tree

    cet escargot this, that snail

3. Distance to the speaker is conveyed in French by adding a hyphen and *-ci* to express closeness to the speaker and distance from the listener; a hyphen and *là,* as in *-là,* express distance from the speaker and closeness to the listener.

    EXAMPLE: *cette table-ci* this table (close to me)

    cette table-là that table (far from me)

B. The demonstrative pronouns are *celui, celle, ceux,* and *celles.* Memorize the following chart of demonstrative pronouns.

Distance	Masculine	Feminine	Plural	English
Not indicated	celui	celle	ceux (masc.)	this one, these ones
Near speaker	celui-ci	celle-ci	ceux-ci (masc.), celles-ci (fem.)	this one, these ones
Far speaker	celui-là	celle-là	ceux-là (masc.), celles-là (fem.)	that one, those ones

1. Demonstrative pronouns refer to something or someone previously mentioned. Demonstrative pronouns translate as the English "this one," "that one," "the one," and their plurals. Demonstrative pronouns agree in number and gender with the nouns they replace.

> EXAMPLE: *J'ai deux clefs, celle qui ouvre* (opens) *l'armoire et celle qui ouvre la chambre.*
>
> I have two keys, the one that opens the wardrobe and the one that opens the room.

2. Closeness and distance are expressed in the same way as with demonstrative adjectives: a hyphen and *-ci (celui-ci)* for closeness and a hyphen and *-là (celui-là)* for distance.

> EXAMPLE: *Celle-ci est pour l'armoire, celle-là est pour la chambre.*
>
> This one is for the wardrobe and that one is for the room.

3. There are three demonstrative pronouns that do not follow any of the preceding rules and that show neither gender nor number. They refer to indefinite things or ideas, and they are: *ceci* (this), *cela* (that), and *ça* (abbreviation of *cela,* and more commonly used).

> EXAMPLE: *Ça ne fait rien = Cela ne fait rien.*
>
> That does not matter.

4. Demonstrative pronouns do not stand by themselves; they need one or the other of the following:

a. A suffix *-ci* or *-là,* as in *J'ai deux clefs, mais je n'ai besoin ni de celle-ci, ni de celle-là.* (I have two keys, but I need neither this one nor that one.)

b. A relative clause, as in *Nous avons besoin de beaucoup de vendeuses* (salesladies), *celles qui travaillent la nuit et celles qui travaillent le jour.* (We need many salesladies, those who work at night and those who work during the day.)

PRACTICE THE DEMONSTRATIVE ADJECTIVES

ANSWERS
pp. 123–124

A. Rewrite the following sentences using the demonstrative adjectives: *ce, cet, cette,* and *ces.*

> *Example:* L'homme est intéressant. *Cet homme est intéressant.*

1. L'avion est immense. _____.
2. Les repas sont délicieux. _____.
3. J'aime la maison. _____.
4. J'achète des escargots. _____.
5. L'armoire n'est pas grande. _____.
6. La fille à la robe verte est ma voisine. _____.
7. Les croissants sont bien chauds. _____.
8. Le lit et le matelas sont neufs. _____.

B. Following the model given, write a full sentence using the same question, *voulez-vous* (do you want), but with the appropriate demonstrative adjective.

Example: Voulez-vous ce livre-ci ou celui-là? (Do you want this book or that book?)

1. Une salade. _____ ou _____

2. Un arbre. _____ ou _____

3. Une taie d'oreiller. _____ ou _____

4. Un lavabo. _____ ou _____

5. Des escargots. _____ ou _____

6. Un gâteau. _____ ou _____

7. Un fauteuil. _____ ou _____

8. Une commode. _____ ou _____

9. Une pizza. _____ ou _____

10. Des bijoux. _____ ou _____

C. Match the two columns.

1. _____ Ça va toujours bien ici.

2. _____ Ce monsieur est mon frère.

3. _____ Je préfère ce poisson-ci à celui-là.

4. _____ Ceci n'est pas à propos.

5. _____ De ces deux films, celui que j'aime est long.

6. _____ Mes enfants sont ceux qui parlent.

7. _____ Que voulez-vous? Cette lampe-ci ou celle-là?

8. _____ Ils ne pensent ni à ceci ni à cela.

9. _____ Ce livre est long, mais celui que je veux est court.

10. _____ Cette pizza-là est délicieuse, mais celle que je mange n'a pas de goût.

A. This book is long, but the one I want is short.

B. Which do you want? This lamp or that one?

C. They think neither of this nor of that.

D. That pizza is delicious, but the one I'm eating has no taste.

E. It's always nice here (goes well).

F. This gentleman is my brother.

G. I prefer this fish to that one.

H. Of these two movies, the one I like is long.

I. This is not the subject (purpose).

J. My children are the ones who are speaking.

7 Une fête d'anniversaire
(A Birthday Party)

les amuse-gueules (masc.)	appetizers	juillet (masc.)	July
l'anniversaire (masc.)	birthday	lundi (masc.)	Monday
		mardi (masc.)	Tuesday
le bavardage	gossip, chatting	le matin	morning
le dimanche	Sunday	le mélange	mix
la fête	party	à la mode	fashionable
le frigo	fridge	le passe-temps	pastimes
le fromage	cheese	le progrès	progress
les glaçons (masc.)	ice cubes	le régime	diet
		les renseignements (masc.)	information
la grève	strike	le rythme	rhythm
l'honneur (masc.)	honor	le sentiment	feeling
		le visage	face
la joie	joy	la voiture	car
		la volonté	will

bavarder	to chat	ressembler	to look like
deviner	to guess	rêver	to dream
fêter	to celebrate	rire	to laugh
gagner	to win, earn	terminer	to end
manquer	to miss, to lack	unir	to unite
remercier	to thank	vouloir bien	to be willing

bavard(e)	talkative	**quelque chose**	something
décontracté(e)	relaxed	**qui**	who, that, which (subject)
dehors	outside		
drôle	funny	**salut!**	hi!
encore	again	**sauvage**	wild
fragile	fragile	**semblable**	similar
occupé(e)	busy	**triste**	sad
passionnant(e)	exciting	**vive!**	long live!
prochain(e)	next	**voyant(e)**	fortune teller
que	whom, which, that (object)	**zut!**	darn it!

PRACTICE THE VOCABULARY

ANSWERS p. 124

Choose the appropriate word to complete the sentences.

1. Lundi matin ma sœur _____ (va, unit, fête) son anniversaire.
2. Les amis arrivent dans une petite _____ (renseignement, régime, voiture).
3. Avant la fête, ma sœur _____ (attend, mange, décore) la maison.
4. La musique et la danse sont des _____ (boisson, trésor, passe-temps).
5. Quand je compose ton numéro de téléphone, la ligne (line) est toujours _____ (complète, passée, occupée).
6. Mardi _____ (meuble, nuageux, prochain) je fête mon anniversaire.
7. Quand les travailleurs ne sont pas satisfaits, ils _____ (font des courses, font le ménage, font la grève).
8. Les invités sont sophistiqués, ils ne sont pas _____ (semblables, passionnants, sauvages).
9. On mange les _____ (fruits, glaces, amuse-gueules) avant les repas.
10. Le contraire de joyeux est _____ (heure, triste, gentil).
11. Say "long live" la musique. _____.
12. La voyante devine _____ (les glaçons, la musique, le futur).
13. Say "darn it" in French. _____.
14. La réception donne les _____ (tables, fruits, renseignements).

DIALOGUE   Juliette a dix-huit ans!

ROBERT: Allô? Pierre?

PIERRE: Bonjour, Robert. Quoi de neuf?

ROBERT: Quelque chose de spécial. Je t'invite à l'anniversaire de ma sœur Juliette.

PIERRE: Je te remercie. J'accepte si je suis disponible. C'est quand?

ROBERT: La fête est fixée pour samedi prochain, le douze mars, à quatre heures de l'après-midi.

PIERRE: J'accepte avec grand plaisir, parce que je ne travaille plus le samedi. Veux-tu que j'apporte quelque chose?

ROBERT: Oui. Attends une minute, je cherche ton nom sur la liste. Voilà. Toi, tu apportes des ballons et des glaçons.

PIERRE: D'accord. À samedi prochain alors?

ROBERT: Attends une minute. Tu sais qu'on va danser et que Jacqueline, ta voisine, va jouer de la guitare, et plus tard, la voyante Madame Soleil va deviner notre futur.

PIERRE: Ceci a l'air d'une grande fête. Peut-on danser avec Madame Soleil?

ROBERT: Bien sûr. C'est un anniversaire spécial, dix-huit ans. C'est l'âge officiel de la majorité où tout est permis!

PIERRE: Écoute, je n'ai pas le temps de faire de la philosophie. Si jamais je ne viens pas, demande à Madame Soleil de deviner la cause de mon absence!

ROBERT: Arrête le sarcasme! Au revoir, Pierre!

DIALOGUE   Juliette Is Eighteen Years Old!

ROBERT: Hello, Pierre?

PIERRE: Good morning, Robert. What's new?

ROBERT: Something special. I'm inviting you to my sister Juliette's birthday.

PIERRE: I thank you. I accept, if I'm available. When is it?

ROBERT: The party is scheduled for Saturday, March twelfth, at four P.M.

PIERRE: I accept with great pleasure, because I no longer work on Saturdays. Do you want me to bring anything?

ROBERT: Yes. Wait a minute, I'm looking for your name on the list. Here it is. You're bringing balloons and ice cubes.

PIERRE: See you next Saturday, then?

ROBERT: Wait a minute. You know, we're going to dance, and Jacqueline, your neighbor, is going to play the guitar, and later the fortune teller, Madame Soleil, is going to guess our future.

PIERRE: This sounds like a big party! May we dance with Madame Soleil?

ROBERT: Of course. Eighteen is a special birthday. It's the official age of majority, where everything is permissible.

PIERRE: Listen, I don't have time to talk philosophy. If I do not come, ask Madame Soleil to guess the reason for my absence!

ROBERT: Stop the sarcasm! Goodbye, Pierre!

NOTES:

1. *Quoi de neuf?* is always "What's new?" It never changes regardless of what comes before or after.

2. *Faire de la philosophie, faire de la psychologie, faire de la morale,* etc. These expressions with *faire* have a sarcastic implication, meaning the *doer* is not

knowledgeable enough in the subject, so *faire de la philosophie* would translate as *to play at talking philosophy*. You can construct your own expressions with this implication (to play at) any time the subject warrants it.

3. The present participles *passionnant* and *voyant* follow the same rules as adjectives.

> EXAMPLE: *Un livre passionnant.*
>
> *Une musique passionnante.*

These participles can also be used as nouns if they are preceded by articles.

> EXAMPLE: *Un voyant* fortune teller (male)
>
> *Une voyante* fortune teller (female)

4. Note that when *le* precedes a day of the week it is translated as *every*, as in: *le lundi* (every Monday), *le dimanche* (every Sunday). French always uses the articles *le, la, les,* and *l'* before the times of the day, to express *in the*.

> EXAMPLE: *Le matin je lis le journal.* I read the paper in the morning.
>
> *L'après-midi je fais la sieste.* I take a nap in the afternoon.
>
> *Le soir je téléphone à mes amis.* I telephone my friends in the evening.

5. *Le matin, l'après midi,* etc., can be placed either at the beginning of a sentence or at the end.

DIALOGUE EXERCISES

A. Answer the following questions with complete sentences, based on the dialog.

1. Comment Robert commence-t-il la conversation au téléphone? _____.
2. Comment Pierre répond-il? _____.
3. Pourquoi Robert téléphone-t-il à Pierre? _____.
4. Est-ce que Pierre accepte l'invitation tout de suite? _____.
5. Pourquoi Pierre accepte-t-il l'invitation? _____.
6. Que doit apporter Pierre? _____.
7. Qui va jouer de la guitare? _____.
8. Qui va lire le futur? _____.
9. Quelle est la date de la fête? _____.
10. Quel est l'âge officiel de la majorité? _____.
11. Est-ce que la question d'âge est importante? _____.
12. Qui veut danser avec Madame Soleil? _____.
13. Pourquoi cette fête d'anniversaire est-elle spéciale? _____.
14. Que doit deviner Madame Soleil? _____.

ANSWERS
p. 124

B. In studying the new vocabulary and the dialogue you will find many words that derive from words familiar to you from previous chapters. Try to find the verbs that derive from the following nouns.

> EXAMPLE: le sentiment—*sentir*
>
> le mélange—*mélanger*

1. la décoration. _____
2. la fête. _____
3. l'occupation. _____
4. le bavardage. _____
5. le progrès. _____
6. l'union. _____
7. la volonté. _____
8. le rêve. _____
9. l'invitation. _____
10. l'organisation. _____

GRAMMAR I   Possessive Adjectives

The chart below lists the possessive adjectives corresponding to the subject pronouns, *je, tu,* etc.

Subject Pronouns	Masculine Singular	Feminine Singular	Plural	English
je	mon	ma	mes	my
tu	ton	ta	tes	your
il, elle, on	son	sa	ses	his, her, its
nous	notre	notre	nos	our
vous	votre	votre	vos	your
ils, elles	leur	leur	leurs	their

NOTES:

1. The possessive adjectives in French agree with not only the possessor, but also with the nouns they modify—with the thing possessed.

   > EXAMPLE: *ma soeur* my sister
   > *mes soeurs* my sisters
   > *mon frère* my brother
   > *mes frères* my brothers

2. The possessive adjectives *mon, ton,* and *son* are masculine. However, when a noun starts with a vowel or a silent *h,* French uses the above adjectives with feminine nouns as well.

   > EXAMPLE: *mon ami* my friend (boy)
   > *mon amie* my friend (girl)
   > *mon auto* my automobile (fem.)
   > *ton histoire* your story (fem.)

3. Notice that *mes, tes, ses, nos, vos,* and *leurs* plural forms are the same for both masculine plural and feminine plural.

    EXAMPLE: *mes soeurs* my sisters (fem.)
                      mes frères my brothers (masc.)

PRACTICE THE POSSESSIVE ADJECTIVES

Complete the sentences with the appropriate possessive adjective.

    Example: Je cherche *mon* (my) stylo.

1. Où est _____ (your) maison?
2. J'organise _____ (our) livres.
3. Nous achetons _____ (his) automobile.
4. Tu ne finis jamais _____ (your) histoire.
5. _____ (My) grand-mère est passionnante.
6. _____ (My) parents sont sévères.
7. _____ (Their) maison est loin d'ici.
8. Vous aimez _____ (your) voisins.
9. Ils veulent garder _____ (their) argent.
10. Nous aimons bien _____ (our) chiens.

EXERCISES

A. Replace each subject with *il* or *elle* and each definite article with a possessive adjective, *son, sa,* or *ses.*

    Example: Marie aime le chat. *Elle aime son chat.*

1. Juliette décore la maison. _____.
2. Robert téléphone à l'ami. _____.
3. Les enfants attendent la mère. _____.
4. Pierre cherche la voiture. _____.
5. La dame veut l'argent. _____.
6. La mère adore les enfants. _____.
7. La femme change les armoires de place. _____.
8. Le chat mange les biscuits. _____.
9. Madame vend les bijoux. _____.
10. Pierre apporte les ballons. _____.

ANSWERS
p. 125

B. Answer the following questions using the appropriate possessive adjective.

> *Example:* Est-ce que c'est l'argent de Jean? *Oui, c'est son argent.*

1. Est-ce que c'est le chien du voisin? _____.
2. Est-ce que ce sont les amis de Jacques? _____.
3. Est-ce que ce sont les fauteuils de Charles? _____.
4. Est-ce que c'est l'amie de Juliette? _____.
5. Est-ce que c'est le cousin de Pierre? _____.
6. Est-ce que ce sont les sœurs de Renée? _____.
7. Est-ce que c'est le mari de la voisine? _____.
8. Est-ce que ce sont les employés des voisins? _____.
9. Est-ce que c'est le chat des amis? _____.
10. Est-ce que c'est l'armoire des parents? _____.

GRAMMAR II   Possessive Pronouns

Study the chart of the possessive pronouns.

Masculine Singular	Feminine Singular	Masculine Plural	Feminine Plural	English
le mien	la mienne	les miens	les miennes	mine
le tien	la tienne	les tiens	les tiennes	yours (*tu* form)
le sien	la sienne	les siens	les siennes	his, hers, its
le nôtre	la nôtre	les nôtres	les nôtres	ours
le vôtre	la vôtre	les vôtres	les vôtres	yours
le leur	la leur	les leurs	les leurs	theirs

NOTES:

1. In English and French, a possessive pronoun replaces a noun modified by a possessive adjective.

> EXAMPLE: *C'est mon livre. C'est le mien.*
>
> It's my book. It's mine.

However, French always uses the definite article, *le, la,* and *les,* with possessive pronouns.

2. In French, possessive pronouns agree in number and gender with the nouns they replace, and not with the possessor as they do in English.

> EXAMPLE: *L'argent de Paul—son argent—le sien.*
>
> *La sœur de Pierre—sa sœur—la sienne.*
>
> *Les bagages des voisins—leurs* (adjective) *bagages—les leurs* (pronouns)

3. Be sure to check the gender of the replaced word before replacing it with a possessive pronoun. It is advisable to base your possessive pronouns on the possessive adjectives, as demonstrated in the above examples. Study the following:

> *Le frère de Jacques—son frère—le sien*
>
> *ton livre—le tien*
>
> *notre maison—la nôtre*

4. Notice the *accent circonflexe* (^) on the o's of *le nôtre, les nôtres, le vôtre,* and *les vôtres.*

5. Be sure to remember the definite article contractions of *de + le = du, de + les = des.* They also apply to *de + mes = des miens, de + tes = des tiens,* and to *de + ton = du tien, etc.*

> EXAMPLE: *le stylo de mon frère* becomes *le stylo du mien*

This rule applies only when *de* is used before the possessive adjective and when you want to replace it with a possessive pronoun.

PRACTICE THE POSSESSIVE PRONOUNS

ANSWERS
p. 126

A. Replace the phrases in italics with the appropriate possessive pronouns. Pay close attention to the gender and number of the nouns.

> *Example:* Ce sont *mes enfants. Ce sont les miens.*

1. Ce sont *tes bagages.* _____.
2. C'est *ta guitare?* _____.
3. Voici *mes billets.* _____.
4. Pourquoi fumez-vous *leurs cigarettes?* _____.
5. Avez-vous *vos bijoux?* _____.
6. Nous avons *nos valises.* _____.
7. Elles cherchent *leurs chambres.* _____.
8. Ce sont *ses amis.* _____.
9. Ce n'est pas *son argent.* _____.
10. Ce ne sont pas *tes sœurs.* _____.
11. Tu as *son adresse.* _____.
12. Cherches-tu *ton hôtel?* _____.
13. Où sont *leurs journaux?* _____.
14. Veux-tu raconter *ton histoire?* _____.
15. Nous ne trouvons pas *notre armoire.* _____.
16. Pourquoi cherchez-vous *votre clef?* _____.
17. Ils ont peur de *leurs parents.* _____.
18. Tu invites *ses amies.* _____.
19. Ta maison est à côté de *mon hôtel.* _____.
20. Nous avons peur de *vos chiens.* _____.

ANSWERS
p. 126

B. Complete the following sentences with the appropriate possessive pronouns in French.

1. Nous achetons nos billets mais pas (yours) _____.
2. Ils trouvent leur chambre mais pas (yours) _____.
3. Tu manges ton repas mais pas (mine) _____.
4. Il arrange son armoire mais pas (hers) _____.
5. Elle décore notre maison mais pas (theirs) _____.
6. Elle aide son frère mais pas (ours) _____.
7. Elle termine ses études (studies) mais pas (mine) _____.
8. Il aime son chat mais pas (ours) _____.
9. Vous inspectez leurs valises mais pas (ours) _____.
10. Vous fumez ses cigarettes mais pas (yours) _____.

GRAMMAR III   Direct Object Nouns and Pronouns

A. Direct object nouns answer the question "what?" or "whom?" In the sentence "Jacques finds the key," *key* is a direct object.

B. A direct object pronoun replaces a direct object noun, as in "Jacques finds *the key*," "Jacques finds *it*." Direct object pronouns replace designated persons, places, objects, or occurrences.

   EXAMPLE: *Je trouve l'adresse. Je la trouve.*

C. All the direct object nouns are preceded by the definite articles *le, la, les, l'*.

   EXAMPLE: Je cherche *le livre*. Je *le* cherche.

D. Direct object nouns can also be used with a demonstrative adjective, or a possessive adjective or proper nouns. Study the following examples:

   Je trouve ma mère. Je la trouve.

   Je cherche cette adresse. Je la cherche.

   J'aime Robert. Je l'aime.

E. It is important to note that in French, as in English, nouns preceded by an indefinite article (*un, une, des*) or a partitive article (*de la, du, des, d'*) *cannot* be replaced with direct pronouns.

F. In French, direct object pronouns are often placed before the verb, and they agree in number and gender with the words they replace.

   EXAMPLE: *Je cherche la clef. Je la cherche.*

   Je cherche les clefs. Je les cherche.

G. The following chart lists the direct pronouns:

Masculine & Feminine		Masculine & Feminine	
Singular	English	Plural	English
me (m')	me	**nous**	us
te (t')	you	**vous**	you
le (l')	him, it	**les**	them
la (l')	her, it		

H. The following examples refer to the chart above:

EXAMPLE: Robert *me* cherche.   (Robert is looking for *me*.)

La concierge *te* demande.   (The concierge is asking for *you*.)

Robert *la* cherche (clef).   (Robert is looking for *it*. [key])

Ses parents *l'*aiment.   (Her parents like *her, him*.)

Il *nous* invite.   (He invites *us*.)

Elle *vous* invite.   (She invites *you*.)

Ils *les* invitent.   (They invite *them*.)

I. Notice how *me, te, le,* and *la* lose their last vowel when they precede a word starting with another vowel.

EXAMPLE: *Ils l'aiment.*   They like *her, him*.

Ils l'honorent.   They honor *her, him*.

PRACTICE THE DIRECT NOUNS AND PRONOUNS

Replace the italicized noun with the appropriate direct object pronoun. Answer in complete sentences.

1. Jacques adore *Josette*. _____.
2. Le propriétaire appelle *le garçon*. _____.
3. Je regarde *le paysage*. _____.
4. Il achète *les glaçons*. _____.
5. Jacques n'a pas *l'argent*. _____.
6. Vous refusez *les conseils* (advice). _____.
7. Nous organisons *nos armoires*. _____.
8. Veux-tu manger *cette viande?* _____.
9. Tu fêtes *ton anniversaire* demain. _____.
10. Ils aiment bien *la publicité*. _____.

11. Elle achète *mes livres.* _____.

12. Je décore *ta maison.* _____.

13. Je loue *l'appartement.* _____.

14. J'invite *vos amis.* _____.

NOTE:

Memorize the following idiomatic expressions that use the direct object pronouns:

me voici	here I am
te voilà	there you are (tu)
la voilà	there she is
le voilà	there he is
les voilà	there they are
nous voilà	there we are
vous voilà	there you are

GRAMMAR IV   The Imperative Form of *être* and *avoir*, and General Rules for Other Verbs

A. The imperative form is used to command, instruct, and give direction. In French, there are three ways in which to command or give instructions:

1. The *tu* form: *mange* eat

2. The *nous* form: *mangeons* let's eat

3. The *vous* form: *mangez* eat

B. The *tu* form is the familiar form we learned in other conjugations. The *nous* form includes the speaker.

C. The imperative uses the same verb forms as those used with *tu, vous,* and *nous,* but without the subject pronoun. Thus, in the case of a regular verb of the *-ER* group like *parler,* the imperative will be:

(*tu*) *parle* (note the *s* from the second person is dropped)

(*nous*) *parlons*

(*vous*) *parlez*

All regular verb conjugations follow this pattern: Remove *tu, vous,* and *nous* from the present indicative of a conjugated verb, and you get the imperative. Let's take the verb *finir:*

finis (tu) finish

finissons (nous) let's finish

finissez (vous) finish

D. The same rule applies with the irregular verbs we have studied. Thus, *aller* will be:

> *va (tu)* go
>
> *allons (nous)* let's go
>
> *allez (vous)* go
>
> *mange (tu)* eat

Note that the *s* of *tu manges* and of *tu vas* is dropped in the imperative form.

E. The verbs *être* and *avoir* have irregular imperative forms. These forms are based on the present subjunctive (which we will study later).

F. Memorize the chart below.

Être	To Be	*Avoir*	To Have
sois (tu)	be	**aie** (tu)	have
soyons (nous)	let's be	**ayons** (nous)	let's have
soyez (vous)	be	**ayez** (vous)	have

G. Study the examples using the imperative forms of *être* and *avoir*:

> *sois aimable*   be pleasant
>
> *soyons aimables*   let's be pleasant
>
> *soyez aimable(s)*   be pleasant
>
> *aie du courage*   have courage
>
> *ayons du courage*   let's have courage
>
> *ayez du courage*   have courage

H. The imperative form in the negative follows the same rule as the present indicative: *subject + ne + verb + pas*

Since the subject is dropped in the imperative we have: *ne + verb + pas,* as in:

> *ne parle pas*   don't speak
>
> *ne fumons pas*   let's not smoke
>
> *ne soyons pas méchant(e)s*   let's not be mean

PRACTICE THE IMPERATIVE

A. Rewrite the following sentences in the imperative form.

1. Nous cherchons Jeanette. _____.
2. Vous ne fumez jamais. _____.
3. Tu es gentille avec moi. _____.
4. Nous avons beaucoup d'argent. _____.
5. Tu n'as pas peur. _____.

6. Vous n'êtes pas triste. _____.

7. Vous faites vos courses le matin. _____.

8. Tu ne vas pas au cinéma aujourd'hui. _____.

9. Vous me racontez une histoire. _____.

10. Vous attendez votre père. _____.

11. Nous choisissons le fauteuil rouge. _____.

12. Tu fais le ménage le lundi. _____.

ANSWERS
p. 126

B. **All the verbs in this exercise are in the infinitive form. Rewrite the sentences in the imperative according to the example:**

   Example: (nous) marcher vite. *Marchons vite.*

1. (tu) être patient. _____.

2. (nous) attendre l'avion. _____.

3. (vous) acheter les meubles. _____.

4. (tu) aller à la plage. _____.

5. (vous) ne pas regarder la télévision. _____.

6. (vous) ne pas faire la sieste. _____.

7. (nous) avoir de la chance maintenant. _____.

8. (vous) ne pas jouer au football. _____.

9. (tu) finir la conversation. _____.

10. (tu) faire attention. _____.

8 L'épicerie du coin
(The Corner Grocery Store)

l'agneau (masc.)	lamb	les haricots verts (masc.)	green beans
l'ail (masc.)	garlic	l'huile (fem.)	oil
l'assiette (fem.)	dish, plate	le jus d'orange	orange juice
le beurre	butter	le lait	milk
le biftek	steak	le marchand	storekeeper
le bœuf	beef	l'œuf (masc.)	egg
la bouteille	bottle	l'oignon (masc.)	onion
le client	customer	le pain	bread
la dinde	turkey	les petits pois (masc.)	(fresh) peas
l'eau minérale (fem.)	mineral water	la poire	pear
les épices (fem.)	spices	le poivre	pepper
la farine	flour	le sel	salt
les fraises (fem.)	strawberries	le sucre	sugar
le gérant	manager		

aiguiser	to sharpen	plaisanter	to joke
s'arrêter	to stop (oneself)	rendre la monnaie	to give back change
bouillir	to boil	servir	to serve
cuire	to cook	supprimer	to suppress
fréquenter	to patronize	tromper	to cheat
gérer	to manage	vendre	to sell
livrer	to deliver	vérifier	to verify, to check
perdre son temps	to waste time	voler	to steal, to fly

à votre service	you're welcome	**souvent**	often
creux, creuse	deep, hollow	**utile**	useful
râpé (masc.)	grated	**vendeur (masc.),**	salesclerk
soudainement	suddenly	**vendeuse (fem.)**	
sous	under, below		

NOTES:

1. In France, the corner grocery store (l'épicerie) and the bakery (la boulangerie) are still the main grocery shopping sites for French homemakers. Both stores are usually located within walking distance of the residential areas and are always crowded before the lunch and dinner hours. Even with supermarkets slowly taking over, the épicerie is still a favorite place to joke with the "épicier," to meet regulars, and to shop in an atmosphere of conviviality.

2. The verb *prendre* is a very useful verb and, as we have seen with *aller* and *faire,* lends itself to several constructions. Study the following:

prendre son temps	to take time (when used sarcastically, it means "taking one's own sweet time!")
prendre un verre	to have a drink
prendre soin de	to take care of
prendre la correspondance	to transfer (airplane, bus, subway)
prendre la retraite	to retire
prendre le soleil	to sunbathe

PRACTICE THE VOCABULARY

ANSWERS p. 127

A. Write the article *le, la, les, l'* as appropriate.

1. _____ sel
2. _____ client
3. _____ eau
4. _____ dinde

5. _____ sucre
6. _____ petits pois
7. _____ pain
8. _____ farine
9. _____ cliente

10. _____ vendeur
11. _____ maison
12. _____ beurre
13. _____ gérante
14. _____ commerçants

ANSWERS p. 127

B. Translate into French:

1. Children are having fun at the grocery store. _____.
2. The storekeeper and the salesclerk work for the manager. _____.
3. When I go to the supermarket, I like to take my time. _____.
4. To make a cake, I need oil, eggs, flour, and sugar. _____.
5. The salesclerk gives me back the change. _____.
6. I often patronize the corner grocery store. _____.
7. My sister can't boil water!_____.
8. When I'm thirsty, I like to have a drink with friends. _____.

DIALOGUE   À l'épicerie du coin

L'ÉPICIER: Bonjour, Madame Simon. Qu'est-ce qu'on désire aujourd'hui?

MADAME SIMON: Un peu de tout. J'ai des invités ce soir. J'ai besoin d'un joli rôti d'agneau, mais alors quelque chose d'extra.

L'ÉPICIER: Chez nous, Madame Simon, tout ce que vous voyez est extra, inclus le vendeur!

MADAME SIMON: Vous avez toujours le cœur à rire, Monsieur. Cela fait plaisir. Bon, j'ai besoin d'un kilo de haricots verts, d'une livre de fromage râpé, et d'une livre de ces belles fraises.

L'ÉPICIER: Je viens de les recevoir. Ces fraises-là sentent encore l'odeur des champs. Tenez, sentez l'arôme.

MADAME SIMON: Vous m'avez toujours dit que c'est mon parfum qui vous redonne votre sens de l'humour. Vous voyez, vous m'avez menti, c'est l'arôme de vos fraises qui vous a mis de bonne humeur. Ah! les hommes sont tous pareils.

L'ÉPICIER   Madame Simon, c'est votre parfum qui a aiguisé mon sens olfactif, et c'est à cause de votre parfum que j'ai pu sentir l'arôme délicat des fraises!

MADAME SIMON: D'accord. Je vous pardonne cette fois-ci. Écoutez, ne me faites pas oublier le sucre et un pot de crème fraîche.

L'ÉPICIER: Je m'excuse, Madame Simon, mais je n'ai pas reçu de crème fraîche. Je l'ai commandée hier, et je n'ai pas encore eu de livraison.

MADAME SIMON: Je ne peux pas perdre de temps alors. Servez-moi vite, s'il vous plaît. Je dois courir à la laiterie.

L'ÉPICIER: Voilà, Mme Simon, c'est deux cent dix francs au total.

MADAME SIMON: Voici trois cents francs.

L'ÉPICIER: Je vous rends quatre-vingt-dix francs de monnaie. Merci, et surtout amusez-vous bien ce soir.

MADAME SIMON: Avec tout le travail à faire? Vous plaisantez! Mes invités sont de Boston, et demain ils veulent voir le Grand Louvre, et surtout la fameuse pyramide.

L'ÉPICIER: Dans ce cas, amusez-vous bien demain aussi.

MADAME SIMON: Merci beaucoup, monsieur, vous êtes si gentil.

DIALOGUE   At the Corner Grocery Store

STOREKEEPER: Good morning, Mrs. Simon. What would we like today?

MRS. SIMON: A little of everything. I'm having guests this evening. I need a pretty lamb roast, but then something special.

STOREKEEPER: At our place, Mrs. Simon, everything you see is special, including the salesman!

MRS. SIMON: You're always happy. That's a pleasure. Well, I need one kilo of green beans, one pound of grated cheese, and one pound of these beautiful strawberries.

STOREKEEPER: I just received them. These strawberries still smell like the fields. Here, smell the aroma.

MRS. SIMON: You've always told me that it is my perfume that gives you back your sense of humor. You see, you lied to me, it's the aroma of your strawberries that puts you in a good mood. Ah! men, they're all alike.

STOREKEEPER: Mrs. Simon, it's your perfume that sharpened my olfactory sense, and it's because of your perfume that I could smell the delicate aroma of the strawberries.

MRS. SIMON: O.K. I forgive you, this time. Listen, don't let me forget sugar and a jar of fresh cream.

STOREKEEPER: I'm sorry, Mrs. Simon, but I have not received any fresh cream. I ordered it yesterday, and I have not yet had a delivery.

MRS. SIMON: I can't waste any time then. Please help me quickly, as I must run to the dairy.

STOREKEEPER: Here, Mrs. Simon, it is a total of two hundred and ten francs.

MRS. SIMON: Here are three hundred.

STOREKEEPER: I'm going to give you back ninety francs in change. Thank you, and have a good time this evening.

MRS. SIMON: With all the work I have to do? You must be joking! My guests are from Boston, and tomorrow they want to see the Grand Louvre, and especially the famous pyramid.

STOREKEEPER: In that case, have a good time tomorrow, too.

MRS. SIMON: Thank you so much, sir, you are so kind!

NOTES:

être de bonne humeur	to be in a good mood
être de mauvaise humeur	to be in a bad mood
avoir le sens de l'humour	to have a good sense of humor
ne pas avoir le sens de l'humour	to have a bad sense of humor (to be without a sense of humor)

The above constructions should be added to your repertoire of expressions with *être* and *avoir.*

CULTURAL NOTE:

When André Malraux was minister of culture in 1960, he decreed that all historic sites and neighborhoods be renovated every fourteen years. In keeping with this tradition, France has seen an extraordinary renovation and expansion of its most cherished museums and monuments, as well as its once-famous commercial and residential quarters.

In the last fifteen years, one of the most ambitious and magnificent renovations was that of the Musée du Louvre, which began in 1981. A controversial and impressive part of this immense effort was the addition of the gigantic pyramid, complete with mini-waterfalls and mesmerizing plays of glittering lights on glass. The renovated wings of the museum did not open to the public until December 21, 1997. "Le Grand Louvre," as the area is now called, has become a minicity with cafés, shops, lounges, and other services open to the public.

DIALOGUE EXERCISES

ANSWERS p. 127

A. Answer the questions with complete sentences, based on the dialogue.

1. Pourquoi Madame Simon fait-elle le marché? _____.
2. Que veut acheter Madame Simon? _____.
3. Comment elle décrit (describes) le rôti d'agneau? _____.
4. Qu'est-ce que Madame Simon ne trouve pas à l'épicerie? _____.
5. Où va Madame Simon après l'épicerie? Pourquoi? _____.
6. Que dit l'épicier au sujet des fraises? _____.
7. Pourquoi Madame Simon pense-t-elle que l'épicier a menti? _____.
8. Qu'est-ce que l'épicier dit au sujet du parfum de Madame Simon? _____.
9. Est-ce que l'épicier plaisante avec Madame Simon? _____.
10. Croyez-vous (do you believe) que Madame Simon fréquente souvent l'épicerie? Pourquoi? _____.

ANSWERS p. 127

B. Match the sentences based on the vocabulary and the dialogue.

1. On a toujours besoin de faire le marché.
2. Les clients et le gérant comptent la monnaie.
3. L'oignon, l'ail, le sel, et le poivre sont des épices.
4. L'épicier est amusant mais il n'a pas une bonne mémoire (memory).
5. La dame est vaine et le monsieur est comme tous les hommes.

A. Onion, garlic, salt, and pepper are spices.
B. The woman is vain and the man is like all men.
C. One always needs to go shopping.
D. The customers and the manager count the change.
E. The grocer is funny, but he does not have a good memory.

GRAMMAR I   *Passé composé* of Regular and Irregular Verbs with *avoir*

A. Study the *passé composée* of *parler,* as shown in the chart below.

Subject	Avoir +	Parler	To Speak
j'(e)	**ai**	parlé	I spoke, have spoken, did speak
tu	**as**	parlé	you spoke, have spoken, did speak
il, elle, on	**a**	parlé	he, she, it, one, spoke (etc.)
nous	**avons**	parlé	we spoke (etc.)
vous	**avez**	parlé	you spoke (etc.)
ils, elles	**ont**	parlé	they spoke (etc.)

B. In French, as in English, there are several ways to express the past. The *passé composé,* the compound past, is the most commonly used past tense in French. The *passé composé* translates as several forms of the past tense in English.

> EXAMPLE: *J'ai parlé* means "I spoke," "I have spoken," and "I did speak."

The *passé composé* is called that because it is "composed" of the main verb and another verb used as an auxiliary. This auxiliary may be either *être* or *avoir,* depending on the main verb. The *passé composé* is obtained by conjugating the verb *être* or *avoir* and adding the past participle of the verb you wish to use. The past participles of the regular verbs in *-er, -ir,* and *-re* are as follows:

1. With regular verbs in *-er* and *-ir,* the *r* is dropped from the infinitive and an acute accent is added to the *e* of the *-er* verbs.

> EXAMPLE: *parler + avoir = j'ai parlé*
>
> *finir + avoir = j'ai fini*

2. With regular verbs in *-re,* the *-re* is dropped and replaced with *u.*

> EXAMPLE: *rendre + avoir = j'ai rendu*

C. Many verbs require irregular past participles. Listed here are the past participles of some verbs that you have learned:

avoir	*j'ai eu*	*pouvoir*	*j'ai pu*
boire	*j'ai bu*	*savoir*	*j'ai su*
croire	*j'ai cru*	*voir*	*j'ai vu*
lire	*j'ai lu*	*vouloir*	*j'ai voulu*

D. The above examples are of irregular verbs used with the auxiliary *avoir.* Most French verbs in the *passé composé* are formed with *avoir.* However, there are some verbs that require the auxiliary *être.* Those verbs are discussed below.

GRAMMAR II   *Passé composé* of Regular and Irregular Verbs with *être*

A. Study the chart below.

Subject	*Être*	*Partir*	To Leave
je	suis	**parti(e)**	I left, have left, did leave
tu	es	**parti(e)**	you left, have left, did leave
il, elle, on	est	**parti(e)**	he, she, it, one left, has left, did leave
nous	sommes	**parti(e)s**	we left, have left, did leave
vous	êtes	**parti(e)s**	you left, have left, did leave
ils, elles	sont	**parti(e)s**	they left, have left, did leave

B. There are two important facts to remember about the French verbs that require *être* in the *passé composé:*

1. They are usually verbs of movement and motion:

   EXAMPLE: *partir, monter, descendre, passer,* etc.

2. Their past participles *always* agree in number and gender with the subject.

   EXAMPLE: *le garçon est parti*   the boy left

   la fille est partie   the girl left

   ils sont partis   they left (masc.)

   elles sont parties   they left (fem.)

C. Below are additional verbs that require *être* in the *passé composé.*

aller   *je suis allé(e)*

arriver   *elle est arrivée*

partir   *ils sont partis*

sortir   *elles sont sorties*

entrer   *il est entré*

venir   *elle est venue*

D. Note that the past participles used with *être* and regular verbs are formed in the same manner as those using *avoir* with regular verbs ending in *-er, -ir,* and *-re.*

EXAMPLE:

j'ai parlé   *(parler + avoir)*

je suis arrivé(e)   *(arriver + être)*

j'ai fini   *(finir + avoir)*

je suis sorti(e)   *(sortir + être)*

j'ai rendu   *(rendre + avoir)*

je suis descendu(e)   *(descendre + être)*

E. Some irregular verbs that we have learned have the following past participles with *être*:

venir	*je suis venu(e)*
devenir (to become)	*je suis devenu(e)*
tenir (to hold)	*je suis tenu(e)*

F. The verbs below form their past participles with *-it*:

écrire	*j'ai écrit*	I wrote, have written, did write
décrire	*j'ai décrit*	I described (etc.)
faire	*j'ai fait*	I did (etc.)
dire	*j'ai dit*	I said (etc.)

G. The following verbs form their past participles with *-is*:

apprendre	*j'ai appris*
mettre (to put, to wear)	*j'ai mis*
comprendre	*j'ai compris*

H. Please note *especially* the following:

    1. The past participle of *être* is "j'ai été."

    2. Negation affects *only* the auxiliary verb.

        EXAMPLE: *J'ai parlé.*   *Je n'ai pas parlé.*

                        Je suis sorti(e).   *Je ne suis pas sorti(e).*

PRACTICE THE *PASSÉ COMPOSÉ* WITH *AVOIR*

A. Rewrite, in the *passé composé*, the following sentences using the auxiliary *avoir*.

    1. J'achète mes meubles au grand magasin. _____.

    2. L'arôme des fraises parfume la cuisine. _____.

    3. Charles voyage avec sa fiancée. _____.

    4. Le douanier peut nous aider. _____.

    5. Nous choisissons la lampe rouge. _____.

    6. La vendeuse nous rend la monnaie. _____.

    7. Juliette veut organiser un pique-nique (picnic). _____.

ANSWERS pp. 127–128

8. Vous avez soif quand il fait chaud. _____.

9. Qu'est ce que Jacques fait quand il boit? _____.

10. Pourquoi Juliette est-elle triste? _____.

ANSWERS
p. 128

B. Rewrite, in the *passé composé*, the following sentences, using the auxiliary *être*.

1. Mes parents reviennent (come back) du restaurant. _____.

2. Il va à New York et elle arrive à Boston. _____.

3. Nous montons au cinquième étage. _____.

4. Vous devenez (devenir) ma belle-soeur. _____.

5. Elle sort avec son mari. _____.

6. Juliette arrive pour l'anniversaire de son frère. _____.

7. Elles restent avec leur tante. _____.

8. Les feuilles (leaves) tombent de l'arbre. _____.

ANSWERS
p. 128

C. Write the following sentences in French, using the *passé composé* with *avoir* and *être*, then say them aloud.

1. I came to see you before leaving. _____.

2. I had money, but I spent it. _____.

3. I have been invited to dinner. _____.

4. You came down to have a drink. _____.

5. I wanted a jar of fresh cream. _____.

6. They left without saying "thank you." _____.

7. We did not lose our keys. _____.

8. They did not drink any wine. _____.

9. He came back with flowers. _____.

10. She liked the music. _____.

GRAMMAR III   Idiomatic Expressions with *avoir, falloir, and valoir*

A. Study the chart listing the impersonal expressions of *avoir* (to have), *falloir* (to require), and *valoir* (to be worth).

Avoir	English	Falloir	English	Valoir	English
il y a	there is	il faut	one must	il vaut	it is worth
il y a	there are	il ne faut pas	one must not	il ne vaut pas	it is not worth
il n'y a pas	there is not, there are not				

B. *Il y a* and *il n'y a pas* are usually followed by nouns with indefinite articles.

> EXAMPLE: *Il y a des fruits dans le frigo.*   There is fruit in the fridge.
>
> *Il y a du vin sur la table.*   There is wine on the table.

Il y a remains the same whether it is used with singular, plural, masculine, or feminine nouns.

C. *Il y a* is always conjugated as the third-person singular of the verb *avoir*. Thus, the passé composé of *il y a* is *Il y a eu.* (There has been.)

> EXAMPLE: *Il y a eu des fraises.*   There have been strawberries.
>
> *Il n'y a pas eu de fraises.*   There have not been any strawberries.
>
> *Il y a eu du vin.*   There has been some wine.
>
> *Il n'y a pas eu de vin.*   There has not been any wine.

D. When we study other tenses of *avoir*, the expression *il y a* will be discussed with the third-person singular of those tenses.

E. When the expression *il faut* is used with infinitives, it translates as the English "It is necessary to."

> EXAMPLE: *Il faut être patient.*   It is necessary to be patient. (One must be patient.)
>
> *Il faut prendre l'avion.*   One must take the plane.

The impersonal pronoun *il* may also be translated *we* or *they*, depending on the context.

> EXAMPLE: *Nous sommes en retard, il faut courir.*
>
> We're late, we must run.

Even when *il faut* is used in the negative form, *il ne faut pas,* the expression still strongly implies the necessity *not to do something.*

> EXAMPLE: *Il ne faut pas fumer.* One must not smoke.

F. *Il vaut* is always used with a qualifying word or phrase such as *la peine de*. Thus we have two idiomatic expressions, one using *mieux* and the other using *la peine*. As long as one adds the qualifying words, many useful expressions can be formed by adding the infinitive.

> EXAMPLE: *Il vaut mieux partir.*   It's better to leave.
>
> *Ça vaut la peine.*   It's worth the trouble.
>
> *Ça vaut la peine d'étudier le français.* It's worth the trouble to study French.

The negative of the above expression is: *Ça ne vaut pas la peine* + infinitive.

> EXAMPLE: *Ça ne vaut pas la peine de rester.* It is not worth the trouble to stay.

G. The impersonal constructions *il faut* and *il vaut* are the third-person singular of *falloir* and *valoir,* and as with *il y a,* they will always be conjugated in the third-person singular in other tenses. Thus, in the passé composé we have:

il a fallu   it was necessary

il a valu   it was worth (it)

When we learn other tenses, the expressions *il faut* and *il vaut* will be pointed out.

PRACTICE THE IMPERSONAL EXPRESSION *IL Y A*

Write, then say, in French:

1. There is much wine in the refrigerator. _____.
2. There is a table, but there are no chairs. _____.
3. There is a manager, but there are no salesclerks. _____.
4. There is no meat with this meal. _____.
5. There is a key for the room, but there is no key for the dresser. _____.
6. There are fruit and vegetables at the grocery store. _____.
7. There has been a birthday party here. _____.

EXERCISE

ANSWERS p. 128

Using *il faut* + infinitive, *il ne faut pas,* or *il a fallu,* rewrite the following sentences.

Example: Nous ne regardons pas la télé. *Il ne faut pas regarder la télé.*

1. Nous ne regardons pas la télé. _____.
2. Vous trouvez les clefs pour l'armoire. _____.
3. Pourquoi avons-nous changé d'avion? _____.
4. Vous organisez le voyage. _____.
5. Nous atterrisons à "Baghdad by the Bay." _____.
6. Il ne perd pas son temps à fumer. _____.
7. On mange quand on a faim. _____.

9 À la banque
(At the Bank)

l'action (fem.)	stock	l'épargne (fem.)	saving(s)
l'actionnaire (masc.)	stockholder	les fonds (masc.)	capital
l'affaire (fem.)	business	le guichet	teller window
l'agent de change (masc.)	broker	l'hypothèque (fem.)	mortgage
le banquier	banker	l'impôt (masc.)	tax
le mandat	money order	l'intérêt (masc.)	interest
la caisse	cashier's office	le carnet de chèques	check book
le caissier (la caissière)	teller	le mois	month
		le montant	amount
le coffre	safe deposit box	le placement	investment
le comptant	cash	le salaire	wages
le crédit	credit	la semaine	week
les devises (fem.)	foreign money	la succursale	branch
l'échange (masc.)	the exchange	le taux	percentage
l'emprunt (masc.)	loan	la valeur	value
		le versement	payment

augmenter	to raise, to increase	laisser	to leave
baisser	to lower	payer comptant	to pay cash
découvrir	to discover	placer	to invest
déposer	to deposit	se plaindre	to complain
économiser	to save	plaire	to please
emprunter	to borrow	prêter	to lend
épargner	to put aside, to spare	tirer	to withdraw
être à sec	to be broke	toucher	to cash (a check)
gagner	to win, earn	valoir	to be worth

annuel (le)	yearly	luxueux (-se)	luxurious
bas (se)	low	mensuel (-le)	monthly
faible	weak	reconnaissant(e)	grateful
fort(e)	strong	satisfaisant(e)	satisfactory
hebdomadaire	weekly	sérieux (-se)	serious

à la fin	at the end	selon	according to
à propos	by the way	surtout	above all
de nouveau	again	vers	toward, about
pour cent	percent		

NOTES:

1. *Les actions* means "stocks." The French equivalent of the Stock Exchange is *La Bourse (de Paris).*

2. *La caisse d'épargne* is the savings bank. The verb *épargner* means "to put aside" when speaking of finances, but *épargner quelqu'un,* when speaking of a person, means "to spare someone," as in *épargnez-moi le bavardage* (spare me the chitchat). *Bavardage* is related to *bavarder* (to chat) and *bavard* (talkative).

3. *Satisfaire* means "to satisfy." From this verb are derived *satisfait* (adjective meaning "satisfied"), *il est satisfait,* and *satisfaisant* (present participle meaning "satisfactory").

4. The verb *plaire* (to please) gives us: *le plaisir* (pleasure) and *plaisanter* (to joke). Such derivatives can greatly enhance your vocabulary. See how many nouns, adjectives, or verbs you can form from vocabulary that you have already learned.

5. *L'année* (year), *l'an* (year), *annuel* (masc.) (yearly) are all related; *l'année* (fem.) denotes a specific year, as in *l'année 1950. L'an* denotes a year in general, as in *Elle a dix ans* (She's ten years old).

PRACTICE THE VOCABULARY

A. Give the feminine form of the following adjectives.

1. fort ____
2. satisfait ____
3. reconnaissant ____
4. sérieux ____
5. mensuel ____
6. annuel ____
7. luxueux ____
8. gagnant ____
9. gentil ____
10. patient ____

11. prudent ____
12. courageux ____
13. vieux ____
14. sportif ____
15. naïf ____

ANSWERS
p. 129

B. Write one or more words that are related to the following words. Your words may be nouns, adjectives, adverbs, verbs, etc.

1. l'emprunt _____   6. satisfaire _____
2. valoir _____   7. placer _____
3. l'action _____   8. plaire _____
4. l'année _____   9. vrai _____
5. bavarder _____   10. fin _____

ANSWERS
p. 129

C. Complete the following sentences using the correct verb tense, and translating into French all English words or expressions. (All verbs are given in the infinitive form.)

1. La banque _____ (fermer) à quatre heures de l'après-midi.
2. La _____ (teller) me _____ (donner) deux cartes _____ (to fill out).
3. Le _____ (rate) dans cette banque est très _____ (low).
4. Il faut payer les _____ (taxes) d'échange à ce guichet.
5. Le _____ (teller window) des _____ (investments) est fermé.
6. À la fin du mois, je _____ (être à sec).
7. Quand j'achète une voiture, je _____ (payer à crédit).
8. À l'épicerie il faut _____ (to pay cash).
9. J'ai deux cent dollars à mon compte à _____ (savings bank).
10. La valeur des _____ (foreign currency, money) baisse ou _____ (rises) selon la Bourse.

DIALOGUE   Une visite à la banque

JACQUES: Bonjour, Madame. Je voudrais ouvrir un compte dans votre banque.

LA CAISSIÈRE: Il faut aller au guichet numéro seize, Monsieur.

JACQUES: Bonjour, Mademoiselle. Je voudrais ouvrir un compte ordinaire.

LA CAISSIÈRE: Monsieur, pour ouvrir un compte, vous avez besoin de remplir ces deux cartes, et n'oubliez pas de signer aux endroits indiqués.

JACQUES: Merci, Mademoiselle. Je dois aussi toucher ce chèque de cinquante dollars. Puis-je faire cela ici?

LA CAISSIÈRE: Oui, c'est possible, mais remplissez les cartes d'abord.

JACQUES: Voici les cartes, signées bien sûr.

LA CAISSIÈRE:	Combien voulez-vous déposer à votre compte? Notre minimum est de vingt-cinq dollars ou cent cinquante francs.
JACQUES:	J'ai un chèque de cent dollars à déposer dans le nouveau compte.
LA CAISSIÈRE:	Pourquoi ne déposez-vous pas vingt-cinq dollars au compte ordinaire et soixante-quinze dollars à un compte de caisse d'épargne? Vous pouvez commencer un compte de caisse d'épargne tout de suite. Les comptes ordinaires ne gagnent pas d'intérêt dans cette banque.
JACQUES:	Très bien, c'est une bonne idée! Quel est le taux d'intérêt dans votre banque?
LA CAISSIÈRE:	Cinq et demi pour cent, Monsieur. Voici une troisième carte à remplir. Aussi il faut endosser les deux chèques, celui de cent dollars à déposer à vos comptes, et celui de cinquante dollars que vous voulez toucher.
JACQUES:	J'ai déjà endossé celui de cent dollars. Le voici. Celui de cinquante dollars n'est pas à mon nom, mais il a été endossé à mon compte.
LA CAISSIÈRE:	Dans ce cas, il faut vérifier votre identité et votre signature.
JACQUES:	Voici ma carte d'identité et mon permis de conduire.
LA CAISSIÈRE:	C'est tout, c'est fait. Voici votre livret de banque et vos chèques provisoires. Dans quinze jours, il faut revenir à la banque pour les chèques imprimés à votre nom.
JACQUES:	J'ai besoin de faire l'échange de cinquante dollars. Je reviens de New York et je n'ai pas un sou français.
LA CAISSIÈRE:	Avec plaisir, monsieur. Je dois vérifier la valeur actuelle du dollar. C'est presque trois cents francs pour vos dollars.
JACQUES:	Très bien. Merci, mademoiselle.
LA CAISSIÈRE:	À votre service, monsieur. Au revoir.

DIALOGUE   A Visit to the Bank

JACQUES:	Good morning. I would like to open a checking account in your bank.
THE TELLER:	You must go to window number sixteen, sir.
JACQUES:	Good morning, Miss. I would like to open a checking account.
THE TELLER:	Sir, for a checking account, you need to fill out these two cards, and don't forget to sign at the designated places.
JACQUES:	Thanks, Miss. I must also cash this fifty-dollar check. Can I do that here?
THE TELLER:	Yes, it is possible, but fill out the cards first.
JACQUES:	Here are the cards, signed, of course.
THE TELLER:	How much do you want to deposit in your checking account? Our minimum is twenty-five dollars or one hundred fifty francs.
JACQUES:	I have a one-hundred-dollar check to deposit in the new account.
THE TELLER:	Why don't you deposit twenty-five dollars in the checking account and seventy-five dollars in a savings account? You can start a savings account right away. In this bank, the checking accounts don't earn any interest.

JACQUES:	Very well, it's a good idea! What is the interest rate at your bank?
THE TELLER:	Five and a half percent, sir. Here's a third card to fill out. Also, you must endorse the two checks, the one-hundred-dollar one for deposit in your accounts, and the fifty-dollar one that you wish to cash.
JACQUES:	I already endorsed the one-hundred-dollar one. Here it is. The fifty-dollar one is not in my name, but it has been endorsed to my account.
THE TELLER:	In that case, I must verify your identity and your signature.
JACQUES:	Here are my identity card and my driver's license.
THE TELLER:	That's all, it's done. Here is your bank book and your temporary checks. In fifteen days, you must come back to the bank for the checks printed with your name.
JACQUES:	I need to exchange fifty dollars. I am back from New York, and I don't have a cent of French money.
THE TELLER:	With pleasure, sir. I have to verify the actual exchange. It's almost three hundred francs for your dollars.
JACQUES:	Very well. Thanks, miss.
THE TELLER:	At your service, sir. Goodbye.

DIALOGUE EXERCISES

A. Answer the questions based on the dialogue, with short complete sentences.

1. Qu'est-ce que Jacques veut commencer? _____
2. Combien de chèques Jacques apporte-t-il à la banque? _____
3. Que fait Jacques avec le chèque de cinquante dollars? _____
4. Où Jacques a-t-il déposé le chèque de cent dollars? _____
5. Que doit faire Jacques avant de déposer un chèque? _____
6. Pourquoi la caissière veut-elle vérifier l'identité de Jacques? _____
7. Quel genre (what kind) de chèques la caissière donne-t-elle à Jacques?

_____
8. Pourquoi Jacques doit-il revenir à la banque? _____
9. Combien d'argent Jacques dépose-t-il à la Caisse d'Épargne? _____
10. Combien d'argent Jacques dépose-t-il à son compte de chèques? _____

B. Match the two columns.

1. _____ Le guichet est fermé.
2. _____ La gérante est occupée maintenant.
3. _____ J'ai perdu mon carnet de banque.
4. _____ Il ouvre un compte de chèques.
5. _____ La banque a baissé le taux d'intérêt.
6. _____ Je suis toujours à sec!

A. He opens a checking account.
B. The bank lowered its interest rate.
C. She wants to cash her paycheck.
D. One must endorse a check.
E. The monthly payment is twenty dollars.
F. The window is closed.

7. ____ Le versement mensuel est de vingt dollars.

8. ____ Le bureau d'échange n'a pas d'agent.

9. ____ Il faut endosser le chèque.

10. ____ Elle veut toucher le chèque de son salaire.

G. The manager is busy now.

H. I lost my bank book.

I. I am always broke.

J. The exchange office has no broker (agent).

GRAMMAR I   Indirect Object Nouns and Pronouns

A. We have seen in Lesson 7 that direct object nouns and pronouns can be used to answer the questions "what" and "whom"; the indirect object nouns and pronouns answer the questions "to what," "for what," "by what," "by whom," "by whose," etc.

> EXAMPLE: *J'ai parlé à la caissière. Caissière* is the indirect object noun.
>
> When you replace *caissière* by *lui*, as in *Je lui ai parlé* (I spoke to her), *lui* is the indirect object pronoun.

B. Indirect object pronouns replace indirect object nouns. They are exactly the same as the direct object pronouns studied in Lesson 7, except for the third-person singular and plural, which are *lui* and *leur*.

C. Study the chart and compare the direct and indirect object pronouns.

Subject	Direct	Indirect	English
je	me	me	me, to me, for me
tu	te	te	you, to you, for you
nous	nous	nous	us, to us, for us
vous	vous	vous	you, to you, for you
il	le, l'	lui	him, her, to him or her, for him or her
elle	la, l'	lui	him, her, to him or her, for him or her
ils	les	leur	them, to them, for them
elles	les	leur	them, to them, for them

NOTES:

1. In French, all indirect object nouns require the preposition *à*. With this fact in mind, it will be easy to replace indirect object pronouns.

> EXAMPLE: *J'ai parlé à Jacques.*   I spoke to Jacques.
>
> *Je lui ai parlé.*   I spoke to him.

2. An important similarity with direct object pronouns is that indirect object pronouns also immediately precede the verb they modify, whether it is conjugated or in the infinitive:

EXAMPLE: *Elle m'a donné le chèque.*   She gave *me* the check.

Elle nous a donné le chèque.   She gave *us* the check.

Je ne veux pas leur donner   I don't wish to give *them* the
le chèque.   check.

EXERCISES

A. Answer the following questions about indirect object nouns and pronouns.

1. What does an indirect object pronoun replace? _____

2. What is the difference between the direct object pronouns and indirect object pronouns? _____

3. What are the third-person singular and plural of the indirect object pronouns? _____

4. What is always required by a French indirect object noun? _____

5. Name one important similarity between the direct object pronouns and the indirect object pronouns. _____

B. Complete the sentences with the appropriate French verb tense and the indirect object pronoun.

Example: Je (give her) *lui donne* la clef.

1. Jacques (asks them) _____ des renseignements.

2. Elle (telephoned me) _____ hier soir.

3. Nous (spoke with him) _____ au restaurant.

4. Il (gives us back) _____ la monnaie.

5. La cliente (asks me) _____ de l'aider.

6. Je (telephoned you) _____ ce matin.

7. Il (showed us) _____ son carnet de chèques.

8. Il (looks like her) _____ en tout.

9. Elle veut (to speak to them) _____ avant de les voir.

10. Il faut (to write to her) _____.

NOTE:
Remember to distinguish between *leur* (them) and *leur, leurs* (their); *leur* (them) always precedes a verb.

EXAMPLE: *Ils cherchent leur valise.*   They're looking for *their* suitcase.

but: *Ils leur donnent leur valise.*   They're giving them their suitcase.

GRAMMAR II   Reflexive Constructions

A. Reflexive means that the action of the verb reflects on the subject, as in *Je me lave* (I wash myself). Reflexive constructions are rare in English, but they are common in French.

B. In reflexive constructions there is always a pronoun that refers to the subject.

> EXAMPLE: I hurt *myself*.
>
> She dresses *herself*.
>
> He sings to *himself*.

The pronouns, myself, herself, and himself, are reflexive pronouns. They can be direct pronouns, as in, "I hurt myself." Or indirect, as in "He sings to himself."

C. In French, the reflexive pronouns are *me, te, se, nous, vous,* and *se.*

D. Study the following chart with *se laver* (to wash oneself).

Subject	Pronoun	*Se laver*	English
je	**me**	lave	I wash myself
tu	**te**	laves	you wash yourself
il, elle, on	**se**	lave	he, she washes himself, herself
nous	**nous**	lavons	we wash ourselves
vous	**vous**	lavez	you wash yourself, yourselves
ils, elles	**se**	lavent	they wash themselves

1. In reflexive constructions, the pronoun subject (*je, tu,* etc.) and the pronoun object both precede the verb.

   EXAMPLE: *Je me lave.* I wash myself.

2. In negative forms, *ne* is placed right after the subject and *pas* is placed after the verb, as usual.

   EXAMPLE: *Je ne me lave pas.* I don't wash myself.

3. In reflexive constructions, the reflexive verb always has a reflexive pronoun that agrees in number and gender with the subject.

   EXAMPLE: *Nous nous lavons.* We wash ourselves.

4. The reflexive pronoun for the third-person singular and the third-person plural is *se,* as in

   > *Il se lave.* He washes himself.
   >
   > *Ils se lavent.* They wash themselves.

PRACTICE THE REFLEXIVE CONSTRUCTIONS

ANSWERS
p. 130

A. Answer the questions.

1. What is a reflexive construction? _____.
2. What is always required in a reflexive construction? _____.
3. How are the pronoun subject and the pronoun object placed in a reflexive construction? _____.
4. Give the negative form of *nous nous amusons*. _____.
5. What kind of reflexive pronoun is in the following construction? *Il se parle.* _____.
6. The reflexive pronoun *se* appears in three reflexive constructions. Name them in the phrase "to wash oneself." _____.
7. Say, and then write, in French, "I am having a good time." _____.
8. Give the first-person plural of the reflexive French verb *s'arrêter*. _____.
9. Give the reflexive construction of "They (masc.) are having a good time." _____.
10. Give the reflexive construction of "You (*tu*) talk to yourself." _____.

ANSWERS
pp. 130–131

B. Using the appropriate reflexive construction, rewrite the following sentences.

1. Ma petite sœur/se lever/tôt le matin _____.
2. Pendant que je/se laver/elle mange _____.
3. Quand j'ai besoin de/se regarder/dans le miroir, elle m'appelle _____.
4. Je/se brosser/les dents après le petit déjeuner _____.
5. Ma petite soeur et moi/s'habiller/en même temps _____.
6. Dès que je finis, je/se préparer/pour sortir _____.
7. Ma soeur et ma voisine/se promener/après mon départ _____.
8. J'ai besoin de/se coucher/de bonne heure ce soir _____.
9. Mes parents/se réveiller/souvent plus tôt que moi _____.
10. Mon ami Mark/se marier/la semaine prochaine _____.

GRAMMAR III   Reflexive Verbs

A. Below is a partial list of the most frequently used reflexive verbs. Please memorize them.

s'appeler	to call oneself	*se coucher*	to go to bed
s'arrêter	to stop	*s'ennuyer*	to be bored
se baigner	to bathe, swim	*se lever*	to get up
		se marier	to get married
se brosser	to brush (one's teeth, hair)	*se reposer*	to rest
		se réveiller	to wake up

B. Many reflexive verbs are also nonreflexive.

> EXAMPLE: *Elle lave ses vêtements.*   She washes her clothes.
>
> *Elle se lave.*   She washes herself.
>
> *Il se réveille à six heures.*   He wakes up at six.
>
> *La radio le réveille à six heures.*   The radio wakes him up at six.

C. Some nonreflexive verbs that we have studied change their meaning when used in reflexive constructions.

> EXAMPLE:
>
> | | | | |
> |---|---|---|---|
> | *demander* | to ask | *se demander* | to wonder |
> | *entendre* | to hear | *s'entendre* | to get along |
> | *tromper* | to deceive | *se tromper* | to be mistaken |
> | *trouver* | to find | *se trouver* | to be located |

D. All reflexive verbs are conjugated in the *passé composé* with *être*. With this in mind, simply determine the past participle of the verb in question and proceed with the conjugation of *être*. The past participle, of course, must agree in gender and number with the reflexive pronoun, which in turn must agree with the subject. Study the chart of *se laver* in the *passé composé*.

Subject	Pronoun	Auxiliary	Verb	English
je	me	suis	lavé(e)	I washed myself
tu	t'	es	lavé(e)	you washed yourself
il, elle	s'	est	lavé(e)	he, she, washes himself, herself
nous	nous	sommes	lavé(e)s	we wash ourselves
vous	vous	étes	lavé(e)s	you wash yourselves
ils, elles	se	sont	lavé(e)s	they wash themselves

NOTES:

1. Whenever the auxiliary *être* is used to form the *passé composé*, the past participle, reflexive or nonreflexive, always agrees in number and gender with the subject and/or the pronoun. In the case of the reflexive *passé composé*, the past participle agrees with both the subject and the reflexive pronoun.

2. In the imperative form, the reflexive verbs follow the rules we have learned. However, the *te* becomes *toi* in the imperative form.

> EXAMPLE: *Tu te laves.—Lave-toi.* Wash yourself.
>
> *Tu t'occupes de ta soeur.—Occupe-toi de ta soeur.*
> Take care of your sister.

EXERCISES

ANSWERS
p. 131

A. Rewrite the following sentences in the reflexive form, according to the example.

   Example: Je me repose, le gérant *se repose aussi.*

1. Elle se réveille tard, nous _____.
2. Je me brosse les dents, ils _____.
3. Tu t'amuses, vous _____.
4. Ils s'excusent et nous _____.
5. Je me couche à minuit, tu _____.
6. Vous vous levez avec peine, ils _____.
7. Ils s'amusent et tu _____.
8. Vous vous reposez et ils _____.
9. Ils s'ennuient et je _____.

ANSWERS
p. 131

B. Rewrite the reflexive sentences in the imperative form.

1. Tu te reposes. _____.
2. Tu te laves. _____.
3. Vous vous dépêchez. _____.
4. Nous nous habillons. _____.
5. Tu te baignes. _____.
6. Vous vous couchez tôt. _____.
7. Vous ne vous ennuyez pas. _____.
8. Nous ne nous arrêtons pas ici. _____.
9. Tu ne t'excuses pas. _____.
10. Vous vous brossez les dents. _____.

NOTE:
Reflexive constructions in the imperative form require *toi* instead of *te* in the second-person singular in the affirmative *only.*

   EXAMPLE: *tu t'excuses—excuse-toi*

10 À la gare
(At the Railroad Station)

le coffre	trunk (car trunk)	l'ouest (masc.)	west
le contrôleur	ticket collector	le panneau	the road sign
la couchette	bunk, berth	le quai	platform
l'endroit (masc.)	place	la route	highway
l'est (masc.)	east	nationale	
l'heure d'affluence	rush hour	la sortie	exit
(fem.)		la station	stop, station (subway)
l'horaire	schedule, timetable	le sud	south
le machiniste	engineer	la vitesse	speed
la malle	trunk (suitcase)	le wagon aux	baggage car
la marque	brand	bagages	
le moyen	the way, means	le wagon-lit	sleeping car
le nord	north	le wagon-restaurant	dining car
la nuit	night		

conduire	to drive	raconter	to tell (story)
courir	to run	rentrer	to return (home)
s'endormir	to fall asleep	repartir	to leave again
être pressé	to be in a hurry	retourner	to return
indiquer	to indicate	se sentir	to feel (oneself)
monter	to go up	tomber	to fall
oublier	to forget		

ensemble	together	incroyable	incredible
à l'étranger	abroad	plusieurs	several
en forme	in shape	plutôt	rather
à l'heure	on time		

NOTES:

1. The prefix *re* in *repartir* (to leave again) designates repetition of the action of the verb *partir* (to leave).

> EXAMPLE: *tomber* to fall   *retomber* to fall again
>
> *venir* to come   *revenir* to come again, to come back
>
> *faire* to do   *refaire* to do again

2. *Heureusement* (happily) is formed with the feminine singular (*heureuse*) of the adjective *heureux* (happy). The *-ment* ending denotes an adverb. All the adverbs ending in *-ment* are usually formed in the above manner. Ex.: *sérieux* (masc.), *sérieuse* (fem.), *sérieusement*, "seriously." We will study more about these adverbs later in Lesson 15.

PRACTICE THE VOCABULARY:

ANSWERS p. 131

A. Write the indefinite articles *un*, *une*, or *des* before the following nouns.

1. _____ couchette
2. _____ wagon aux bagages
3. _____ horaire
4. _____ rails
5. _____ malle

6. _____ train
7. _____ unit
8. _____ marque
9. _____ quais
10. _____ moyen

11. _____ endroit
12. _____ panneau
13. _____ route
14. _____ coffres
15. _____ station

ANSWERS p. 131

B. Write the opposite of the following words.

1. le départ _____
2. le nord _____
3. l'est _____
4. monter _____
5. se réveiller _____

6. la sortie _____
7. gagner _____
8. payer à crédit _____
9. faible _____
10. baisser _____

ANSWERS p. 132

C. Fill in the blanks with the *passé composé* of the given verbs.

1. Les horaires (changer) _____ hier.
2. Le taux d'intérêt (augmenter) _____ de cinq pour cent.
3. Le train de six heures du soir (arriver) _____ à l'heure.
4. Juliette et moi (oublier) _____ de remercier la concierge.
5. Charles (repartir) _____ en France.
6. Heureusement que la semaine (finir) _____.
7. La caissière (être) _____ gentille avec moi.
8. Nous (avoir) _____ de la chance de trouver un taxi.

9. Ils (envoyer) _____ un mandat international de cent dollars.

10. Vous (avoir) _____ raison d'être heureux.

DIALOGUE   À la gare Saint Lazare

JULIETTE: Ah! Voilà Charles. Il a l'air un peu perdu! Charles, par ici!

CHARLES: Salut, Juliette! Attends une minute, je voudrais dire au revoir à Monsieur Legrand.

JULIETTE: As-tu fait un bon voyage? Pour quelqu'un qui a passé la nuit dans le train, tu as l'air bien reposé.

CHARLES: Oui, je me sens en forme. J'avais la couchette supérieure dans le wagon-lit, et après le dîner au wagon-restaurant, j'ai pris un verre avec Monsieur Legrand. Ensuite je suis monté à ma couchette et quand je me suis réveillé, nous étions à la gare!

JULIETTE: C'est parfait, parce que j'ai plusieurs projets pour notre premier jour ensemble à Paris.

CHARLES: Très bien, attends ici une minute, je vais aller trouver ma malle, regarde s'il y a un taxi près d'ici.

JULIETTE: D'accord, j'y vais tout de suite. Vous êtes libre, monsieur?

LE CHAUFFEUR: Oui, mademoiselle, c'est pour vous?

JULIETTE: Oui, et pour mon ami. Il arrive avec sa malle.

LE CHAUFFEUR: Excusez-moi, je dois ouvrir le coffre.

JULIETTE: Ta malle a l'air vraiment lourde. Heureusement que j'ai trouvé un taxi tout près.

CHARLES: Oui, nous avons de la chance. Les taxis ne sont pas toujours libres pendant les heures d'affluence.

(Juliette et Charles sont à l'intérieur du taxi)

CHARLES: La première chose que je veux faire demain c'est d'acheter trois cartes, et faire tout Paris et économiser de l'argent en même temps.

JULIETTE: Et quelles sont ces trois cartes, mon cher ami?

CHARLES: La Carte Paris-Visite, la Carte Musées-Monuments, et la Télécarte.

JULIETTE: Tu sais, il y a aussi une nouvelle carte: la Carte Le Menu.

CHARLES: Regarde, nous sommes arrivés; le temps passe si vite quand je suis avec toi!

DIALOGUE   At the Saint-Lazare Train Station

JULIETTE: Ah! There's Charles. He seems a little lost. Charles, over here!

CHARLES: Hi, Juliette! Wait a minute, I would like to say goodbye to Mr. Legrand.

JULIETTE:	Did you have a good trip? For someone who spent the night on a train, you look well rested.
CHARLES:	Yes, I feel in good shape. I had the upper bunk (berth) in the sleeping car, and after dinner I had a drink with Mr. Legrand in the dining car. Then I went up to my bunk and when I woke up, we were at the train station!
JULIETTE:	That's perfect, because I have several things in mind for our first day in Paris together.
CHARLES:	Very well, wait here a minute, I'm going to go find my trunk. See if there is a taxi nearby.
JULIETTE:	Agreed, I'm going there right away. Are you available, sir?
THE CHAUFFEUR:	Yes, miss. Is it for you?
JULIETTE:	Yes, and my friend. He's coming (arriving) with his trunk.
THE CHAUFFEUR:	Excuse me, I have to open the car trunk.
JULIETTE:	The trunk seems really heavy. Fortunately I found a taxi nearby.
CHARLES:	Yes, we are lucky. Taxis are not always available during rush hour.
	(Juliette and Charles are inside the taxi)
CHARLES:	The first thing I want to do tomorrow is to buy three cards, do all of Paris, and save money at the same time.
JULIETTE:	And what are these three cards, my friend?
CHARLES:	La Carte Paris-Visite, la Carte Musées-Monuments, and la Télécarte.
JULIETTE:	You know there is also a new card: La Carte Le Menu.
CHARLES:	Look, we've arrived; time goes so fast when I'm with you!

NOTES:

1. *La Gare Saint-Lazare* is one of the most important train stations in Paris. It is also a subway stop and is connected to the government-regulated SNCF, which stands for the Société Nationale des Chemins de Fer. All the railroads in France are controlled by the SNCF, which started in 1938. *La Gare Saint-Lazare* is said to serve thirteen hundred travelers a minute during the evening peak hours.

2. *Le coffre* refers to the trunk, in the case of cars. It is a safety deposit box, when the subject is a bank.

3. *Y* is a pronoun replacing a place, as in *Es-tu allé au cirque? Oui, j'y suis allé.* Yes, I went there.

4. *L'heure d'affluence* literally means "the hour of the crowd" (otherwise known as the rush hour) and is usually used in the plural.

5. *Libre:* free (taxi), does not mean *gratis,* but available. Free of charge is translated in French by *gratuit* (masc.) or *gratuite* (fem.).

CULTURAL NOTE:

It is no secret that the costly renovation of historic sites and neighborhoods undertaken by the French government was to make France the place of choice for those who search for the ultimate vacation. And to make things more inviting, there are all sorts of cards simply called Les Cartes. The Carte Paris-Visite allows one to navigate through Paris as a Parisian, with unlimited travel by métro and bus. Then there is the Carte Musées-Monuments, which allows the carrier admittance to sixty-five museums and monuments inside and outside Paris. There is also the Télé-carte, which is the only "coin" accepted in the high-tech French public telephone system. These cards are available at métro stations, museums, and certain other locations. The Carte Le Menu™ will introduce both the gourmet and the gourmand to a variety of French cuisines in distinctive settings. Card carriers will be able to enjoy chef's specials at a number of selected restaurants throughout the city at prices ranging from moderate to expensive.

DIALOGUE EXERCISES

ANSWERS p. 132

Answer the questions based on the dialogue.

1. Où est Juliette? _____.

2. Que dit Juliette quand elle voit Charles? _____.

3. Que répond Charles? _____.

4. À qui Charles voudrait-il dire au revoir? _____.

5. Où Charles a-t-il passé la nuit? _____.

6. Quel est l'opposé (opposite) de *fatigué*? _____.

7. Pourquoi Charles est-il en forme? _____.

8. Qu'est-ce que Charles fait après le dîner? _____.

9. Que fait le chauffeur quand Charles arrive? _____.

10. Combien de cartes Charles veut-il acheter? _____.

11. Quelles sont ces cartes? _____.

GRAMMAR I   The Imperfect Indicative (*imparfait*)

A. Study the imperfect endings in the chart below.

Subject	Verb: *Trouver*	Imperfect Ending	English
je	**trouv**	ais	I used to find
tu	**trouv**	ais	you used to find
il, elle, on	**trouv**	ait	he, she, it used to find
nous	**trouv**	ions	we used to find
vous	**trouv**	iez	you used to find
ils, elles	**trouv**	aient	they used to find

NOTE:

The stem for the imperfect of the -*ir* verbs is the same as that used for the plural forms in the present indicative.

> *je finissais, nous réussissions*

1. The *imparfait* (imperfect) has several English equivalents: *il trouvait* can mean "he found," "he was finding," and "he used to find."

2. The imperfect is used to describe continuous or habitual actions that occurred over indefinite periods of time. This, in fact, is the reason that this tense is called imperfect—we never know when the action in the imperfect began, nor when it ended.

> EXAMPLE: *Elle regardait la télévision tous les soirs.* She watched television every night. (habitual, repetitious)
>
> *La maison était grande et belle.* The house was large and beautiful. (description)

3. The imperfect is also used to describe emotions and feelings; it is used to state a date, time of day, or someone's age in the past.

4. A verb having -*ier* in the infinitive, such as *associer* (to associate) or *étudier* (to study)—in which the first-person plural is *nous associons* and *nous étudions*—has *associ* and *étudi* as the stem when we drop the -*ons*. The imperfect will then be *nous associions* and *nous étudiions,* with the *i* doubled in the first and second persons of the plural.

> EXAMPLE: *nous associiions, nous étudiions*
>
> *vous associiez, vous étudiiez*

B. Memorize the imperfect of *être,* the only exception to the rule for forming the imperfect of all French verbs.

Subject	Imperfect of *Être*	English
j'	étais	I was, used to be, was being
tu	étais	you were, used to be, etc.
il, elle, on	était	he, she, it was, used to be, etc.
nous	étions	we were, used to be, etc.
vous	étiez	you were, etc.
ils, elles	étaient	they were, etc.

EXERCISES

ANSWERS
p. 132

A. Rewrite the following sentences in the imperfect indicative.

1. Ils ont réussi à faire des économies (savings). _____.
2. Mes parents et moi sommes d'accord sur ce sujet (subject). _____.
3. Les voisins ont commencé à nous inviter. _____.
4. La route nationale est pleine (full) de panneaux. _____.
5. Nos amis n'ont pas hésité une minute. _____.
6. Vous m'encouragez tous les jours. _____.
7. Il est midi pile et il ne déjeune pas. _____.
8. À minuit nous entendons des bruits (noises). _____.
9. Nous pouvons sortir plus tard. _____.
10. Il veut faire la connaissance de Juliette. _____.

ANSWERS
p. 132

B. Write complete sentences using the imperfect indicative and adding necessary connecting words, articles, and prepositions.

1. nous/avoir/plusieurs/heures/route nationale _____.
2. mon mari/donner/argent/pendant/semaine _____.
3. chaque (every) jour/voisin/inviter/ma sœur _____.
4. nous/partir/en vacances/ensemble _____.
5. ces garçons/être/Amérique/Canada _____.
6. nous/faire/promenade/le soir _____.
7. après le travail/je/faire/des courses _____.
8. ils/rentrer/souvent/très tard _____.
9. nous/être/avec/Jean/jour/fête _____.
10. nous/être/heureux/avec/voisins _____.

ANSWERS
p. 133

C. Rewrite the following paragraph, replacing all the verbs with the imperfect indicative, then read the new paragraph aloud.

Je fais mes débuts en français, les leçons sont parfois difficiles, mais je fais mon possible pour les comprendre. Je suis occupé l'après-midi, mais j'étudie le matin et quelquefois (sometimes) j'essaie de finir les exercices le soir. La leçon cinq est très longue parce qu'elle a plusieurs pages de révision (review). Je veux bien continuer l'étude du français parce que j'aime beaucoup la langue, et parce que j'ai envie d'aller en France.

GRAMMAR II   Comparing the *imparfait* and *passé composé*

A. The two main verb tenses in French are the *imparfait* (imperfect) and the *passé composé* (compound past). We have just learned that the *imparfait* is used in descriptive past actions conveying repetition, habit, and continuity. The *passé composé,* which we have also learned, differs from the *imparfait* in that it is used in actions that are neither continuous nor descriptive.

B. The *passé composé* conveys something that began and ended in the past, without any consideration as to how long that action lasted.

> EXAMPLE: *J'ai fini mon travail.* (I started *mon travail* and completed it.)

> The main distinction, then, could be summarized this way:

> a. *imparfait* past continuous action with no specific beginning nor end.

> b. *passé composé* past completed action without continuity or duration.

C. The *passé composé* can also convey a one-time event that happened in the past, as in *J'ai visité Versailles l'année dernière* (last year).

D. Remember that the *imparfait* always relates what was going on and how things were, while the *passé composé* interrupts these continuous, repetitious, habitual situations:

> EXAMPLE: *Il est venu pendant que je mangeais.* He came while I was eating.

NOTE:
The imperfect reflexive verbs follow the same pattern as the nonreflexive constructions.

> EXAMPLE: *Nous nous lavons. Nous nous lavions.*

> (We were washing ourselves.)

EXERCISES

A. Write complete sentences using the *imparfait* and *passé composé,* as appropriate. Follow the example.

> *Example: Juliette était gentille, mais hier elle m'a blessé* (she hurt me).

1. Juliette/venir/toujours à midi, mais aujourd'hui elle/venir/en retard _____
_____.

2. Elle/croire/à mes promesses, mais soudainement (suddenly) elle/changer _____
_____.

3. Elle/penser/toujours à moi, mais lundi elle/oublier/mon anniversaire _____
_____.

4. Elle/aimer/mes histoires, mais hier elle/trouver/ma plaisanterie (joke) ennuyeuse (boring) _____
_____.

5. Le soir elle/étudier/mais hier elle/sortir/avec Pierre _____
_____.

6. Elle me/téléphoner/le matin, mais aujourd'hui elle/ne pas me téléphoner _____
   _____.

7. Juliette/vouloir/aller camper mais elle/refuser/d'aller avec moi _____
   _____.

8. Juliette/pouvoir/me faire rire, mais hier elle me/faire/pleurer (to cry) _____
   _____.

9. Elle m'/attendre/toujours, mais aujourd'hui elle/décider/de partir sans moi (without
   me) _____.

10. Elle/être/souvent polie, mais hier elle/insulter/ma sœur _____
    _____.

ANSWERS p. 133

B. Complete the sentences using the *imparfait* and/or the *passé composé,* as required.
Remember to use the *imparfait* in descriptive past actions (habitual, continuous,
repetitious) and the *passé composé* in past completed actions (actions begun and
ended in the past).

> *Example:* Je ne (aller) _____ au cinéma hier, je (rester)
> _____ à la maison. Je ne <u>suis pas allé(e)</u> au cinéma hier, je <u>suis</u>
> <u>resté(e)</u> à la maison.

1. Juliette (vouloir) _____ faire la connaissance d'Antoine, mais il n(e)
   (venir) _____ avec Charles.

2. Ma sœur et moi (faire) _____ une promenade quand nous (rencontrer)
   _____ Jacques.

3. J' (avoir) _____ froid quand je (retourner) _____ de l'aéroport.

4. J' (avoir) _____ faim alors j(e) (manger) _____ tout (all) le
   pain.

5. Hier, j(e) (rester) _____ au lit parce que j(e) (être) _____
   malade (ill).

6. Je (s'ennuyer) _____ alors mon ami m(e) (raconter) _____
   une histoire.

7. J(e) (monter) _____ dans ma couchette et j(e) (commencer)
   _____ à lire.

8. L'heure d'affluence (être) _____ toujours entre quatre heures et cinq
   heures.

9. Le contrôleur (vérifier) _____ nos billets pendant que (while) nous
   (manger) _____.

10. Nous (aller) _____ à l'étranger l'année dernière (last year).

GRAMMAR III   The Days of the Week, Months of the Year, Dates, and Ordinal Numbers 1–100

A. *Les jours de la semaine* (days of the week):

In French, the days of the week begin with *Monday,* are *not capitalized,* and are all masculine.

B. *Les mois de l'année* (the months of the year):

The months of the year are *not capitalized* in French and are also masculine.

C. Memorize the chart below.

Les Jours (Days)	English	*Les Mois* (Months)	English
lundi	Monday	janvier	January
mardi	Tuesday	février	February
mercredi	Wednesday	mars	March
jeudi	Thursday	avril	April
vendredi	Friday	mai	May
samedi	Saturday	juin	June
dimanche	Sunday	juillet	July
		août	August
		septembre	September
		octobre	October
		novembre	November
		décembre	December

NOTES:

1. In French, to ask what day it is, we say,

   Quel jour sommes-nous? What day is it?

   Then we answer either by simply stating the day, *lundi, mardi,* etc., or by repeating the verb *être, nous sommes mardi.*

2. Remember that *le,* before any day of the week, means that the action takes place every week on that same day.

   EXAMPLE: *Le dimanche ils vont à l'église.*

   On Sunday they go to church (every Sunday).

   Le is also used when a specific date is called for.

   EXAMPLE: *Le 20 décembre nous partons en vacances.*

3. The adjective *prochain*(e) is used to indicate the next day, week, month, or year.

   EXAMPLE: *la semaine prochaine*   next week

   lundi prochain   next Monday

   février prochain   next February

   l'année prochaine   next year

4. French uses the day of the week alone, when English would use "this," "that," "on," etc.

   EXAMPLE: *Jeudi, il va faire des courses.*

   (This) Thursday, or (On) Thursday, he's going shopping.

5. In French, the months are expressed either alone, when used with *prochain*, or with *en*, to translate as the English *in*, as in "in February," *en février*. We also may say *au mois de février*—in the month of February. However, *en* is the more common usage.

> EXAMPLE: En septembre nous allons à Paris.
> En juillet nous allons à Nice.

It's not incorrect to say *au mois de septembre* and *au mois de juillet.*

D. Ordinal numbers 1–100.

1. Ordinal numbers are formed by adding *-ième* to the cardinal number, except for one (*un*) and first (*premier, première*, fem.).

> EXAMPLE: *un, premier*(e)   first
>
> *deux, deuxième* second (the *x* of *deuxième* is pronounced *z*)
>
> *trois, troisième*   third

2. When a cardinal number ends with *e* as in *quatre*, the *e* is dropped and we have

   quatrième, fourth

NOTES:

1. The *x*'s in *sixième* and *dixième* are pronounced *z*.

2. The *f* in *neuf* becomes *v* in *neuvième*.

3. The *x* in *soixante* is pronounced *ss*.

4. After *soixante*, the ordinal number is indicated by *dix*, as in *soixante-dix, soixante-dixième*. The same applies to *quatre-vingt-dix* (90), *quatre-vingt-dix-ième*.

5. Ordinal numbers can also be written by adding *è* or *ème* to Arabic numbers: 1*er*, 2*è*, 3*ème*, 5*è*, 6*ème*, etc.

CULTURAL NOTE:

The French enjoy more holidays than Americans, because most French holidays are religious in nature. Thus, besides *la Fête Nationale,* which is the 14th of July, *la Fête de la Victoire* (Armistice Day), which is November 11th, and *la fête du Premier Mai,* which is their Labor Day, the French have the following holidays:

> *Le jour de l'An* (New Year's Day)—1er janvier.
> *Le lundi de Pâques* (Easter Monday)—mars ou avril.
> *L'Ascension* (Ascension Day)—mai, jeudi
> *L'Assomption* (Assumption Day)—15 août.
> *La Toussaint* (All Saints Day)—1er novembre.
> *Noël* (Christmas)—25 décembre.

Note also that when French people take a long holiday weekend (four days), they say *"Faire le pont."* Literally, it means "to make the bridge."

EXERCISES

ANSWERS
pp. 133–134

A. Practice the days of the week and the months of the year.

1. What is the difference between the days of the week in French and in English?
_____.

2. With what day does the French week start? _____.

3. What is the gender of days and months in French? _____.

4. What does the definite article *le,* before a weekday, mean? _____.

5. How do we translate "this Saturday," "on Thursday," "that Friday" into French?
_____.

6. Write in French, "next Sunday" _____, "next July" _____,
"next year" _____.

7. How is the French ordinal number formed?_____.

8. With which ordinal numbers is *x* pronounced like *z?*_____.

9. With which ordinal number is *x* pronounced like *ss?*_____.

10. Say, and then write, in French: "The first day of the week is Monday."

ANSWERS
p. 134

B. Translate into French.

1. Next week we are going to buy some furniture. _____.

2. The second week in July, my friend went to Nice. _____.

3. In March we drove to the airport together. _____.

4. The ninth month of the year is September. _____.

5. Every Tuesday I take piano lessons. _____.

6. Next October my husband is leaving for Paris. _____.

7. The hundredth passenger won the jackpot! _____.

ANSWERS   LESSONS 6–10

Lesson 6

Vocabulary

Practice

A. 1. beau

   2. compose

   3. montagnes

   4. disponible

   5. aimable

   6. la commode

   7. clef

   8. tapageurs

B. 1. I

   2. H

   3. G

   4. B

   5. A

   6. J

   7. C

   8. D

   9. E

   10. F

Dialogue Exercises

A. 1. Ils sont à l'Hôtel Rivoli.

   2. Il parle à la concierge.

   3. Il est à Nice.

   4. Ils veulent une chambre à deux lits.

   5. Odette est la fiancée de Jacques.

   6. La chambre est parfaite.

   7. Elle donne sur la plage.

B. 1. grande et belle

   2. sarcastiques

   3. est beau

   4. bijoux

   5. heureuse, affamée

Grammar I and II

Practice

A. 1. to be

   2. pouvoir, vouloir

   3. verb and noun

   4. check a dictionary

   5. verb + direct inf.

      verb + prep. *de*

      verb + prep. *à*

   6. conseiller, défendre, demander, ordonner, suggérer

   7. no

B. 1. Nous avons faim aujourd'hui.

   2. Odette a peur de Jacques.

   3. J'ai envie de danser.

   4. La concierge a l'air gentille.

   5. J'ai soif quand je suis ici.

   6. J'ai besoin de faire des courses.

   7. J'ai l'intention de réussir.

   8. Nous avons de la chance d'être ici.

Grammar III

Practice

A. 1. Cet avion est immense.

   2. Ces repas sont délicieux.

3. J'aime cette maison.
4. J'achète ces escargots.
5. Cette armoire n'est pas grande.
6. Cette fille à la robe verte est ma voisine.
7. Ces croissants sont bien chauds.
8. Ce lit et ce matelas sont neufs.

B. 1. cette salade-ci ou cette salade-là
2. cet arbre-ci ou cet arbre-là
3. cette taie-ci ou cette taie-là
4. ce lavabo-ci ou ce lavabo-là
5. ces escargots-ci ou ces escargots-là
6. ce gâteau-ci ou ce gâteau-là
7. ce fauteuil-ci ou ce fauteuil-là
8. cette commode-ci ou cette commode-là
9. cette pizza-ci ou cette pizza-là
10. ces bijoux-ci ou ces bijoux-là

C. 1. E   6. J
2. F   7. B
3. G   8. C
4. I   9. A
5. H   10. D

Lesson 7

Vocabulary

Practice
1. fête
2. voiture
3. décore
4. passe-temps
5. occupée
6. prochain
7. font la grève
8. sauvages
9. amuse-gueules
10. triste
11. Vive la musique
12. le futur
13. Zut!
14. renseignements

Dialogue Exercises

A. 1.   Allô? Pierre est là s'il vous plaît?
2.   Bonjour, Robert, quoi de neuf?
3.   Robert téléphone à Pierre pour l'inviter à l'anniversaire de Juliette.

4.   Non, il n'accepte pas tout de suite.

5.   Pierre accepte l'invitation parce qu'il ne travaille pas le samedi.

6.   Pierre doit apporter des ballons et des glaçons.

7.   Jacqueline va jouer de la guitare.

8.   La voyante Madame Soleil va lire le futur.

9.   La date de la fête est le samedi, douze mars.

10.   L'âge officiel de la majorité est dix-huit ans.

11.   Non, la question d'âge n'est pas importante.

12.   Pierre veut danser avec Madame Soleil.

13.   Cette fête d'anniversaire est spéciale parce que c'est l'âge officiel de la majorité.

14.   Madame Soleil doit deviner la raison de l'absence de Pierre.

B. 1. décorer

2. fêter

3. occuper

4. bavarder

5. progresser

6. unir

7. vouloir

8. rêver

9. inviter

10. organiser

Grammar I

Practice

1. votre (ta)

2. nos

3. son

4. ton

5. Ma

6. Mes

7. Leur

8. vos

9. leur

10. nos

Exercises

A. 1. Elle décore sa maison.

2. Il téléphone à son ami.

3. Ils, elles attendent leur mère.

4. Il cherche sa voiture.

5. Elle veut son argent.

6. Elle adore ses enfants.

7. Elle change ses armoires de place.

8. Il mange ses biscuits.

9. Elle vend ses bijoux.

10. Il apporte ses ballons.

B. 1. Oui, c'est son chien.

2. Oui, ce sont ses amis.

3. Oui, ce sont ses fauteuils.

4. Oui, c'est son amie.

5. Oui, c'est son cousin.

6. Oui, ce sont ses sœurs.

7. Oui, c'est son mari.

8. Oui ce sont leurs employés.

9. Oui c'est leur chat.

10. Oui, c'est leur armoire.

Grammar II

Practice

A.
1. Ce sont les tiens.	11. . . . la sienne.
2. . . . la tienne.	12. . . . le tien?
3. . . . les miens.	13. . . . les leurs.
4. . . . les leurs.	14. . . . la tienne.
5. . . . les vôtres.	15. . . . la nôtre.
6. . . . les nôtres.	16. . . . la vôtre?
7. . . . les leurs.	17. . . . des leurs.
8. . . . les siens.	18. . . . les siennes.
9. . . . le sien.	19. . . . du mien.
10. . . . les tiennes.	20. . . . des vôtres.

B.
1. les vôtres.	6. le nôtre.
2. la vôtre.	7. les miennes.
3. le mien.	8. le nôtre.
4. la sienne.	9. les nôtres.
5. la leur.	10. les vôtres.

Grammar III

Practice

1. Jacques l'adore.	8. Tu veux la manger?
2. Le propriétaire l'appelle.	9. Tu le fêtes demain.
3. Je le regarde.	10. Ils l'aiment bien.
4. Il les achète.	11. Elle les achète.
5. Il ne l'a pas.	12. Je la décore.
6. Vous les refusez.	13. Je le loue.
7. Nous les organisons.	14. Je les invite.

Grammar IV

Practice

A.
1. Cherchons Jeanette.	7. Faites vos courses le matin.
2. Ne fumez jamais.	8. Ne va pas au cinéma aujourd'hui.
3. Sois gentille avec moi.	9. Racontez-moi une histoire.
4. Ayons beaucoup d'argent.	10. Attendez votre père.
5. N'aie pas peur.	11. Choisissons le fauteuil rouge.
6. Ne soyez pas triste.	12. Fais le ménage le lundi.

B.
1. Sois patient.	6. Ne faites pas la sieste.
2. Attendons l'avion.	7. Ayons de la chance maintenant.
3. Achetez les meubles.	8. Ne jouez pas au football.
4. Va à la plage.	9. Finis la conversation.
5. Ne regardez pas la télévision.	10. Fais attention.

Lesson 8

Vocabulary

Practice

A. 1. le   5. le   10. le

2. le   6. les   11. la

3. l'   7. le   12. le

4. la   8. la   13. la

9. la   14. les

B. 1. Les enfants s'amusent à l'épicerie.

2. L'épicier et le vendeur (la vendeuse) travaillent pour le gérant.

3. Quand je vais au supermarché, j'aime prendre mon temps.

4. Pour faire un gâteau, j'ai besoin d'huile, d'oeufs, de farine, et de sucre.

5. Le vendeur (la vendeuse) me rend la monnaie.

6. Je fréquente souvent l'épicerie du coin.

7. Ma sœur ne sait pas (ne peut pas) faire bouillir l'eau.

8. Quand j'ai soif, j'aime prendre un verre avec des amis (des amies).

Dialogue Exercises

A. 1. Elle fait le marché parce qu'elle a des invités.

2. Elle veut acheter un peu de tout.

3. Elle dit un joli rôti d'agneau, quelque chose d'extra.

4. Elle ne trouve pas la crème fraîche.

5. Elle va à la laiterie pour acheter la crème fraîche.

6. Elles sentent encore l'odeur des champs.

7. Elle pense que l'epicier a menti parce que l'arôme des fraises a parfumé l'épicerie.

8. Il dit qu'il a aiguisé son sens olfactif.

9. Oui, il plaisante avec elle.

10. Oui, parce qu'elle plaisante avec l'épicier.

B. 1. C

2. D

3. A

4. E

5. B

Grammar I and II

Practice

A. 1. J'ai acheté mes meubles au grand magasin.

2. L'arôme des fraises a parfumé la cuisine.

3. Charles a voyagé avec sa fiancée.

4. Le douanier a pu nous aider.

5. Nous avons choisi la lampe rouge.

6. La vendeuse nous a rendu la monnaie.

7. Juliette a voulu organiser un pique-nique.

8. Vous avez eu soif quand il a fait chaud.

9. Qu'est-ce que Jacques a-t-il fait (a fait)? quand il a bu?

10. Pourquoi Juliette a été (a-t-elle été) triste?

B. 1. Mes parents sont revenus du restaurant.

2. Il est allé à New York et elle est arrivée à Boston.

3. Nous sommes montés (montées) au cinquième étage.

4. Vous êtes devenue ma belle-sœur.

5. Elle est sortie avec son mari.

6. Juliette est arrivée pour l'anniversaire de son frère.

7. Elles sont restées avec leur tante.

8. Les feuilles sont tombées de l'arbre.

C. 1. Je suis venu(e) vous voir avant de partir.

2. J'ai eu de l'argent, mais je l'ai dépensé.

3. J'ai été invité(e) au dîner *(or)* à dîner.

4. Vous êtes descendu(e) prendre un verre.

5. J'ai voulu un pot de crème fraîche.

6. Ils sont partis sans dire "merci."

7. Nous n'avons pas perdu nos clefs.

8. Ils n'ont pas bu de vin.

9. Il est revenu avec des fleurs.

10. Elle a aimé la musique.

Grammar III

Practice

1. Il y a beaucoup de vin dans le frigo.

2. Il y a une table, mais il n'y a pas de chaises.

3. Il y a un gérant mais il n'y a pas de vendeuses.

4. Il n'y a pas de viande avec ce repas.

5. Il y a une clef pour la chambre, mais il n'y a pas de clef pour la commode.

6. Il y a des fruits et des légumes à l'épicerie.

7. Il y a eu une fête d'anniversaire ici.

Exercise

1. Il ne faut pas regarder la télé.

2. Il faut trouver les clefs pour l'armoire.

3. Pourquoi a-t-il fallu changer d'avion?

4. Il faut organiser le voyage.

5. Il faut atterrir à "Baghdad by the Bay."

6. Il ne faut pas perdre son temps à fumer.

7. Il faut manger quand on a faim.

Lesson 9

Vocabulary

Practice

A. 1. forte
   2. satisfaite
   3. reconnaissante
   4. sérieuse
   5. mensuelle
   6. annuelle
   7. luxueuse
   8. gagnante
   9. gentille
   10. patiente
   11. prudente
   12. courageuse
   13. vieille
   14. sportive
   15. naïve

B. 1. emprunter
   2. valeur
   3. actionnaire
   4. annuelle
   5. bavard
   6. satisfait
   7. place
   8. plaisanter
   9. vraiment
   10. finir

C. 1. ferme
   2. caissière me donne . . . à remplir
   3. taux . . . bas.
   4. impôts
   5. guichet des investissements
   6. suis à sec
   7. paie à crédit
   8. payer comptant
   9. la caisse d'epargne
   10. devises . . . augmente

Dialogue Exercises

A. 1. Il veut ouvrir un compte.
   2. Jacques apporte deux chèques.
   3. Il le touche.
   4. Il le dépose dans les nouveaux comptes.
   5. Il doit l'endosser.
   6. Parce que le chèque est déjà endossé.
   7. Elle lui donne des chèques provisoires.
   8. Pour les chèques imprimés à son nom.
   9. Il dépose soixante-quinze dollars.
   10. Il dépose vingt-cinq dollars.

B. 1. F
   2. G
   3. H
   4. A
   5. B
   6. I
   7. E
   8. J
   9. D
   10. C

Grammar I

Exercises

A. 1. an indirect object noun
   2. direct object answers: what, whom; indirect object answers: to what, to whom, of what, etc.
   3. *lui* and *leur*
   4. the preposition *à*
   5. They immediately precede the verb.

B. 1. leur demande
   2. m'a téléphoné
   3. lui avons parlé
   4. nous rend
   5. me demande
   6. vous ai téléphoné
   7. nous a montré
   8. lui ressemble
   9. leur parler
   10. lui écrire

Grammar II

Practice

A. 1. When the action of a verb reflects on the subject.
   2. The verb always has a reflexive pronoun.
   3. They both precede the verb.
   4. *Nous ne nous amusons pas.*
   5. indirect object pronoun
   6. *il se lave, ils se lavent, se laver* (infinitive)
   7. Je m'amuse.
   8. Nous nous arrêtons.
   9. Ils s'amusent.
   10. Tu te parles.

B. 1. Ma petite sœur se lève tôt le matin.
   2. Pendant que je me lave, elle mange.
   3. Quand j'ai besoin de me regarder dans le miroir, elle m'appelle.

4. Je me brosse les dents après le petit déjeuner.

5. Ma petite sœur et moi nous nous habillons en même temps.

6. Dès que je finis, je me prépare pour sortir.

7. Ma sœur et ma voisine se promènent après mon départ.

8. J'ai besoin de me coucher de bonne heure ce soir.

9. Mes parents se réveillent souvent plus tôt que moi.

10. Mon ami Mark se marie la semaine prochaine.

Grammar III

Exercises

A. 1. nous réveillons tard aussi.

2. se brossent aussi.

3. vous amusez aussi.

4. nous excusons aussi.

5. te couches aussi.

6. se lèvent aussi.

7. t'amuses aussi.

8. se reposent aussi.

9. m'ennuie aussi.

B. 1. Repose-toi.

2. Lave-toi.

3. Dépêchez-vous.

4. Habillons-nous.

5. Baigne-toi.

6. Couchez-vous tôt.

7. Ne vous ennuyez pas.

8. Ne nous arrêtons pas ici.

9. Ne t'excuse pas.

10. Brossez-vous les dents.

Lesson 10

Vocabulary

Practice

A.
1. une	6. un	11. un
2. un	7. une	12. un
3. un	8. une	13. une
4. des	9. des	14. des
5. une	10. un	15. une

B. 1. l'arrivée

2. le sud

3. l'ouest

4. descendre

5. se coucher

6. l'entrée

7. perdre

8. payer comptant

9. fort

10. augmenter

C. 1. ont changé
  2. a augmenté
  3. est arrivé
  4. avons oublié
  5. est reparti
  6. est finie
  7. a été
  8. avons eu
  9. ont envoyé
  10. avez eu

Dialogue Exercises

1. Juliette est à la gare.
2. Juliette dit, "Ah! voilà Charles."
3. Charles répond, "Salut, Juliette!"
4. Charles voudrait dire "Au revoir" à Monsieur Legrand.
5. Charles a passé la nuit dans le train.
6. L'opposé de "fatigué" est "reposé."
7. Charles est en forme parce qu'il a bien dormi.
8. Après le dîner, Charles prend un verre avec Monsieur Legrand.
9. Quand Charles arrive, le chauffeur ouvre le coffre.
10. Charles veut acheter trois cartes.
11. Ces cartes sont: la Carte Paris-Visite, la Carte Museés-Monuments, et la Télécarte.

Grammar I

Exercises

A. 1. Ils réussissaient à faire des économies.
  2. Mes parents et moi étions d'accord sur ce sujet.
  3. Les voisins commençaient à nous inviter.
  4. La route nationale était pleine de panneaux.
  5. Nos amis n'avaient pas hésité une minute.
  6. Vous m'encouragiez tous les jours.
  7. Il était midi pile et il ne déjeunait pas.
  8. À minuit nous entendions des bruits.
  9. Nous pouvions sortir plus tard.
  10. Il voulait faire la connaissance de Juliette.

B. 1. Nous avions plusieurs heures de route nationale.
  2. Mon mari me donnait de l'argent pendant la semaine.
  3. Chaque jour le voisin invitait ma sœur.
  4. Nous partions en vacances ensemble.
  5. Ces garçons étaient de l'Amérique et du Canada.
  6. Nous faisions une promenade le soir.
  7. Après le travail je faisais des courses.
  8. Ils rentraient souvent très tard.
  9. Nous étions avec Jean le jour de la fête.
  10. Nous étions heureux avec nos voisins *(or)* avec les voisins.

C. Je faisais mes débuts en français, les leçons étaient parfois difficiles, mais je faisais mon possible pour les comprendre. J'étais occupé(e) l'après-midi, mais j'étudiais le matin et quelquefois j'essayais de finir les exercices le soir. La leçon cinq était très longue parce qu'elle avait plusieurs pages de révision. Je voulais continuer l'étude du français parce que j'aimais beaucoup la langue, et parce que j'avais envie d'aller en France.

Grammar II

Exercises

A. 1. Juliette venait toujours à midi, mais aujourd'hui, elle est venue en retard.
    2. Elle croyait à mes promesses, mais soudainement, elle a changé.
    3. Elle pensait toujours à moi, mais lundi elle a oublié mon anniversaire.
    4. Elle aimait mes histoires, mais hier elle a trouvé ma plaisanterie ennuyeuse.
    5. Le soir elle étudiait, mais hier elle est sortie avec Pierre.
    6. Elle me téléphonait le matin, mais aujourd'hui elle ne m'a pas téléphoné.
    7. Juliette voulait aller camper, mais elle a refusé d'aller avec moi.
    8. Juliette pouvait me faire rire, mais hier elle m'a fait pleurer.
    9. Elle m'attendait toujours, mais aujourd'hui elle a décidé de partir sans moi.
    10. Elle était souvent polie, mais hier elle a insulté ma sœur.

B. 1. Juliette voulait faire la connaissance d'Antoine, mais il n'est pas venu avec Charles.
    2. Ma sœur et moi faisions une promenade quand nous avons rencontré Jacques.
    3. J'avais froid quand je suis retourné(e) de l'aéroport.
    4. J'avais faim, alors j'ai mangé tout le pain.
    5. Hier, je suis resté(e) au lit parce que j'étais malade.
    6. Je me suis ennuyé(e), alors mon ami(e) m'a raconté une histoire.
    7. Je suis monté(e) dans ma couchette et j'ai commencé à lire.
    8. L'heure d'affluence était toujours entre quatre heures et cinq heures.
    9. Le contrôleur vérifiait nos billets pendant que nous mangions.
    10. Nous sommes allé(e)s à l'étranger l'année dernière.

Grammar III

Exercises

A. 1. Days are not capitalized in French.
    2. Monday
    3. masculine
    4. every
    5. samedi, jeudi, vendredi
    6. dimanche prochain, juillet prochain, l'année prochaine
    7. cardinal number + -ième
    8. deux, six, dix

      9. soixante

    10. Le premier jour de la semaine est lundi.

B.   1. La semaine prochaine nous allons acheter des meubles.

     2. Mon ami est allé(e) à Nice la deuxième semaine de juillet.

     3. Nous avons conduit ensemble à l'aéroport en mars.

     4. Le neuvième mois de l'année est septembre.

     5. Je prends des leçons de piano le mardi.

     6. Mon mari part à Paris le mois d'octobre prochain (*or*) en octobre prochain.

     7. Le centième passager a gagné le gros lot!

Note: In answers 2, 3, and 5, the months and days could also start the sentence, as in *Le mardi je prends. . . .*

REVIEW EXAM   LESSONS 6–10

PART I: VOCABULARY

ANSWERS
p. 138

A. Match the two columns.

1. _____ l'eau
2. _____ le matelas
3. _____ le loyer
4. _____ la grève
5. _____ les glaçons
6. _____ les renseignements
7. _____ l'épicier
8. _____ le gérant
9. _____ les œufs
10. _____ le guichet
11. _____ le coffre
12. _____ le comptant
13. _____ le montant
14. _____ le panneau
15. _____ le quai
16. _____ le nord
17. _____ l'heure d'affluence
18. _____ le mécanicien

A. C'est ce qu'on paie au propriétaire
B. Dans les boissons
C. À demander pour savoir quelque chose
D. Propriétaire d'une épicerie
E. Directeur
F. Pour faire une omelette
G. Est sur le lit
H. La caissière
I. Nécessaire quand on a soif
J. Le droit des travailleurs
K. Le total de l'addition
L. Indique la route
M. Les passagers attendent là
N. Il contrôle le train
O. C'est le contraire de "crédit"
P. Dans une banque pour garder les bijoux
Q. Le contraire de sud
R. Il y a beaucoup de voitures

ANSWERS
p. 138

B. Write the opposite of the following words.

1. froid _____
2. heureux _____
3. comptant _____
4. ouvrir _____
5. vendre _____
6. gagner _____
7. faible _____
8. dépenser _____
9. se coucher _____
10. monter _____

ANSWERS
p. 138

C. Complete the following sentences with the correct word.

1. La caissière m'a donné des _____ à remplir pour ouvrir un compte de chèques.
2. Le train de Paris-Marseille n'a pas de _____ alors je n'ai pas dormi.
3. J'étais invité à dîner chez Marie et _____ bien amusé.
4. Quand j'ai de l'argent _____ à la caisse d'épargne.
5. La banque de notre ville avait un taux d'intérêt très _____.
6. Quand je vais à l'étranger je dois acheter des _____.
7. Les enfants de ma tante sont mes _____ et mes _____.

8. Le mari de ma sœur est mon _____ et la femme de mon frère est ma _____.

9. Il faut toujours _____ un chèque avant de le toucher.

10. L'agneau, le bœuf ne sont pas des poissons, ce sont des _____.

D. Circle the best answers to complete the statements below.

1. L'hôtel où nous sommes restés est très beau;
   - a. il a des fenêtres.
   - b. il donne sur la plage.
   - c. les meubles sont vieux.
   - d. il n'y a pas un lit.

2. Quand la famille est ensemble
   - a. nous allons à la banque.
   - b. nous cherchons un hôtel.
   - c. nous nous amusons bien.
   - d. nous sommes fatigués.

3. Il vaut mieux voyager par avion.
   - a. quand il fait beau.
   - b. à la fin de l'année.
   - c. quand on est pressé.
   - d. quand on n'a pas de voiture.

4. Quand les travailleurs veulent une augmentation de salaire et ne la reçoivent pas,
   - a. ils font la grève.
   - b. ils ne sont pas à sec.
   - c. ils dépensent beaucoup d'argent.
   - d. ils ouvrent des comptes ordinaires.

5. Il vaut mieux voyager par train
   - a. quand on veut apprécier le paysage.
   - b. quand on n'a pas d'avion.
   - c. quand on est en retard.
   - d. quand on a beaucoup de bagages.

PART II: GRAMMAR

A. Write the correct form of the *imparfait* (imperfect) in the following sentences.

1. Les enfants _____ (jouer) dans le jardin.

2. Les frères _____ (être) très aimables, et les sœurs _____ (vouloir) nous aider aussi.

3. À la banque, ils _____ (pouvoir) nous vendre des actions.

4. Le gérant du supermarché _____ (chercher) la caissière.

5. L'hôtel _____ (être) grand et il y _____ (avoir) un jardin où _____ (pousser) (to grow) de belles fleurs exotiques.

6. Nous _____ (pouvoir) aller à pied à la plage.

7. Nous _____ (étudier) le français tous les soirs.

8. Mon frère _____ (manger) le petit déjeuner quand je _____ (faire) mes devoirs (homework).

9. Nous _____ (danser) et nous _____ (être) heureux avec nos amis.

10. Il y _____ (avoir) beaucoup de travail à faire.

ANSWERS
p. 138

B. Rewrite the verbs, in the following text, in the past tense, using the *imparfait* or the *passé composé* as verb actions dictate.

Nous arrivons à Nice à quatre heures de l'après-midi. Nous sommes fatigués, mais il fait beau et nous marchons vers la plage. Les baigneuses (swimmers, fem.) ressemblent à des vedettes de cinéma (movie stars). Nous avons soif et nous voulons nous asseoir; nous cherchons un restaurant, alors nous trouvons un petit "snack bar." Nous commandons deux bières et deux sandwiches. Nous finissons, nous nous levons et nous continuons notre promenade.

ANSWERS
p. 139

C. Write the appropriate words in French to complete the following sentences.

Example: (Her) vêtements sont neufs.

Ses vêtements sont neufs.

1. Le 20 juin _____ (I went) au théâtre.
2. (These) _____ exercises sont faciles.
3. J'aime mon repas et toi, aimes-tu _____ (yours)?
4. Les enfants amusent souvent _____ (their) parents.
5. Il a choisi cette couchette-ci, et j'ai choisi _____ (that one).
6. Nous avons ouvert (opened) un compte de chèques et ils ont fermé _____ (theirs).
7. Il vaut mieux prendre l'avion de huit heures que _____ (the one) de dix heures.
8. Nous avons habité _____ (this) ville pendant cinq ans.
9. (It is not allowed) _____ de fumer dans le wagon-lit.
10. (My) _____ parents et _____ (those) de mon mari sont partis en vacances ensemble.
11. Les légumes que _____ (I bought) au supermarché sont dans le frigo.
12. Quand tu es pressé _____ (you don't walk) _____ (you must, one must run).
13. La couchette supérieure est _____ (for him) et la couchette inférieure est _____ (for her).

ANSWERS   REVIEW EXAM

Lessons 6–10

Vocabulary

A. 1. I   7. D   13. K
   2. G   8. E.   14. L
   3. A   9. F   15. M
   4. J   10. H   16. Q
   5. B   11. P   17. R
   6. C   12. O   18. N

B. 1. chaud   6. perdre
   2. triste   7. fort
   3. crédit   8. économiser
   4. fermer   9. se réveiller
   5. acheter   10. descendre

C. 1. cartes   6. devises
   2. couchettes (or) wagon-lits   7. cousins et mes cousines
   3. je me suis   8. mon beau-frère . . . , ma belle-sœur
   4. je le dépose   9. endosser
   5. bas (or) haut   10. viandes

D. 1. b
   2. c
   3. c
   4. a
   5. d (or) a

Grammar

A. 1. jouaient   6. pouvions
   2. étaient . . . voulaient   7. étudiions
   3. pouvaient   8. mangeait . . . faisais
   4. cherchait   9. dansions . . . étions
   5. était . . . il y avait . . . poussaient   10. avait

B. Nous sommes arrivés à Nice à quatre heures de l'après-midi. Nous étions fatigués, mais il faisait beau et nous marchions vers la plage. Les baigneuses ressemblaient à des vedettes de cinéma. Nous avions soif et nous voulions nous asseoir; nous cherchions un restaurant, alors nous avons trouvé un petit "snack bar." Nous avons commandé deux bières et deux sandwiches. Nous avons fini, nous nous sommes levés et nous avons continué notre promenade.

C.   1. Le 20 juin, je suis allé(e) au théâtre.

2. Ces exercises sont faciles.

3. J'aime mon repas et toi, aimes-tu le tien?

4. Les enfants amusent souvent leurs parents.

5. Il a choisi cette couchette-ci, et j'ai choisi cette couchette-là.

6. Nous avons ouvert un compte de chèques et ils ont fermé le leur.

7. Il vaut mieux prendre l'avion de huit heures que celui de dix heures.

8. Nous avons habité cette ville pendant cinq ans.

9. Il est défendu de fumer dans le wagon-lit.

10. Mes parents et ceux de mon mari sont partis en vacances ensemble.

11. Les légumes que j'ai achetés au supermarché sont dans le frigo.

12. Quand tu es pressé tu ne marches pas, tu cours. (*or*) Il ne faut pas marcher, il faut courir.

13. La couchette supérieure est pour lui, et la couchette inférieure est pour elle.

11 Les parties du corps
(Parts of the Body)

la barbe	beard	la gorge	throat
la bouche	mouth	la jambe	leg
le bras	arm	la langue	tongue
le casse-pieds	pest	la main	hand
les cheveux (masc.)	hair	le menton	chin
la cheville	ankle	le nez	nose
le cil	eyelash	l'œil (masc.)	eye
le conseil	advice	l'oreille (fem.)	ear
le corps	body	le pied	foot
le cou	neck	la poitrine	chest
la dent	tooth	le poumon	lung
le doigt	finger	la santé	health
le dos	back	le sourcil	eyebrow
l'épaule (fem.)	shoulder	le sourire	smile
l'estomac (masc.)	stomach	le ventre	belly, abdomen
le foie	liver	le visage	face
le front	forehead	les yeux (masc.)	eyes
le genou	knee		

casser	to break	se sentir	to feel
guérir	to heal	soigner	to take care
poser	to put	tomber malade	to get sick
se reposer	to rest	tousser	to cough
reposer	to put back	trébucher	to trip over
respirer	to breathe	se trouver	to find oneself
se réveiller	to wake up		

blond(e)	blond, blonde	**lentement**	slowly
brun(e)	brown, brunette	**lourd(e)**	heavy
donc	therefore	**mal**	evil, badly
droit	right	**malade**	sick
en plus	in addition	**mieux**	better
gauche	left	**souple**	supple
imprévu(e)	unexpected	**trop**	too much
léger (-ère)	light		

NOTES:

1. All the verbs in the above vocabulary except *tomber malade* and *trébucher* can be either reflexive or nonreflexive. When some of them change into reflexive, they also change their meaning. One such verb is *sentir*—"to smell" (nonreflexive) and *se sentir*—"to feel" (reflexive); others simply mean what reflexive constructions imply: that the action reflects back to the subject.

    EXAMPLE: *guérir quelqu'un* = to heal someone

    se guérir = to heal oneself

    trouver = to find (something, someone)

    se trouver = to find oneself, as in *Je me trouve à Paris.*
    (I find myself in Paris).

2. *Le mal* literally means "evil," as in *Le bien et le mal,* "good and evil." It is also used as an adverb, as in *C'est très mal fait* (It is very badly [poorly] done). *Malade* means "sick" (adjective), and with the article it becomes a noun.

    EXAMPLE: *le malade, la malade* the sick one

3. When the adverb *mal* is preceded by *avoir,* it means "to hurt," as in *J'ai mal aux pieds.* (My feet hurt.)

    Thus, by using *avoir mal* and adding the affected part of the body, we can make as many sentences as we wish.

    EXAMPLE: *Il a mal à la gorge.* He has a sore throat.

    Note that the expression *avoir mal à* is followed by *à la* for feminine nouns, *au* for masculine singular, and *aux* for both feminine and masculine plurals, as in:

    Elles ont mal aux jambes (fem. pl.). Their legs hurt.

    Il a mal aux bras. (masc. pl.). His arms hurt.

PRACTICE THE VOCABULARY

A. Name all the pairs of the parts of the body, following the example.

Example: J'ai *deux mains* (hands).

1. J'ai _____ (eyes).
2. J'ai _____ (ears).
3. J'ai _____ (feet).
4. J'ai _____ (legs).
5. J'ai _____ (ankles).

6. J'ai _____ (knees).
7. J'ai _____ (shoulders).
8. J'ai _____ (lungs).
9. J'ai _____ (eyebrows).
10. J'ai _____ (arms).

ANSWERS
p. 193

B. Translate the following sentences into French.

1. They got sick yesterday. _____.
2. Where do you hurt? _____.
3. Was the suitcase heavy? _____.
4. He feels weak. _____.
5. We are able to heal ourselves. _____.
6. Take good care of yourself. _____.
7. How are you? Are you better today? _____.
8. I feel much better when I rest. _____.
9. Give me your hand, I want to see it. _____.
10. I have been sick for a week. _____.

DIALOGUE   Un portrait

Le téléphone sonne. Je prends le récepteur. C'est mon frère.

CHARLES: Allô? C'est Charles. Je voulais te dire que ma nouvelle voisine est d'une beauté rare.

MOI: C'est formidable. Est-elle blonde, brune, grande, petite? Dis-moi tout.

CHARLES: D'abord, elle a les cheveux longs et frisés qui lui touchent les épaules. Elle est blonde bien sûr!

MOI: Pourquoi, bien sûr? Qu'est-ce que tu veux dire par là?

CHARLES: Je veux te rappeler, que je ne regarde presque jamais une brune. Bien sûr, je ne parle pas des membres de la famille!

MOI: Heureusement que tu as ajouté ces mots-là. J'allais t'arrêter tout de suite!

CHARLES: Bon, laisse-moi continuer. Elle a une petite bouche, des dents légèrement imparfaites, et un corps de sportive.

MOI: Elle t'a parlé? Comment as-tu découvert que ses dents étaient imparfaites?

CHARLES: Elle ne m'a pas parlé, mais elle m'a fait un grand sourire.

MOI: Tu as l'intention de faire sa connaissance bientôt, n'est-ce pas? Dans ce cas, je te conseille de surveiller ta langue. Surtout ne parle pas de ses cheveux blonds!

CHARLES: Pourquoi pas? Quel mal y a-t-il à cela?

MOI: Peut-être qu'elle était brune dans l'autre monde.

CHARLES: Quel autre monde?

MOI: Le monde où les hommes ont du tact!

CHARLES: Tu es vraiment aimable, chère sœur!

MOI: Je suis en colère parce que tu m'as réveillée.

CHARLES: Mais il est midi et demi. Tu n'es pas malade, j'espère!

MOI: Je ne suis pas malade, mais je ne me sens pas très bien. En plus j'ai le droit de dormir tard, le dimanche.

CHARLES: Excuse-moi et merci pour ton conseil!

MOI: Au revoir, Charles, bonne chance avec ta blonde!

DIALOGUE   A Portrait

(The telephone rings. I pick up the receiver. It's my brother.)

CHARLES: Hello! It's Charles. I wanted to tell you that my new neighbor is a rare beauty.

ME: That's great! Is she blond, brunette, tall, petite? Tell me everything.

CHARLES: First, she has long curly hair, which touches her shoulders. She is blond, of course!

ME: Why, of course? What do you mean by that?

CHARLES: I want to remind you that I almost never look at a brunette. Of course, I'm not speaking about members of the family!

ME: It's fortunate that you added those words. I was going to cut you off right away!

CHARLES: Well, let me continue. She has a small mouth, teeth slightly imperfect, and the body of an athlete.

ME: Did she talk to you? How did you discover her teeth were imperfect?

CHARLES: She didn't speak to me, but she gave me a big smile.

ME: You intend to meet her soon, don't you? In that case, I advise you to watch your tongue. Most of all, don't talk about her blond hair!

CHARLES: Why not? What is the harm in that?

ME: Perhaps she was a brunette in some other world!

CHARLES: What other world?

ME: A world where men have some tact!

CHARLES: You are truly kind, dear sister!

ME: I am angry because you woke me.

CHARLES: But it's half past noon. You're not sick, I hope!

ME: No, I'm not sick, but I don't feel very well. Also, I have the right to sleep late
             on Sunday!

CHARLES: Excuse me, and thanks for your advice!

ME: Goodbye, Charles, and good luck with your blonde!

DIALOGUE EXERCISES

ANSWERS
p. 193

A. Based on the dialogue, answer the following questions with complete sentences.

1. Qui est Charles? _____

2. Que voulait-il dire? _____

3. Les cheveux de la voisine sont _____, _____ et
    _____.

4. Pourquoi la sœur de Charles est-elle en colère? _____

5. Est-ce que les cheveux de "Moi" sont blonds? _____

6. Pourquoi "Moi" a-t-elle dormi tard? _____

7. À quelle heure le téléphone a-t-il sonné? _____

8. Est-ce que "Moi" est polie, aimable, sarcastique? _____

9. De quel monde est Charles? _____

10. Comment sont les dents de la voisine? _____

11. Est-ce que la voisine a parlé à Charles? _____

12. Comment la voisine a-t-elle montré ses dents? _____

13. Est-ce que "Moi" est malade? _____

14. Est-ce que Charles a fait la connaissance de la voisine? _____

ANSWERS
p. 194

B. Complete the following sentences, following the example.

   Example: Nous sautons (jump) avec *les jambes.*

1. Nous marchons avec _____.

2. Nous regardons avec _____.

3. Nous sentons avec _____.

4. Nous entendons avec _____.

5. Nous écrivons avec _____.

6. Nous mangeons avec _____.

7. Nous mâchons (chew) avec _____.

8. Nous touchons avec _____.

GRAMMAR I   Comparisons of Inequality

A. Study the following table.

French	English
plus + adjective + **que**	more + adjective + than
moins + adverb + **que**	less + adverb + than
plus de + noun	more + noun
moins de + noun	less + noun

B. Where the English adjective takes the comparative ending *-er* or *more* + the adjective + *than*, French always uses the expression *plus . . . que* and *plus de . . . que*. French uses *plus . . . que* with adverbs or adjectives.

> EXAMPLE: *Elle est plus riche que lui*   She is richer than he (is).
>
> *Il sort plus souvent qu'elle.*   He goes out more often than she (does).

C. With nouns expressing numbers or amounts, French uses *plus de . . . que*.

> EXAMPLE: *J'ai plus d'argent que lui.*   I have more money than he (does).
>
> *J'ai plus d'amis que lui.*   I have more friends than he.

D. The expressions *moins . . . que* and *moins de . . . que* follow the same rules as *plus . . . que* and *plus de . . . que*. With adjectives and adverbs of inequality, the English equivalent of *moins de . . . que* is "fewer than."

E. The expression *moins de . . . que* is used with nouns expressing numbers and amounts, like *plus de . . . que* above.

> EXAMPLE: *Il a moins de problèmes que moi.*   He has fewer problems than I.
>
> *Nous avons moins de patience que vous.*   We have less patience than you.

F. *Plus . . . que* and *moins . . . que* are always placed *after* the verb.

> EXAMPLE: *Elle gagne plus que lui.*   She earns more than he.
>
> *Ils mangent moins que nous.*   They eat less than we.

PRACTICE THE COMPARATIVES

ANSWERS
p. 194

A. Complete the following exercise.

1. The expressions *plus . . . que* and *moins . . . que* are used with verbs, adverbs, and _____.

2. The expressions *plus de . . . que* and *moins de . . . que* are only used with _____.

3. What expression is used with numbers and amounts? _____.

4. The English comparatives *-er than* and *more than* are translated into French by _____ and _____.

5. The English equivalent of *less than* in French is _____.

6. How do you say in French: "He is more serious than she"? _____.

7. Say and then write in French: "She has less than twenty dollars." _____.

8. Say and then write in French: "We talk more seriously than you." _____.

9. Where are the comparatives *plus . . . que* and *moins . . . que* placed in relation to the verb? _____.

10. When does French use *moins de . . . que?* _____.

ANSWERS
p. 194

B. Complete the sentences with the appropriate comparative.

1. Elle s'est réveillée (later than) _____ lui.

2. En magique, la main est (quicker than) _____ l'œil.

3. Payer comptant est (easier than) _____ payer à crédit.

4. En general les malles sont (heavier than) _____ les valises.

5. Ils voyagent à l'étranger (more often than) _____ nous.

6. Les femmes sont (more sociable than) _____ nous.

7. Les petites filles sont (less talkative than) _____ les petits garçons.

8. Le nez de Pinocchio est (longer than) _____ le mien.

9. Elle dépense (more money than) _____ lui.

10. Elle est (less intelligent than) _____ vous.

GRAMMAR II   Comparisons of Equality • Superlatives

A. Study comparisons of equality with adjectives and adverbs.

French	English
aussi + adjective + **que**	as + adjective + as
aussi + adverb + **que**	as + adverb + as

NOTE:
Following are examples.

> EXAMPLE: *Elle est aussi intelligente que moi* (adj).
> She is as intelligent as I.
>
> *Elle parle aussi bien que moi* (adv.). She speaks as well as I.

B. Study comparisons of equality with verbs and nouns.

French uses *autant . . . que* and *autant de . . . que* with verbs and nouns to translate the English "as much . . . as" or "as many . . . as."

> EXAMPLE: *Il parle autant que moi* (verb). He talks as much as I do.
>
> *Il a autant d'amis que moi* (noun). He has as many friends as I do.

Notice that *autant de . . . que* is used in French only with nouns expressing amounts and numbers (just like *plus de . . . que* and *moins de . . . que*), while in English "as much" and "as many" are used with verbs as well as with nouns.

C. French superlatives are formed by adding *le, la,* or *les* to the comparative of the adjective, thus agreeing in number and gender with the nouns they modify.

> EXAMPLE: *Il est intelligent.*   He is intelligent.
> *Il est plus intelligent.*   He is more intelligent.
> *Il est le plus intelligent.*   He is the most intelligent.

D. There are some French adjectives and adverbs that have irregular comparatives and superlatives. Study the following chart.

Adjective/Adverb	Comparative	Superlative	English
bon	meilleur	le meilleur	good, better, the best
bien	mieux	le mieux	well, better, the best
mal	pire	le pire	bad, worse, the worst

NOTE:
1. The feminine of the adjective *bon* is *bonne,* the masculine plural is *bons,* and the feminine plural is *bonnes.*

> EXAMPLE: *La salade est bonne.*
> *Le vin est bon.*
> *La salade et le vin sont bons.*
> *Les salades sont bonnes.*
> *Les vins sont bons.*

2. The superlatives *le (la, les) meilleur (e, s, es)* also agree in number and gender with the nouns they modify.

> EXAMPLE: *J'ai mangé la meilleure salade.*
>
> *J'ai bu le meilleur vin.*
>
> *J'ai bu les meilleurs vins.*
>
> *J'ai mangé les meilleures salades.*

PRACTICE THE GRAMMAR

ANSWERS
pp. 194–195

Practice the comparative of equality and the superlative in the following exercise.

1. What are the French equivalents of "as . . . as" and "as much as" and "as many as"? _____.
2. When does French use *autant de . . . que*? _____.
3. How is *autant de . . . que* translated in English? _____.
4. What does French use to form the superlative of an adjective? _____.
5. What is important about the formation of French superlatives? _____.
6. Give the French equivalent of "the best books." _____.
7. Say and then write in French, "Their books are better." _____.
8. Say and then write in French, "They speak better." _____.
9. Say and then write in French, "He feels worse." _____.
10. Say and then write in French, "He feels as bad as you do." _____.

EXERCISE

ANSWERS
p. 195

Change the expressions *plus . . . que, plus de . . . que* into *moins . . . que* and *moins de . . . que*. Follow the example.

> *Example:* Il y a plus de garcons que de filles.
>
> *Il y a moins de filles que de garçons.*

1. Nous avons plus de courage que vous. _____.
2. Jean et Juliette attendent plus longtemps (longer) que vous. _____.
3. Les voisins sont plus charmants que vous. _____.
4. La concierge est plus sérieuse que la téléphoniste. _____.
5. La banque est plus près que la caisse d'épargne. _____.
6. Les enfants sont plus bavards que les parents. _____.

GRAMMAR III   Future Indicative of Regular and Irregular Verbs

A. Study the forms of the future indicative of regular verbs shown on the chart below.

Subject	*Parler*	*Choisir*	*Attendre*
je	parler ai	choisir ai	attendr ai
tu	parler as	choisir as	attendr as
il, elle, on	parler a	choisir a	attendr a
nous	parler ons	choisir ons	attendr ons
vous	parler ez	choisir ez	attendr ez
ils, elles	parler ont	choisir ont	attendr ont

1. The future tense in French is formed by adding the future tense endings to the infinitive of the verbs. These endings are: *-ai, -as, -a, -ons, -ez,* and *-ont.*

2. The final *e* of the verbs ending in *-re* is dropped, as with *attendre-ai.* The endings for the future tense of regular verbs are always regular.

> EXAMPLE: *manger   je manger-ai*
> *finir   je finir-ai*
> *prendre   je prendr-ai*

B. Some verbs have stem changes or irregular stems. These irregularities are also found in the future tense. For example, we have already studied spelling changes in the verbs *acheter* and *payer.* The future tense of these verbs is:

> *acheter: j'achèterai*
> *tu achèteras,* etc.
> *payer: je paierai*
> *tu paieras,* etc.

C. Study the verbs with irregular stems.

aller	j'irai	tu iras	il, elle ira	etc.
avoir	j'aurai	tu auras	il, elle aura	etc.
devoir	je devrai	tu devras	il, elle devra	etc.
être	je serai	tu seras	il, elle sera	etc.
faire	je ferai	tu feras	il, elle fera	etc.
pouvoir	je pourrai	tu pourras	il, elle pourra	etc.
savoir	je saurai	tu sauras	il, elle saura	etc.
venir	je viendrai	tu viendras	il, elle viendra	etc.
voir	je verrai	tu verras	il, elle verra	etc.
vouloir	je voudrai	tu voudras	il, elle voudra	etc.

1. The verbs listed in the chart all have very irregular stems. Once you've memorized the stems, however, you'll find that the future endings follow the regular pattern.

2. The future tense, in French, is used in the same way as in English. However, French uses the future tense with dependent clauses, starting with *quand* (when), *lorsque* (when), and *dès que* (as soon as), whereas English uses the present tense.

   EXAMPLE: *Je te raconterai une histoire quand je reviendrai.*
   I'll tell you a story when I come back.

   Je pourrai te parler lorsque je finirai mon travail.
   I'll be able to talk to you when I finish my work.

   Je téléphonerai dès que je rentrerai.
   I will telephone (you) as soon as I return.

PRACTICE THE FUTURE TENSE

1. Write the endings of the future tense: _____, _____, _____, _____, _____, _____.
2. To what verb form does French add these endings in order to form the future tense? _____.
3. Do the future tense endings ever change? _____.
4. Do the future tense stems change with irregular verbs? _____.
5. Where does French use the future tense where English does not? _____.
6. Say and then write in French, "They will be able to." _____.
7. Say and then write in French, "They will know more than we." _____.
8. What is the future tense of *il faut*? _____.
9. What is the future tense of *il vaut mieux*? _____.
10. Say and then write in French, "He will eat as soon as he comes back." _____.

EXERCISE

Rewrite the sentences below in the future tense.

1. Ma sœur est invitée chez la voisine. _____
2. Nous trouvons un petit hôtel charmant. _____
3. Vous pouvez m'aider à préparer le dîner. _____
4. Juliette travaille à la banque. _____
5. Nous allons à Paris après la fête de Noël. _____
6. Elle apprend à jouer de la harpe. _____
7. Nous savons écrire le chinois (Chinese). _____

12 À la pharmacie
(At the Drugstore)

l'alimentation (fem.)	food	la goutte	drop
la balance	scale	la lame (de rasoir)	blade
le barbier	barber	le peigne	comb
la boucherie	butcher's	la pipe	pipe
la boulangerie	bakery	le plâtre	plaster
la brosse (à dents, à cheveux)	brush (tooth-, hair-)	le plombage	filling (tooth)
		la poissonnerie	fish market
le calmant	sedative	la poudre	powder
le compte-goutte	eyedropper	le rasoir	razor
la crise	attack, crisis	le régime	diet
la diète	diet	le soulagement	relief
la drogue	drug	le syrop	syrup
l'espoir (masc.)	hope	le talc	talcum

abuser	to abuse	grossir	to gain weight
alimenter	to feed	s'habituer	to get used to
avaler	to swallow	(se) passer	to pass
devoir . . . à	to owe to	plomber	to fill (tooth)
durer	to last	se raser	to shave
écouter	to listen	répondre	to answer
équilibrer	to balance	(se) soulager	to relieve

compliqué(e)	complicated	maigre	thin, skinny
grâce à	thanks to	mince	slender
gras, grasse	fat	pendant	during, for
gros, grosse	fat	sain(e)	healthy
inoxidable	rustproof	sévère	strict
longtemps	long time	simple	uncomplicated

NOTES:

1. *Devoir* means "to have to," as in *Je dois manger.* (I must eat.) *Devoir . . . à* means "to owe (something) to someone."

> EXAMPLE: *Je te dois dix francs.*   I owe you ten francs.
>
> *Combien je vous dois?*   How much do I owe you?

Notice that the indirect pronoun is required (*me, te, lui, elle,* etc.)

2. *La diète* means a low-calorie diet, *se mettre à la diète* means to put oneself on a low-calorie diet, *diète absolue* is a starvation diet. *Régime* also means "diet," but could imply other restrictions (salt, sugar, butter, etc.).

3. *Gros, grosse* means fat (adj.) as in *Cet homme est gros* (This man is fat). *Gras, grasse* also means "fat" (adj.), but when applied to people, it carries a pejorative meaning. When we speak of foods or things, *gras(se)* means greasy, as in *Cette soupe est grasse* (This soup is greasy).

CULTURAL NOTE:

The local *pharmacie* and the *pharmacien* (pharmacist) are where the French search for advice and remedies for minor ailments. The doctor is called upon only in serious cases. The local *pharmacien* becomes a trusted friend whose advice and treatment are taken very seriously. These professionals know their over-the-counter drugs very well and are able to help their clients make the best decisions for whatever ails them. What ails most French people is their liver—*le foie.* The French *ont mal au foie* as often as Americans get headaches. The only difference is that the French blame all their discomforts on their liver.

PRACTICE THE VOCABULARY

A. Write *un* or *une* before the following nouns.

1. _____ talc	6. _____ diète	11. _____ compte-goutte
2. _____ brosse	7. _____ rasoir	12. _____ régime
3. _____ pipe	8. _____ lame	13. _____ calmant
4. _____ drogue	9. _____ boulangerie	14. _____ balance
5. _____ peigne	10. _____ plâtre	15. _____ narcotique

B. Which words from the vocabulary are related to the following?

1. grossir _____
2. calmer _____
3. le dentifrice _____
4. la barbe _____
5. le poisson _____

6. plomber _____

7. balancer _____

8. alimenter _____

9. rasoir _____

10. maigrir _____

ANSWERS
p. 196

C. Review the future tense by completing the sentences with the appropriate future forms.

1. Mon mari _____ (se raser) avant de sortir.

2. Si elle ne mange pas aujourd'hui, elle _____ (maigrir).

3. Le calmant que le docteur m'a prescrit ne _____ (être) pas prêt demain.

4. Il _____ (faut) acheter un compte-goutte.

5. Elle _____ (user) toute la pâte dentifrice en une semaine.

6. Juliette n'aime pas les médicaments, elle _____ (avaler) le syrop malgré elle.

7. Ils _____ (perdre) leurs privilèges dès qu'ils les _____ (abuser).

DIALOGUE   La pharmacie du coin

LE PHARMACIEN: Bonjour, Madame Bellan. Comment allez-vous aujourd'hui?

MME BELLAN: Pas très bien. J'ai eu une crise de foie ce matin et je n'avais plus de pilules pour me soulager. Vous savez de quoi je parle, n'est-ce pas?

LE PHARMACIEN: C'était par ordonnance, Madame Bellan?

MME BELLAN: Oui, c'était l'ordonnance du docteur Blanchard.

LE PHARMACIEN: Ah! La voilà. C'était un calmant, c'est ce que je pensais.

MME BELLAN: Vous croyez que c'est sain de prendre ces pilules trois fois par jour?

LE PHARMACIEN: Cela ne vous fera pas de mal si vous vous arrêtez dès que votre crise de foie sera passée. Vous savez que le meilleur conseil en médecine est: "user sans abuser."

MME BELLAN: Vous donnez toujours de bons conseils. C'est grâce à vous que ma grippe est passée en deux jours, alors que ma fille a gardé le lit pendant une semaine.

LE PHARMACIEN: Voilà votre médicament, Madame Bellan.

MME BELLAN: Je voudrais aussi un tube de pâte dentifrice, des losanges pour la gorge et un paquet de lames de rasoir.

LE PHARMACIEN: Voici le tout. Passez à la caisse, s'il vous plaît.

MME BELLAN: Combien je vous dois pour le tout?

LE PHARMACIEN: Ça vous fait un total de soixante francs. Merci, Madame Bellan. J'espère que votre crise de foie passera vite.

DIALOGUE   The Corner Drugstore

THE PHARMACIST: Good morning, Mrs. Bellan. How are you today?

MRS. BELLAN: Not very well. I had a liver attack this morning and I had no more pills to relieve me. You know what I'm talking about, don't you?

THE PHARMACIST: Was it by prescription, Mrs. Bellan?

MRS. BELLAN: Yes, it was Dr. Blanchard's prescription.

THE PHARMACIST: Ah! There it is. It was a sedative, just what I thought.

MRS. BELLAN: Do you believe it's safe to take these pills three times a day?

THE PHARMACIST: That will not do you any harm, if you stop as soon as your liver attack is gone. You know that the best advice in medicine is "use without abuse."

MRS. BELLAN: You always give good advice. Thanks to you my flu was gone in two days, while my daughter stayed in bed for a week.

THE PHARMACIST: There's your medicine, Mrs. Bellan.

MRS. BELLAN: I would also like a tube of toothpaste, throat lozenges, and a pack of razor blades.

THE PHARMACIST: Here's everything. Go to the cash register, please.

MRS. BELLAN: How much do I owe you for everything?

THE PHARMACIST: It comes to a total of sixty francs. Thank you, Mrs. Bellan. I hope your liver attack will go away quickly.

NOTE:

The verb *passer* means "to pass," but depending on the context it may mean "to walk over to" as in *passer à la caisse,* or "to go away" as in *la crise passera. Se passer* means "to be happening" as in *Qu'est-ce qui se passe?* (What's happening?)

DIALOGUE EXERCISES

A. Answer the following questions in short complete sentences.

1. Pourquoi Mme Bellan est-elle allée à la pharmacie? _____.

2. Qu'est-ce qui soulage Mme Bellan? _____.

3. Qui est-ce qui a prescrit les pilules? _____.

4. Quel genre de médicament est-ce? _____.

5. Pourquoi Mme Bellan est-elle inquiète? _____.

6. Quel est le meilleur conseil du pharmacien? _____.

7. How do you say in French "That won't hurt you"? _____.

8. Mme Bellan voudrait aussi un _____, des _____, et des _____.

9. Quel est le prix de tout ce que Mme Bellan a acheté? _____.

10. Quelle autre maladie Mme Bellan et sa fille avaient-elles avant la crise de foie? _____.

ANSWERS p. 196

B. Review the rules of the *passé composé* and the *imparfait* for this summary of the dialogue. Fill in the blanks with the appropriate form of each verb.

Madame Bellan ne se _____ (sentir) pas bien, alors elle _____ (aller) voir son pharmacien. Le pharmacien lui _____ (conseiller) de prendre le calmant que le docteur a prescrit. Elle _____ (acheter) le médicament et elle _____ (payer) soixante francs. Mme Bellan _____ (faire) d'autres (other) achats. Avant la crise de foie Mme Bellan _____ (avoir) la grippe pendant deux jours, mais sa fille _____ (garder) le lit pendant une semaine. Mme Bellan _____ (soulager) de savoir que le médicament ne lui fera pas mal.

ANSWERS p. 196

C. Match the two columns.

1. _____ Le pharmacien donne de bons conseils.
2. _____ Elle est un peu bavarde.
3. _____ Les médicaments ne sont pas chers.
4. _____ La crise du malade passera vite.
5. _____ Le secret est de ne rien abuser.
6. _____ La grippe peut durer très longtemps.
7. _____ Parfois les parents sont trop sévères.
8. _____ Le calmant soulagera la malade.

A. The secret is to abuse nothing.
B. The sedative will relieve the sick lady.
C. The flu can last a long time.
D. Sometimes parents are too strict.
E. The medicines are not expensive.
F. The pharmacist gives good advice.
G. She is a bit talkative.
H. The sick man's attack will go away quickly.

GRAMMAR I   Present Subjunctive of Regular Verbs

So far, most of the verb tenses you've learned were in the indicative, which, as its name implies, is used to indicate facts, ask questions, or make statements. We need the subjunctive to express moods, feelings, desires, attitudes, or opinions about people, things, and actions.

A. French uses the subjunctive more frequently than English. Note that the subjunctive requires a dependent clause beginning with *que* (that). Study the present subjunctive of the regular verbs below.

Subject	*Parler*	*Choisir*	*Attendre*
que je	parle	choisisse	attende
que tu	parles	choisisses	attendes
qu'il, elle, on	parle	choisisse	attende
que nous	parlions	choisissions	attendions
que vous	parliez	choisissiez	attendiez
qu'ils, elles	parlent	choisissent	attendent

NOTES:
The subjunctive endings are the same for all French verbs except *avoir* and *être*.

These endings are: *-e, -es, -e, -ions, -iez,* and *-ent*.

For the regular verbs ending in: *-er, -ir,* and *-re,* the subjunctive stem is the same as the *imparfait* stem, which is formed by dropping the *-ons* from the *nous* form of the present indicative and adding *-ions,* as in *nous parlions.*

EXAMPLE: nous choisiss/ons   choisissions

nous attend/ons   attendions

The subjunctive *-er, -ir,* and *-re* stems are:

parl	e, es, e, ions, iez, ent
choisiss	e, es, e, ions, iez, ent
attend	e, es, e, ions, iez, ent

B. Uses of the subjunctive.

1. The subjunctive is used to express the speaker's opinions, or attitudes, about an action.

2. The French subjunctive has several English equivalents.

EXAMPLE: *que tu parles* may be translated: "that you speak," "that you may speak," "that you are speaking," "that you do speak," "that you will speak," or "you to speak," as in *je veux que tu parles* (I want you to speak).

3. The subjunctive is used to express personal feelings such as emotions, doubts, uncertainty, possibility, and volition.

4. The subjunctive is used to express subjective views about actions, as well as the concept of necessity:

EXAMPLE: *Je veux que tu partes.* I want you to leave. (volition, command)

Il faut que tu partes. You must leave. (necessity)

Il doute que tu sortes. He doubts that you will leave. (doubt)

C'est possible que nous partions. It is possible that we will leave. (possibility)

PRACTICE THE SUBJUNCTIVE PRESENT

ANSWERS
pp. 196–197

A. Answer the following questions.

1. How do you form the subjunctive stem of a French verb? _____.

2. Give the subjunctive form of *nous formons.* _____.

3. Name two French verbs that do not follow the rule for the subjunctive endings: _____ and _____.

4. What is the French equivalent of "that he will finish"? _____.
5. How do you say in French, "I want you to wait here"? _____.
6. What kinds of clauses does the subjunctive require? _____.
7. In a subjunctive sentence, the independent clause is in what form? _____.
8. How do you say in French, "It's possible that she may leave"? _____.
9. The subjunctive is used to express personal feelings. Name two: _____ and _____.
10. How do you say in French, "We want you to listen"? _____.

ANSWERS
p. 197

B. Express wishes in the following sentences, according to the example.

Example: Le docteur veut que *tu gardes* (garder) le lit.

1. Il veut que nous _____ (acheter) les médicaments.
2. Il est content que je _____ (finir) de parler.
3. Nous désirons que tu _____ (attendre) ton ami.
4. Il faut que vous _____ (demander) une augmentation.
5. Elle insiste que nous _____ (refuser) de sortir.

GRAMMAR II   Present Subjunctive of Stem-Changing Verbs: *essayer, appeler, commencer,* and *manger*

Study the stem-changing verbs in the following chart.

Subject	*Essayer*	*Appeler*	*Commencer*	*Manger*
j'(e)	essai e	appelle	commence	mange
tu	essai es	appelles	commences	manges
il, elle, on	essai e	appelle	commence	mange
nous	essay ions	appelions	commencions	mangions
vous	essay iez	appeliez	commenciez	mangiez
ils, elles	essai ent	appellent	commencent	mangent

NOTES:

1. In Lesson 5, we listed the categories of stem-changing verbs for which *g* and *c* sounds in *manger* and *commencer* needed an *e* and a cedilla in the present indicative of the *nous* forms to keep the softer sounds of those consonants. In the subjunctive of such verbs, neither an *e* nor a cedilla is needed because we already have the vowels *e* and *i* throughout the conjugated forms. Indicative: *nous mangeons, nous commençons;* subjunctive: *nous mangions, nous commencions.*

2. In the verb category of *appeler*, as in *j'appelle,* the *e* of the stem is pronounced as if it had an accent grave (`) every time it is followed by a double *l*.

3. The verb category of *essayer* reflects the same changes occurring in the indicative. Notice, however, that the *nous* and *vous* forms in the subjunctive are the same as the *imparfait*. Only the meaning of the sentence can alert you to the form of the verb. Study this example.

> *Quand nous étions* (imparfait)   *jeunes, nos parents voulaient*
> *que nous essayions* (subjunctive)   *beaucoup de choses.*

PRACTICE

ANSWERS
p. 197

A. Practice the present subjunctive of the stem-changing verbs.

1. Name two verbs in the same category as *appeler*: _____ and _____.

2. Name two verbs in the same category as *manger*: _____ and _____.

3. Name two verbs in the same category as *essayer*: _____ and _____.

4. Why are the *cedilla* in *nous commençons* and the *e* in *nous mangeons* necessary? _____.

5. Which two verb forms are the same in the *imparfait* indicative and present subjunctive of the *essayer* verb category? _____.

6. How do you say in French, "I want you to pay your bills"? _____.

7. How do you say in French, "They may want you to call a doctor"? _____.

8. How do you say in French, "She may insist I stay in bed"? _____.

9. How do you say in French, "I want you to start studying French"? _____.

ANSWERS
p. 197

B. Write the subjunctive forms of the following:

1. nous _____ (voyager)

2. tu _____ (partager)

3. nous _____ (épeler—to spell)

4. vous _____ (employer)

5. nous _____ (acheter)

6. nous _____ (balancer)

7. ils _____ (acheter)

8. vous _____ (changer)

9. tu _____ (rappeler)

10. je _____ (payer)

GRAMMAR III   Present Subjunctive with Impersonal Expressions: *il faut, il vaut mieux,* etc.

A. The subjunctive occurs after impersonal expressions that express the same conditions in which the subjunctive is used: doubt, uncertainty, possibility, necessity, volition, etc. The subjunctive occurs after an impersonal expression followed by *que.* Study the following examples.

> EXAMPLE: Il faut *que tu partes.* (necessity)
>
> Il est douteux *que tu paies* ta facture. (bill) (doubt)
>
> Il vaut mieux *que vous partiez.* (subjective opinion)
>
> Il est possible *que vous appeliez* la police. (possibility)

B. The subjunctive is not used in impersonal expressions that convey certainty or probability.

> EXAMPLE: *Il est certain qu'elle va partir. Il est vrai qu'elle partira bientôt.*

C. The subjunctive has no future tense, so the present tense refers to both present and future. This was mentioned earlier in the possible English translations of the present subjunctive.

> EXAMPLE: *Il est bon qu'elle parte.* It's good for her to leave (now or later).

D. Memorize the following impersonal expressions requiring the subjunctive.

1. Expressions of doubt:

   il est douteux que . . .

2. Expressions of necessity:

   il faut que . . .
   il est nécessaire que . . .
   il est exigé (required) que . . .

3. Expressions with a subjective view of action:

   il est temps que . . .
   il est important que . . .
   il est juste que . . .
   il vaut mieux que . . .
   il est bon que . . .
   il est naturel que . . .

PRACTICE

ANSWERS
p. 197

A. Rewrite the following sentences using the present subjunctive or present indicative, introducing your sentences with the impersonal expression in parentheses.

Example: Nous ne fumons pas. (il est necessaire)

Il est necessaire que nous ne fumions pas.

1. Elle parle souvent. (il faut) _____.
2. Vous vous reposez. (il est bon) _____.
3. Nous essayons tout. (il est important) _____.
4. Vous commencez votre travail à l'heure. (il est naturel) _____.
5. Elle ne jugera personne. (il est certain) _____.
6. Vous voyagerez en France bientôt. (il est juste) _____.
7. Nous ne répondons pas souvent. (il est nécessaire) _____.
8. Notre réputation grandit à travers la ville. (il est temps) _____.
9. Nous finirons cet exercice aujourd'hui. (il vaut mieux) _____.
10. Nous payerons notre facture demain. (il est douteux) _____.

ANSWERS
p. 198

B. Write the given verbs in the required mood and form according to the meaning of the sentence.

Example: Il est vrai qu'elle (partir) _____ demain.

Il est vrai qu'elle *partira* demain. (No subjunctive is required in certainty clauses)

1. Nous doutons beaucoup que vous _____ (finir) cette bouteille de vin.
2. Vos parents sont heureux que vous _____ (réussir) à vos examens.
3. Nous pensons que c'est juste que vous _____ (payer) vos impôts (taxes).
4. Nous sommes sûrs que vous _____ (aller) demain à la plage.
5. Il est vrai que nous _____ (être) toujours avec vous.
6. Il est important que vous _____ (partager) votre argent avec moi.
7. Mes parents sont contents que je _____ (partir) en France.
8. Nous doutons que les voisins _____ (acheter) notre voiture.
9. Il vaut mieux que nous _____ (commencer) à économiser de l'argent.
10. Il est certain que tu _____ (payer) ta facture bientôt.

13 La voiture
(The Automobile)

l'accélérateur (masc.)	accelerator	le feu	stoplight
		le frein	brake
l'agent (masc.)	policeman	l'indicateur (masc.)	signal
l'aile (fem.)	fender		
l'arrière (masc.)	back	la jauge	gauge
		le klaxon	horn
l'avant (masc.)	front	lampe de poche	flashlight
la batterie	battery	le moteur	motor
le bouton	button	la panne	car breakdown
le capot	hood	le pare-brise	windshield
la carte grise	title	le phare	headlight
la carte routière	road map	la plaque	license plate
la ceinture	belt	la plaque d'immatriculation	license plate
le chauffage	heating		
la contravention	traffic ticket	le pneu	tire
la crevaison	flat tire	la roue	wheel
le démarreur	starter	la station service	gas station
l'embrayage (masc.)	clutch	le trottoir	pavement
		la vitesse	speed
l'essuie-glace (masc.)	windshield wiper	le volant	steering wheel
éteindre	to turn off	remorquer	to tow
faire le plein	to fill the tank	stationner	to park
freiner	to brake	tomber	to fall
gonfler	to inflate		
allumer	to turn on a light	guider	to guide
capoter	to turn over	heurter	to hit, run into

161

défendu	forbidden	marcher	to work (machine)
dégonfler	to deflate	nettoyer	to clean
démarrer	to start	ralentir	to slow down
dépanner	to repair (on the spot)	reculer	to back up

assuré(e)	insured	sec, sèche	dry
luxueux (-euse)	luxurious	selon	according
manuel(le)	manual	usé(e)	used, worn out
d'occasion	secondhand	volontiers	gladly, willingly
sans cesse	constantly		

NOTES:

1. *L'arrière* (the back of the car) and *l'avant* (the front) are both masculine, because the word *le côté* is understood: *le côté avant* and *le côté arrière. Arrière* is also used with *pneu* and *aile. L'aile* literally means "the wing of a bird," but in cars it refers to "the fender," as in *l'aile arrière* (rear fender).

2. *Marcher* means "to walk." However, when speaking of machines, motors, or anything that works with motors, *marcher* means "to work."

   EXAMPLE: *Ma montre marche bien.* My watch works well.

   Familiar expressions heard frequently are:

   > *Comment ça marche?* How are things?
   >
   > *Tout marche très bien.* All is very well.

3. *Être en panne* and *tomber en panne* are two expressions that mean "to have car trouble" (breakdown). *Avoir une panne sèche* means to be out of gas.

4. *Allumer* means "to light." When we say *allumer les phares,* it means "to turn on the headlights." *Les allumettes* (matches) is the noun derived from *allumer. Volontiers* (willingly, gladly) derives from *la volonté* (will), *vouloir* (to want).

CULTURAL NOTE:

In the past ten years, owning a car has become such a top priority for the typical French family that today, France ranks third in Europe—after Germany and Sweden—in private car ownership. France also boasts some 54,000 miles of well-kept national highways and allows its citizens to drive at a speed limit of 80 miles per hour on superhighways (55 miles per hour everywhere else). France is also known for its high-speed trains called TGV (trains à grande vitesse). These trains whisk passengers along at incredible speeds, making travel between major cities astonishingly fast. In fact, the TGV from Paris to London takes only three hours.

PRACTICE THE VOCABULARY

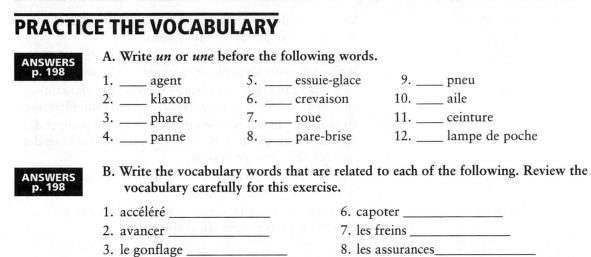

ANSWERS p. 198

A. Write *un* or *une* before the following words.

1. ____ agent
2. ____ klaxon
3. ____ phare
4. ____ panne

5. ____ essuie-glace
6. ____ crevaison
7. ____ roue
8. ____ pare-brise

9. ____ pneu
10. ____ aile
11. ____ ceinture
12. ____ lampe de poche

ANSWERS p. 198

B. Write the vocabulary words that are related to each of the following. Review the vocabulary carefully for this exercise.

1. accéléré _____
2. avancer _____
3. le gonflage _____
4. chauffer _____
5. dépanner _____

6. capoter _____
7. les freins _____
8. les assurances _____
9. le stationnement _____
10. la lumière _____

DIALOGUE   Jacques est en panne

JACQUES:	Marc, tu voudrais attendre à côté de la voiture? Je vais essayer de téléphoner à mon mécanicien; je reviens tout de suite.
MARC:	D'accord, mais ne tarde pas, et si tu peux, apporte-moi quelque chose à boire. J'ai vraiment soif.
	(quelques minutes plus tard)
JACQUES:	Je n'ai pas trouvé mon mécanicien, alors un employé de garage a offert de nous aider.
MARC:	C'est parfait. Où est ma boisson?
JACQUES:	Ah! Excuse-moi, j'ai complètement oublié.
L'EMPLOYÉ (LE GARAGISTE):	Voyons, d'abord il faut lever le capot, ensuite, dites-moi exactement ce qui s'est passé pendant que je vérifie les choses.
JACQUES:	Je conduisais comme d'habitude, et tout d'un coup le moteur a commencé à ralentir. Je pousse sur l'accélérateur et rien n'arrive. Alors j'ai tourné le volant à droite et je me suis stationné ici à côté du trottoir.
LE GARAGISTE:	Allumez les phares, s'il vous plaît; tout marche bien de ce côté-là. Eteignez-les maintenant. Voyons, les freins sont bons, les indicateurs marchent bien. Avez-vous fait un réglage récemment?
JACQUES:	Oui, le mois dernier exactement.
LE GARAGISTE:	La seule chose qui reste à vérifier c'est l'essence et l'huile.

JACQUES:	Vous savez, depuis que mon jauge d'essence ne marche plus, j'ai été en panne à trois reprises.
LE GARAGISTE:	C'est ça alors, c'est une panne sèche; c'est facile à vérifier. Je vais retourner au garage et apporter un bidon d'essence.
MARC:	Tu devrais faire réparer ta jauge? Ce n'est pas amusant pour deux docteurs de gaspiller une heure si stupidement.
JACQUES:	Tu as raison, mais j'ai si peu de temps pour m'occuper de ma voiture. Tu sais comment c'est, on travaille comme des esclaves dans cette profession.
MARC:	Eh bien, alors tu pourrais dire que tu n'as pas gaspillé une heure; tu t'es reposé une heure.
JACQUES:	Avoir une panne sèche n'est pas le genre de repos que j'ai l'intention de recommencer, crois-moi.

DIALOGUE   Jacques's Car Breaks Down

JACQUES:	Marc, would you wait next to the car? I'm going to try to call my mechanic; I'll be right back.
MARC:	O.K., but don't be long, and if you can, bring me something to drink. I'm really thirsty.
	(a few minutes later)
JACQUES:	I did not find my mechanic, so the garage attendant offered to help us.
MARC:	That's perfect. Where is my drink?
JACQUES:	Ah! I'm sorry, I completely forgot.
GARAGE ATTENDANT:	Let's see, first we have to raise the hood, then tell me exactly what happened while I check things.
JACQUES:	I was driving as usual, and all of a sudden the motor started to slow down. I pushed on the gas pedal, and nothing happened. So I turned the steering wheel to the right and parked next to the pavement.
GARAGE ATTENDANT:	Turn the headlights on, please; all is working well from that side. Turn them off now. Let's see, the brakes are good, the signals are working well. Have you checked your car recently?
JACQUES:	Yes, last month, exactly.
GARAGE ATTENDANT:	The only thing left to check is the gas and the oil.
JACQUES:	You know, since my gas gauge broke, I've had car trouble on three occasions.
GARAGE ATTENDANT:	That's it, then, you're out of gas; that's easy to check. I'm going to go back to the garage and bring a gas can.
MARC:	You should have your gas gauge repaired. It's not amusing for two doctors to waste one hour so foolishly!

JACQUES: You are right, but I have so little time to take care of my car. You know how it is, we work like slaves in this profession.

MARC: Well then, you could say that you did not waste one hour; you rested for one hour!

JACQUES: Being out of gas is not the kind of rest I intend to repeat, believe me.

NOTES:

1. *La révision* means review (studies, accounts, etc.). *La révision* is a car check, *la révision générale* is a tune-up.

2. *Faire* + infinitive, such as *faire nettoyer, faire réparer,* means to have someone else do the work and is translated in English by "to have" + past participle. *(Le) faire réparer* (to have [it] repaired), *(le) faire nettoyer* (to have [it] cleaned).

DIALOGUE EXERCISES

ANSWERS p. 198

A. Answer the following questions with short and specific answers.

1. Où Marc doit-il attendre Jacques? _____.

2. Quelle est la profession de Jacques et de Marc?_____.

3. Pourquoi Jacques est-il revenu avec un employé de garage, et non avec son mécanicien?_____.

4. Qu'est-ce que Jacques a oublié de faire?_____.

5. Quelles sont les trois choses que le garagiste a vérifiées?_____, _____, et _____.

6. Pourquoi le moteur a-t-il ralenti?_____.

7. Où Jacques a-t-il stationné la voiture?_____.

ANSWERS p. 198

B. Review the subjunctive.

Suppose that Marc is giving some advice to Jacques on how to take better care of himself and his car. All the verbs given are regular. Write their appropriate subjunctive forms.

All sentences start with: *Jacques, il faut que* . . .

1. tu _____ (commencer) à prendre soin de ta santé.

2. tu _____ (se reposer) plus souvent.

3. tu _____ (partir) en vacances bientôt.

4. tu _____ (garder) ta voiture en meilleur état.

5. tu _____ (essayer) de quitter ton travail plus tôt.

6. tu _____ (s'arrêter) de rester tard dans ton bureau.

7. tu _____ (gaspiller) moins de temps.

8. tu _____ (surveiller) ta santé plus sérieusement.

GRAMMAR I Present Subjunctive of Irregular Verbs

A. Study the chart below with the subjunctive of *avoir, être,* and *savoir.*

Subject	Avoir	Être	Savoir
que je (j')	aie	sois	sache
que tu	aies	sois	saches
qu'il, elle, on	ait	soit	sache
que nous	ayons	soyons	sachions
que vous	ayez	soyez	sachiez
qu'ils, elles	aient	soient	sachent

NOTE:
Except for the *nous* and *vous* forms of *avoir* and *être,* the other subjunctive stem endings are all regular.

B. Study the present subjunctive of the irregular verbs *aller, connaître,* and *faire.*

Subject	Aller	Connaître	Faire
je (j')	aille	connaisse	fasse
tu	ailles	connaisses	fasses
il, elle, on	aille	connaisse	fasse
nous	allions	connaissions	fassions
vous	alliez	connaissiez	fassiez
ils, elles	aillent	connaissent	fassent

NOTES:
1. Notice that when irregularities occur within subjunctive stems, they usually occur in the *nous* and *vous* forms.
2. The *nous* and *vous* forms *allions, alliez, connaissions,* and *connaissiez* are identical to the *nous* and *vous* forms of the *imparfait* (imperfect indicative) of those verbs.

C. Study the present subjunctive of the irregular verbs *pouvoir* and *vouloir.*

Subject	Pouvoir	Vouloir
que je	puisse	veuille
que tu	puisses	veuilles
qu'il, elle, on	puisse	veuille
que nous	puissions	voulions
que vous	puissiez	vouliez
qu'ils, elles	puissent	veuillent

NOTES:

1. Notice that the *nous* and *vous* forms of *vouloir* are identical to the *imparfait* (imperfect indicative) forms.

2. The most commonly used form of the imperative of *vouloir* is *veuillez,* which is often found in the closing words of business letters. Most French business letters close with *Veuillez agréer nos salutations les plus distinguées* (Kindly accept our most distinguished greetings).

EXERCISE

ANSWERS
pp. 198–199

Rewrite the following sentences, using *il faut que, il est important que, il est nécessaire que,* or *il est douteux que* so that each sentence makes sense.

Example: 1. Marc doit attendre. *Il faut que Marc attende.*

1. La voiture est en panne. Marc doit attendre. _____.
2. Marie va au cinéma sans son fiancé. _____.
3. Monsieur Bertrand connaît les projets de Jacques. _____.
4. Vous devez aller chercher un mécanicien. _____.
5. Nous avons besoin d'avoir du courage. _____.

GRAMMAR II   Comparing the Indicative and the Subjunctive

A. The uses of the indicative and subjunctive:

1. Most of the verbs you have learned in previous lessons have been in the indicative. We use the indicative to make statements and to ask questions, while we need the subjunctive to express opinions, attitudes, and feelings, rather than facts.

2. A sentence requiring the subjunctive has two clauses: an independent one requiring the indicative, and a dependent one with *que* (that) requiring the subjunctive.

    EXAMPLE: *Je veux qu'elle fasse le ménage.* I want (*indicative*) her to do (that she does) (*subjunctive*) the housework.

3. However, if the main clause contains an expression of fact or certainty, the verb in the dependent (subordinate) clause will require the indicative.

    EXAMPLE: *Je sais qu'il partira demain.* I know he will leave tomorrow.

    You have studied many verbs and expressions in the previous lessons and dialogues. Now, review the following table, which lists more of the verbs and expressions that use the indicative.

communiquer	to communicate	**il est certain**	it's certain
déclarer	to declare	**il est clair**	it's clear
écrire	to write	**il est sûr**	it's sure
informer	to inform	**il est vrai**	it's true
lire	to read	**il est évident**	it's evident
reconnaître	to recognize		

B. The subjunctive after verbs of command, wishing, etc.

1. The subjunctive is required if the main clause (independent) contains a verb expressing an opinion, a wish, a feeling, or something that is not a fact. Included in this category are verbs of command, forbidding, wishing, volition, doubt, request, suggestion, possibility, etc.

> EXAMPLE: *J'exige qu'il sorte* I require that he leave (I require him to leave.)

You recall that the subject of the independent clause is frequently different from that of the dependent clause. However, if the subject is the same, the infinitive is used.

> EXAMPLE: *Je veux partir* I want to leave.

2. In Lesson 12 you studied several verbs and expressions of command, doubt, volition, possibility, etc. The following table lists other verbs and expressions that use the subjunctive.

conseiller	to advise	**il est défendu**	it's forbidden
défendre	to forbid	**il est impératif**	it's imperative
demander	to ask	**il est important**	it's important
désirer	to desire	**il est inutile**	it's useless
préférer	to prefer	**il est utile**	it's useful
regretter	to regret		

C. Verbs using both the subjunctive and indicative forms.

1. The verbs *croire* (to believe) and *penser* (to think), when used in an affirmative main clause (independent), are followed by an indicative subordinate clause (dependent).

> EXAMPLE: *Je pense qu'elle est gentille* I think she's kind.
>
> *Je crois qu'elle est gentille* I believe she's kind.

2. However, when *croire* and *penser* are used in an interrogative or negative independent clause, they are followed by a subjunctive subordinate (dependent) clause.

> EXAMPLE: *Penses-tu qu'elle soit gentille?* Do you think she's kind?
>
> *Je ne pense pas qu'elle soit gentille.* I don't think she's kind.
>
> *Croyez-vous qu'elle soit gentille?* Do you believe she's kind?

Vous ne croyez pas qu'elle soit gentille. You don't believe she's kind.

3. The verb *dire* (to say, to tell) may use both indicative and subjunctive forms. *Dire* with the indicative relates a fact, while *dire* with the subjunctive may suggest an order or a command. Study the two examples.

EXAMPLE: *Je lui ai dit qu'il est gentil.* I told him that he is kind.

Je lui ai dit qu'il soit gentil; or . . . *qu'il faut qu'il soit gentil.* I told him to be kind.

PRACTICE

A. **Show your understanding of the distinction between the indicative and the subjunctive by completing the following exercise.**

1. Name one major difference between the indicative and the subjunctive.

   _____.

2. When is the infinitive used instead of the subjunctive in a sentence with two clauses?

   _____.

3. Write a French sentence using the infinitive. _____

   _____.

4. Rewrite this sentence using the subjunctive: *Ils pensent que nous aimons le vin blanc.*

   _____.

5. When do the verbs *croire* and *penser* require the subjunctive? _____

   _____.

6. What is the French equivalent of "I don't think he can (is able to) change"? _____

   _____.

7. Which verb may be followed by either the indicative or the subjunctive, depending on its intended meaning in the sentence? _____.

8. Rewrite this sentence using the subjunctive: *Vous lui dites qu'il est sage.* _____

   _____.

B. **Use the indicative or the subjunctive for the verbs in parentheses, depending on the meaning of the sentence.**

Example: Nous savons que vous *êtes* (être) français.

1. Ils doutent toujours que nous _____ (pouvoir) finir notre travail à l'heure.
2. Il est vrai que les parents n(e) _____ (avoir) pas toujours la meilleure réponse.
3. Pourquoi pense-t-il que les femmes ne _____ (être) pas sûres de leurs talents?
4. Il est préférable que les politiciens _____ (faire) moins de publicité.
5. On dit que la patience _____ (pouvoir) former le caractère.
6. Nous sommes certains que les médicaments _____ (aller) guérir le malade.
7. Nous ne doutons pas que les voyageurs _____ (connaître) bien leur itinéraire.

GRAMMAR III   Review of the Subjunctive and Impersonal Expressions

A. In reviewing the differences between the subjunctive and the indicative forms, the most important point to remember is that information (fact) = indicative versus influence (emotion) = subjunctive. In a subjunctive sentence, the speaker voices an opinion, an attitude, a wish, a doubt, a concern, a denial, and other personal expressions of emotion. In a subjunctive sentence, the main clause is in the indicative; the dependent clause is always introduced by *que*.

Main Clause	Dependent Clause
subject + verb (indicative) + *que*	subject + verb (subjunctive)

B. The subjunctive is used in all the impersonal expressions you have learned except those expressing certainty, fact, or information.

C. Review the following examples of subjunctive usage.

1. Emotion   *Le malade est heureux que le médicament le guérisse.*

2. Doubt, uncertainty   *Nous ne sommes pas sûrs que nous puissions venir demain.*

3. Desire, volition   *Le patron veut que tu fasses bien ton travail.*

4. Necessity   *Il est nécessaire que tu saches ce qu'on dit.*

5. Regret   *Je regrette que vous soyez malade.*

6. Demand, command   *J'exige que vous me rendiez mon argent.*

D. Study the following examples of the use of the indicative and subjunctive with *penser* and *croire*.

1. *Penser* + affirmative + indicative: *Je pense qu'il est gentil.*

2. *Penser* + interrogative, negative + subjunctive:

    a. *Penses-tu qu'il soit gentil?*

    b. *Je ne pense pas qu'il soit gentil.*

3. *Croire* + affirmative + indicative: *Je crois qu'il est gentil.*

4. *Croire* + interrogative, negative + subjunctive:

    a. *Crois-tu qu'il soit gentil?*

    b. *Je ne crois pas qu'il soit gentil.*

E. Review the following table of impersonal expressions requiring the subjunctive.

Desire, Necessity	Emotion	Doubt, Possibility
il est important que	il est bon que	il est normal que
il est nécessaire que	il est dommage que (it's too bad that)	il est possible que
il est essentiel que	il est juste que	il semble que
il est exigé que	il est préférable que	
(it's required that)	il est utile, inutile que	
	il vaut mieux que	

F. Review the following impersonal expressions requiring the indicative.

il est certain que   il est probable que

il est clair que   il est sûr que

il est évident que   il est vrai que

NOTE:
Anytime any of the above expressions are in the negative or interrogative form, the subjunctive is required, because the certainty becomes doubt and the probability becomes a possibility.

EXAMPLE: *Il n'est pas sûr qu'il puisse finir demain.*

Est-il sûr qu'il puisse finir demain?

REVIEW EXERCISE

ANSWERS p. 199

In the sentence *Je veux que vous sachiez tout,* replace the *Je veux* with the given expressions and complete the sentences with the appropriate form of the indicative or the subjunctive.

Example: Je pense *Je pense que vous savez tout.*

1. Je sais _____.
2. Crois-tu _____.
3. Il est évident _____.
4. Nous savons _____.
5. Il est certain _____.
6. Il est probable _____.
7. Il est impossible _____.
8. Je ne crois pas _____.
9. Je suis sûr _____.
10. Il est défendu _____.

14 L'ordinateur et les périphériques
(The Computer and the Peripherals)

l'alimentation (fem.)	supply	l'ingénieur (masc.)	engineer
la bande	tape	le logiciel	software
le bilan	outcome, balance sheet	la machine à écrire	typewriter
		le magnétophone	tape recorder
la carte perforée	punch card	le marteau	hammer
la cassette	cassette tape	le matériel	hardware
le circuit	circuit	le mensuel	monthly
le clavier	keyboard	le modem	modem
la colle	glue	numéro vert	toll-free number
la configuration	configuration	l'ordinateur (masc.)	computer
le crayon	pencil	le papier	paper
le critère	criterion	parasurtenseur	surge protector
la dactylo	typist	la puce	chip
le dessin industriel	industrial design	le régistre	register
l'écran (masc.)	screen	le ruban	ribbon
l'ensemble (masc.)	together, whole, entirety	le schéma	diagram, sketch
		la sortie	exit (output)
l'entrée (fem.)	entrance (input)	la souris	mouse
l'explorateur (masc.)	scanner	le stylo	pen
l'imprimante (fem.)	printer	le stylo lumineux	light pen
l'informatique	computer science	le tournevis	screwdriver

accéder	to reach	manier	to handle
brancher	to connect	marchander	to haggle over
coller	to glue, stick	perforer	to pierce
enseigner	to teach	résoudre	to solve
falloir	to have to	réussir	to succeed
imprimer	to print	sur-le-champ	on the spot
rattacher	to connect	taper à la machine	to type

NOTES:

1. Although the French government recently imposed a law that requires the use of French terms in computer language, there are no words in French for BUS, ROM, RAM, and REM. The use of existing French words as applied to computers is not without humor. Consider the word *la puce* (the flea), that small exasperating insect that bites everywhere with the assurance it will not be caught. *La puce* (the flea) is now "the chip" in computer lingo.

2. *L'imprimante* (the printer) is derived from the word *imprimer* (to print); *imprimant* is the present participle—corresponding to the *-ing* ending in English. This participle is also used as an adjective in French and as such agrees with the noun it precedes.

   EXAMPLE: *thé-dansant* (tea party with dancing), *soirée-dansante* (evening party with dancing).

3. *Ensemble* is an adverb as well as a noun. When used with an article, it is a noun, as in *l'ensemble des questions* (all the questions together); when used with verbs it is an adverb, as in *nous sommes tous ensemble* (we are all together). *Ensemble* is also used as a noun when speaking of matching pieces of women's clothing.

   EXAMPLE: *L'ensemble bleu est très joli.* (The blue suit is very pretty.)

   A man's suit is called *un costume.*

4. *Coller,* "to stick" or "to glue together," relates to the noun *la colle,* which means "glue." This word is found in several expressions.

   EXAMPLE: *Ça colle?* Is everything O.K.?

   Ça ne colle pas avec ma sœur, avec lui, avec elle, etc.

   Le collant, as a noun, means "tights" (gym tights or panty hose).

   Collant, used as a present participle, translates as "clinging" or "tight," when speaking about clothes.

   EXAMPLE: *Une robe collante,* a clinging dress, or a tight dress.

CULTURAL NOTE:

Since the founding of the Académie Française in 1635, France has nurtured an obsessive desire to keep the French language free of foreign intrusion. We all remember the uproar in French circles about the "Frenglish" of the 1980s, when words such as *le drugstore* and *le shopping* infiltrated the French vocabulary. After all, French is the language of diplomacy, one of only six official languages at the U.N.! French is also the language of the intellectual and scientific elite in many countries, as well as in eighteen countries in Africa alone, so it comes as no surprise that Franglais was perceived as a real threat to the French culture.

Today, France is experiencing a major cultural challenge with the Internet, where English is the lingua franca. Nevertheless, France is embracing the information revolution and vows to make computer literacy an integral part of French life, a daunting task since only 2 percent of the population is presently connected to the Internet. Many in France believe that for now, the French will have to contend with an English-dominated Internet until they can find alternatives for *le surf, le web, le CD-ROM,* and so on.

PRACTICE THE VOCABULARY

**ANSWERS
p. 200**

A. Indicate the gender of the following nouns.

> *Example:* le clavier *masc.*

1. clavier _____
2. listing _____
3. vidéo _____
4. tournevis _____
5. marteau _____
6. cassette _____
7. ruban _____
8. stylo _____
9. sortie _____
10. entrée _____
11. puce _____
12. ordinateur _____
13. bande _____
14. papier _____
15. logiciel _____
16. crayon _____
17. bilan _____

**ANSWERS
p. 200**

B. Write verbs related to the following nouns.

> *Example:* le comptable *compter*

1. la solution _____
2. l'imprimante _____
3. la colle _____
4. l'écriture _____
5. le dessin _____
6. la branche _____
7. la sortie _____
8. l'entrée _____
9. la vente _____
10. l'amour _____
11. l'allumette _____
12. la comptabilité _____
13. la conduite _____
14. la décision _____
15. la transformation _____

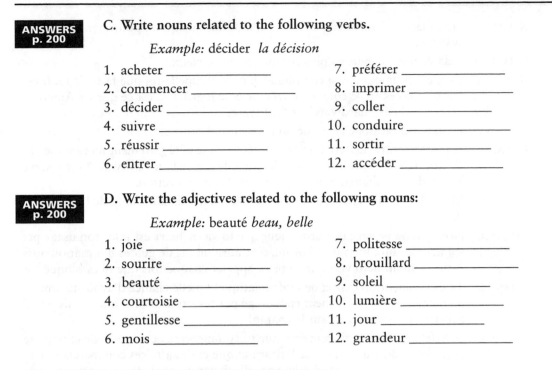

ANSWERS
p. 200 **C.** Write nouns related to the following verbs.

Example: décider *la décision*

1. acheter _____
2. commencer _____
3. décider _____
4. suivre _____
5. réussir _____
6. entrer _____

7. préférer _____
8. imprimer _____
9. coller _____
10. conduire _____
11. sortir _____
12. accéder _____

ANSWERS
p. 200 **D.** Write the adjectives related to the following nouns:

Example: beauté *beau, belle*

1. joie _____
2. sourire _____
3. beauté _____
4. courtoisie _____
5. gentillesse _____
6. mois _____

7. politesse _____
8. brouillard _____
9. soleil _____
10. lumière _____
11. jour _____
12. grandeur _____

DIALOGUE   Une idée excellente!

(Charles décide d'acheter un ordinateur et demande à son ami Roland de lui donner des conseils. Roland vient de terminer des études d'informatique.)

CHARLES: Ça y est! J'ai décidé d'économiser mon argent et d'acheter un ordinateur.

ROLAND: Idée excellente, mon ami! C'est un appareil fascinant! Mais je t'avertis, c'est très cher.

CHARLES: Oui, je sais. C'est pour cela que j'ai fait des économies toute l'année.

ROLAND: Très bien. Je connais quelqu'un qui travaille dans l'informatique.

CHARLES: C'est chouette! Alors viens avec moi, présente-moi à ton ami, et sois mon professeur d'informatique pour quelques heures.

ROLAND: Il y a longtemps que je n'ai parlé à cet ami-là, mais allons-y quand même. Je suis sûr qu'il sera content de nous voir.

CHARLES: Regarde cette machine, quelle beauté!

ROLAND: Cet appareil que tu vois n'est qu'un des périphériques. Il y a un tas d'autres pièces nécessaires au fonctionnement complet de ce que tu appelles "la machine."

CHARLES: Explique-moi, s'il te plaît.

ROLAND: Voilà, regarde le schéma sur cette feuille volante: l'ordinateur c'est l'unité centrale qui est rattachée à l'écran-vidéo, au clavier, à la cassette, au disque, à la table traçante et au listing. Sans tous ces accessoires, ou périphériques, l'unité centrale n'est qu'une machine sourde et muette.

CHARLES: Tu veux dire que ce sont ces périphériques qui permettent à l'ordinateur de communiquer avec l'extérieur?

ROLAND: Oui, mais seulement en partie, car il faudrait quelqu'un pour manier le système.

CHARLES: Cela devient de plus en plus compliqué, mon vieux.

ROLAND: Ce n'est vraiment pas si compliqué que ça. Rappelle-toi que faire de l'informatique nécessite le côté matériel et le côté logiciel. C'est ce que les Américains appellent "hardware" et "software."

CHARLES: Le matériel est donc l'opposé du logiciel?

ROLAND: Oui, en effet. Le matériel ou "hardware" est le côté purement mécanique et électronique de l'informatique, alors que le logiciel ou "software" est réservé à l'art de faire dialoguer les appareils de la configuration.

CHARLES: Mais alors il faut être ingénieur et écrivain à la fois pour faire de l'informatique?

ROLAND: Non, pas dans ton cas, l'ordinateur que tu vas acheter est pour ton usage personnel. Ensuite, ton nouvel ordinateur aura un tas de guides d'initiation aussi bien qu'un numéro vert que tu peux appeler chaque fois que tu es bloqué.

CHARLES: Tu es vraiment un expert de l'informatique! Quelle chance d'avoir un ami comme toi! Je suis tellement encouragé par tes explications, que je suis prêt à acheter mon ordinateur sur le champ!

ROLAND: Je te félicite, cher ami. Peut-être que tu commenceras une nouvelle entreprise et tu deviendras un expert de l'informatique et des affaires commerciales en même temps. Et surtout n'oublie pas d'acheter un parasurtenseur pour éviter les court-circuits.

CHARLES: Tu es formidable, Roland. Tu penses toujours à tout!

ROLAND: Avec ta nouvelle entreprise et ton nouvel ordinateur, tu seras obligé de penser à tout.

CHARLES: De nos jours, avec l'Internet, les possibilités sont énormes. Merci beaucoup, cher ami.

DIALOGUE   An Excellent Idea!

(Charles decides to buy a computer and asks his friend Roland to give him advice. Roland has just finished data processing school.)

CHARLES: That's it! I have decided to save my money and buy a computer.

ROLAND: Excellent idea, my friend! It's a fascinating gadget. But I warn you, it's very expensive.

CHARLES: Yes, I know. That is the reason I saved all year.

ROLAND: Very well, I know someone who works in computer science.

CHARLES: That's super! Come with me, then, introduce me to your friend, and be my data processing teacher for a few hours.

ROLAND: It's been a long time since I have spoken to that friend, but let's go anyway. I am sure he will be happy to see us.

CHARLES: Look at this beauty of a machine!

ROLAND: That apparatus you see is just one of the peripherals. There are a whole lot of parts necessary for the complete functioning of what you call "the machine."

CHARLES: Explain, please.

ROLAND: Here, look at the sketch on this flier: the computer is the central processing unit, which is connected to the screen, the keyboard, and the printer. Without all these accessories, or peripherals, the central processing unit is nothing but a deaf and mute machine.

CHARLES: You mean that these peripherals allow the computer to communicate with people?

ROLAND: Yes, but only in part, for it would need someone to make the system work.

CHARLES: This is becoming more and more complicated, my friend.

ROLAND: It's not really that complicated. Remember that data processing involves hardware and software. It is what the Americans call "hardware" and "software."

CHARLES: Hardware is the opposite of software?

ROLAND: Yes, in fact hardware is the part of data processing that is purely mechanical and electronic, while software is the art of making the system's parts talk to one another.

CHARLES: You have to be an engineer and a writer at the same time.

ROLAND: Not in your case, since the computer you want to buy is for your personal use. In addition, your new computer will have a lot of tutorials as well as a toll-free number you can call every time you are stuck.

CHARLES: You are truly a computer expert! What luck to have a friend like you! I am so encouraged by your explanations that I am ready to buy my computer on the spot.

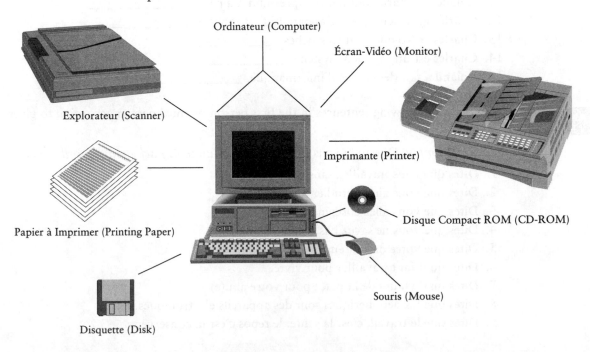

Ordinateur (Computer)

Écran-Vidéo (Monitor)

Explorateur (Scanner)

Imprimante (Printer)

Papier à Imprimer (Printing Paper)

Disque Compact ROM (CD-ROM)

Souris (Mouse)

Disquette (Disk)

ROLAND: I congratulate you, my friend. Perhaps you will begin a start-up company and become an expert in computers and in business at the same time. And above all, don't forget to buy a surge protector to avoid short circuits.

CHARLES: You are terrific, Roland. You always think of everything!

ROLAND: With your new start-up company and your new computer, you will be forced to think of everything.

CHARLES: Nowadays, with the Internet the possibilities are enormous! Thank you very much, dear friend.

DIALOGUE EXERCISES

ANSWERS p. 200

A. Answer True (T) or False (F).

1. Charles veut acheter un ordinateur. _____
2. Roland ne sait rien au sujet de l'informatique. _____
3. Roland est un ami de Charles. _____
4. Charles sait beaucoup de choses au sujet des ordinateurs. _____
5. Roland et Charles sont allés au cinéma. _____
6. Roland n'aime pas l'informatique. _____
7. Charles n'achètera jamais d'ordinateur. _____
8. Roland vient d'acheter un ordinateur. _____
9. Charles a acheté beaucoup d'accessoires. _____
10. Charles demande à Roland de l'aider. _____
11. Roland et Charles ont passé l'après-midi au parc. _____
12. Charles est fasciné par les appareils d'informatique. _____
13. Charles et Roland sont très riches. _____
14. Charles est un ingénieur-système. _____
15. Roland a fait des études d'informatique. _____

ANSWERS p. 201

B. Write the following sentences in the first person or third person according to given text.

Example: Dites que vous acheterez un ordinateur. *J'achèterai un ordinateur.*

1. Dites que vous travaillez sans cesse.
2. Dites que vous aimez étudier l'informatique.
3. Dites que vous allez enseigner la biologie.
4. Dites que vous ne savez pas conduire.
5. Dites que votre ordinateur marche très bien.
6. Dites qu'il faut travailler pour vivre.
7. Dites qu'il y aura de la place pour votre ami(e).
8. Dites que les périphériques sont des appareils électroniques.
9. Dites que le travail, c'est la santé; le repos c'est la conserver.

10. Dites que la puce de l'ordinateur est une des parties essentielles de l'informatique.

11. Dites que vous venez de rentrer d'un long voyage.

12. Dites que vous allez faire des versements mensuels.

13. Dites que le matériel est aussi compliqué que le logiciel.

GRAMMAR I   Immediate Past: *venir de* with the Infinitive

Besides the *imparfait* and the *passé composé,* which convey the past tense, French has an additional past tense called "the immediate past." The English equivalent is a verb used with the adverb "just," as in "I just finished my lunch." To translate the immediacy of a past action as a second action is taking place, French uses a present tense form of *venir de* followed by the infinitive of the action verb.

> EXAMPLE: *Il vient de rentrer.*   He just came back.
>
> *Nous venons de finir notre leçon.*   We just finished our lesson.

Venir de is conjugated as the verb *venir* would be. *Venir de* in the imperfect becomes the English pluperfect.

> EXAMPLE: *Elle vient de partir.*   She just left.
>
> *Elle venait de partir.*   She had just left.

PRACTICE THE IMMEDIATE PAST

Write complete sentences in French, with the appropriate verb form.

1. (He just telephoned you.) _____.

2. (We just sent) votre lettre. _____.

3. (They just bought) une voiture. _____.

4. (I just connected) la table traçante. _____.

5. (She just went out.) _____.

6. (You just solved) notre problème. _____.

GRAMMAR II   Immediate Future: *aller* with the Infinitive

A. In French, there is an additional future tense that is formed with *aller* (to go), followed by the infinitive of the action verb.

> EXAMPLE: *Je vais faire le marché.* I'm going grocery shopping.

This is the French equivalent of the English "to be going to" with the infinitive.

Note that the French does not use the same verb form *-ant,* which would be the literal English translation of "-ing."

EXAMPLE: *Je vais acheter un stylo.* I'm going to buy a pen.

Ils vont apprendre l'informatique. They're going to learn data processing.

B. An important rule to remember here is that when one verb follows another, the second verb is always an infinitive.

EXAMPLE: *Il veut chanter à l'opéra.* He wants to sing at the opera.

Elle aime faire du ski. She likes to ski.

PRACTICE THE IMMEDIATE FUTURE

**ANSWERS
p. 201**

Translate the following sentences into French.

1. (I'm going to sell my car.) _____.
2. (He was going to have lunch) avec nous. _____.
3. (Are you going to drive) jusqu'à New York? _____?
4. (Are you going to teach) à Los Angeles? _____.
5. (Are they going) rester avec nous? _____?
6. (You are going to use) votre ordinateur. _____.

GRAMMAR III   Impersonal Expressions

A. Remember how we stressed the absence of the English *it* as a neuter gender of nouns? Well, in French we do have this neuter gender, but only in connection with the verbs that are called impersonal *(expressions impersonnelles)*. These impersonal expressions are always used in the third-person singular. They are *il faut* (one must, one has to), *c'est* (it's), and *il y a* (there is, there are).

EXAMPLE: *Il faut travailler.* One has to work.

C'est gentil à vous. It's nice of you.

Il y a des gens chez vous. There are people at your home.

B. These expressions follow the rules of the regularities or irregularities of their verbs. For example, *il faut* is the third-person singular of the verb *falloir*. It is important to note that this verb is used *only* in the third person. As a result, it is doubly impersonal since it can't be used with any other pronoun besides *il*.

EXAMPLE: *il faut* one must, has to

il fallait one had to

il faudra one will have to

il faudrait one would have to

C. Unlike *falloir,* which can be used only with the third-person singular *il,* the verbs *être* (to be) and *avoir* (to have) are conjugated in all persons, singular and plural. However, in the two impersonal ways they are used here, *c'est* (it's) and *il y a* (there is, there are), they always remain in the third-person singular.

> EXAMPLE: *C'est dommage.* It's a pity.
>
> *C'était dommage.* It was a pity.
>
> *Il y a du bruit.* There is noise.
>
> *Il y avait du bruit.* There was noise.

D. Since *il y a* and *c'est* are formed with the verbs *avoir* and *être,* they follow the rules of their respective conjugations in all forms and tenses.

> EXAMPLE: *Il y aura de la place.* There will be room.
>
> *Ce sera dommage.* It will be a pity.

NOTE:
The *c'* in *c'est* is *ce + est.* The first vowel is always dropped when the following word starts with a vowel or a mute *h.* Thus, *ce est* becomes *c'est,* *le homme* becomes *l'homme.* In other constructions, the *c'* regains its vowel, as in *ce sera* (it will be), *ce serait* (it would be).

EXERCISES

ANSWERS
pp. 201–202

A. Practice the impersonal expressions with *falloir* and *devoir* by translating the expression in parentheses, using the tense indicated.

> *Example:* <u>Il fallait</u> (had to) acheter du pain.

Note: The negative form takes on a slightly different meaning. *Il ne faut pas* is equivalent to *défense de* + infinitive, as in *défense de fumer* (no smoking, no smoking allowed).

1. _____ (did not have to) acheter du pain.
2. _____ (will have to) être gentil.
3. _____ (would have to) suivre les règles.
4. _____ (has to) se reposer.
5. _____ (had to drive) doucement.
6. _____ (has had to) finir le travail.
7. _____ (does not have to) être méchant.
8. _____ (would not have to) rester debout.
9. _____ (will not have to) s'asseoir par terre.
10. _____ (has to learn) ses leçons.

ANSWERS
p. 202

B. Practice the impersonal expressions with *être* by translating the expressions in parentheses, using the tense indicated.

    Example: (It's difficult.) *C'est difficile.*

1. (It's a pity.) _____.
2. (It will be nice.) _____.
3. (It will be correct.) _____.
4. (It is not) _____ votre faute.
5. (It was a pity.) _____.
6. (It was nice.) _____.
7. (It was not necessary.) _____.
8. (It will not be) _____ compliqué.
9. (It has been a pleasure.) _____.
10. (It has not been) _____ comme d'habitude.

ANSWERS
p. 202

C. Practice the impersonal expressions with *avoir* by translating the expressions in parentheses, using the tense indicated.

    Example: (There will be room.) *Il y aura de la place.*

1. (There are a lot of people.) _____.
2. (There is enough sun.) _____.
3. (There will be a rainbow.) _____.
4. (There is some kindness.) _____.
5. (There are not enough computers.) _____.
6. (There will be a contract.) _____.
7. (There has been noise.) _____.
8. (There will be a new screen.) _____.
9. (There were enough accessories.) _____.
10. (There are many French people in San Francisco.) _____.

15 Mots apparentés et faux amis
(Cognates and False Friends)

This chapter is the culmination of your newly acquired French vocabulary and grammar. It's intended to remind you that you have a chance to enrich your French vocabulary, on your own, through some 2,000 cognates.

Cognates are words that may have similar sounds, spellings, and meanings as known English words. Many will resemble so closely the English words that by applying the rules set forth in this chapter, you will be able to form your own French equivalents. This chapter will not overlook *les faux amis* (false friends)—these are French words that have exactly the same spelling as English words, but convey a completely different meaning. The French word *sensible*, for example, means "sensitive," or "touchy," while in English it conveys common sense. This chapter will list the most frequently used *faux amis*.

Cognates such as *garage, automobile, vague, vain,* and *primordial* belong to the category of hundreds of cognates that have the same meaning, spelling, and sound as in English. There are, however, hundreds of other cognates that have the same meaning conveyed by the English words but are not spelled exactly like them. These cognates are found as nouns, adjectives, verbs, and adverbs. While it will be impossible to list all English cognates, the following pages will provide the necessary guidelines to assist you in converting your own English words into new French ones.

FRENCH NOUNS WITH ENGLISH ENDINGS

Please study the charts and word ending conversion below.

French Nouns	French Endings	English Endings	
l'anatomie (fem.)	**-ie**	(anatomy)	**-y**
la chambre	**-re**	(chamber)	**-er**
le dictionnaire	**-aire**	(dictionary)	**-ary**
la liberté	**-té**	(liberty)	**-y**
le moteur	**-eur**	(motor)	**-or**
la république	**-que**	(republic)	**-ic**
le snobisme	**-isme**	(snobism)	**-ism**
l'urgence (fem.)	**-ence**	(urgency)	**-ency**

NOTE:
Notice that all word transformations take place in the word endings.

FRENCH ADJECTIVES WITH ENGLISH ENDINGS

French Adjectives	French Endings	English Endings	
américain	**-ain**	(American)	**-an**
canadien	**-ien**	(Canadian)	**-ian**
comique	**-ique**	(comical)	**-ical**
contraire	**-aire**	(contrary)	**-ary**
délicieux	**-eux**	(delicious)	**-ous**
pessimiste	**-iste**	(pessimistic)	**-istic**
populaire	**-aire**	(popular)	**-ar**
progressif	**-if**	(progressive)	**-ive**

NOTE:
Notice that both French adjectives and nouns ending in *-aire* correspond to the English ending "*-ary,*" and that both French adjectives and nouns ending in *-iste* have the English ending "ist" for nouns and "istic" for adjectives.

FRENCH VERBS WITH ENGLISH ENDINGS

French Verbs	French Endings	English Endings	
admirer	**-er**	(to admire)	**-e**
analyser	**-yser**	(to analyze)	**-yze**
célébrer	**-er**	(celebrate)	**-ate**
finir	**-ir**	(to finish)	**-ish**
organiser	**-iser**	(to organize)	**-ize**

FRENCH ADVERBS WITH ENGLISH ENDINGS

French adverbs ending in *-ment*, as in *directement, sérieusement,* etc., correspond to the English ending "-ly," as in "directly," "seriously." All the French adjectives ending in *-eux (euse),* which have the English ending "-ous," follow the *-ment,* "-ly," equivalent in the respective adverbs.

> EXAMPLE: *délicieux, délicieusement,* delicious, deliciously

NOTES:

1. Both French and English have identical scientific and technical terms. The spelling may vary slightly from French into English, but all words are easily recognized.

   > EXAMPLE: *analyse, artère, ordre, alcali, acide, angle, triangle, vitamine, protéine, oxygène,* etc.

2. French nouns ending in *-ance, -ence, -able, -ible, -sion, -tion, -ude, -ure, -ment* are similar in both languages.

   > EXAMPLE: *élégance, différence, agréable, précision, éducation, certitude, culture, département.*

Certain months of the year are also easily recognizable.

> EXAMPLE: *septembre, octobre, novembre, décembre, mars, avril, mai.*

French *Faux Amis*

As stated earlier, there are many French words that can be misleading, thus their nickname of "false friends." Below is a short list of such *faux amis.*

French *Faux Amis*	Translation	English False Friends
anniversaire	birthday	not: anniversary
assister (à)	to attend	not: to help or assist
la cave	cellar	not: a cave
commander	to order (meal, etc.)	not: to command
demander	to ask for	not: to demand
la dent	the tooth	not: the dent
la lecture	reading	not: a lecture, lesson
la location	rent, renting	not: a location, place
rester	to stay, to remain	not: to rest
sensible	sensitive	not: sensible

There are no set rules for *faux amis.* You should, however, be aware of their existence. When a phrase does not make sense with a cognate, you know it's a false friend.

The following is a summary of cognate endings in nouns, adjectives, adverbs, and verbs.

French Endings	Equivalent English Endings
-ie, géographie	-y, geography
-té, possibilité	-y, possibility
-eur, labeur (noun)	-or, labor
-ique, logique	-ic, logic
-isme, optimisme	-ism, optimism
-iste, chimiste	-ist, chemist
-ien, musicien	-ian, musician
-ain, africain	-an, African
-eux, furieux	-ous, furious
-if, décisif	-ive, decisive
-iste, optimiste (adj.)	-istic, optimistic
-er, arriver	-e, to arrive
-er, célébrer	-ate, to celebrate
-ier, simplifier	-y, to simplify
-ir, nourrir	-ish, to nourish
-iser, organiser	-ize, to organize
-yser, analyser	-yze, to analyze
-ment, arrangement (n.)	-ment, arrangement
-ment, immédiatement (adj.)	-ly, immediately

UNDERSTANDING COGNATES

ANSWERS p. 202

A What are the English cognates for the following words?

1. capacité _____
2. géométrie _____
3. analogie _____
4. monstre _____
5. ordinaire _____
6. ferveur _____
7. musique _____
8. estuaire _____
9. sérieux _____
10. logique _____
11. australien _____
12. abusif _____
13. actif _____
14. modérer _____
15. temporaire _____
16. affirmer _____
17. bannir _____
18. chimiste _____
19. offrir _____
20. absolument _____
21. dangereux _____
22. cultiver _____
23. irriter _____
24. multiplier _____

GRAMMAR I   Conditional Form of Regular Verbs

A. To form the conditional of a regular verb in French, we add the endings of the *imparfait* to the infinitive. Study the chart below.

Subject	*Parler*	*Choisir*	*Attendre*
je	parler ais	choisir ais	attendr ais
tu	parler ais	choisir ais	attendr ais
il, elle, on	parler ait	choisir ait	attendr ait
nous	parler ions	choisir ions	attendr ions
vous	parler iez	choisir iez	attendr iez
ils, elles	parler aient	choisir aient	attendr aient

1. The verb stem of the conditional is the infinitive, just as we have seen in the future tense.

2. To this stem are added the conditional endings, which are the same as those of the *imparfait: -ais, -ais, -ait, -ions, -iez,* and *-aient*. These endings are added to the infinitives of regular verbs. If a verb has an *e* in the infinitive, this vowel is dropped, as in *apprendre.*

   EXAMPLE: *j'apprendr-ais* I would learn.
   tu apprendr-ais You would learn.

B. Uses of the *conditionnel* (conditional).

1. The conditional is used with wishes and requests. Using the conditional makes a request softer and more polite. Compare these two examples:

   (a) *Je voudrais un livre.* I would like a book.
   (b) *Je veux un livre.* I want a book.

   The request in example *a* is more polite than *b*.

2. The conditional is also used to indicate a projected action that is to occur sometime in the future.

   EXAMPLE: *Elle savait qu'il téléphonerait après le dîner.* She knew he would call after dinner.

3. English uses the conditional to express habits that occurred in the past. This form is rendered in French by *l'imparfait.*

   EXAMPLE: *À Paris, je me promenais toujours le matin.* In Paris, I would always take a walk in the morning.

PRACTICE THE GRAMMAR

A. Answer the following questions about the use of the conditional.

1. What is the verb stem of the conditional in French? _____

2. In English, the conditional is formed by *would* + infinitive. How is it formed in French? _____

3. When is the conditional used to convey politeness? _____

4. What tense does French use to convey the English conditional expressing habits occurring in the past? _____

5. Give the conditional form of *ils* _____ *(finir)* and of *elle* _____ *(rendre)*.

**ANSWERS
p. 203**

B. Change the verb forms from the *passé composé* to the conditional.

1. j'ai acheté _____

2. nous avons examiné _____

3. nous sommes partis _____

4. ils sont sortis _____

5. elle a mangé _____

6. nous avons admiré _____

7. elle a appris _____

8. il a fini _____

9. tu as préparé _____

10. tu t'es ennuyé(e) _____

**ANSWERS
p. 203**

C. Change the verb forms from the present to the conditional.

1. nous partons _____

2. elle joue _____

3. vous sortez _____

4. il s'amuse _____

5. tu attends _____

6. ils achètent _____

7. tu manges _____

8. nous finissons _____

9. elle admire _____

10. ils aiment _____

GRAMMAR II Comparing the Future and the Conditional of Irregular Verbs

A. Memorize the following chart with *être* and *avoir*.

Subject	Future (*Être*)	Conditional (*Être*)	Future (*Avoir*)	Conditional (*Avoir*)
je	serai	serais	aurai	aurais
tu	seras	serais	auras	aurais
il, elle, on	sera	serait	aura	aurait
nous	serons	serions	aurons	aurions
vous	serez	seriez	aurez	auriez
ils, elles	seront	seraient	auront	auraient

NOTES:

1. All irregular verbs in the future tense are irregular in the conditional. This means that the list of irregular verbs given in Lesson 11 will have the same irregular changes, to which are added the regular conditional endings.

2. The same rules apply in changes of spelling or accentuation in stem-changing verbs such as *acheter* (to buy) or *appeler* (to call).

    EXAMPLE: *acheter, j'achèterai, j'achèterais,* etc.

    appeler, j'appellerai, j'appellerais, etc.

B. Memorize the irregular verbs in the future and conditional forms below.

Infinitive	Future	Conditional
aller	j'irai	j'irais
devoir	je devrai	je devrais
faire	je ferai	je ferais
pouvoir	je pourrai	je pourrais
savoir	je saurai	je saurais
venir	je viendrai	je viendrais
voir	je verrai	je verrais
vouloir	je voudrai	je voudrais

C. Study the irregular impersonal expressions in the future and conditional forms.

Impersonal	Future	Conditional
il faut	il faudra	il faudrait
il vaut	il vaudra	il vaudrait

PRACTICE

A. Practice the irregular future and conditional forms.

1. All the verbs that are irregular in the future are also irregular in _____.
2. The conditional of *savoir* is je _____.
3. If the future of *il peut* is *il pourra*, what is the conditional? _____.
4. If the future of *nous apprenons* is *nous apprendrons*, what is the conditional? _____.
5. If the future of *tu sais* is *tu sauras*, what is the conditional? _____.
6. If the future of *il doit* is *elle devra*, what is the conditional? _____.
7. If the future of *tu fais* is *tu feras*, what is the conditional? _____.
8. If the future of *vous voyez* is *vous verrez*, what is the conditional? _____.
9. If the future of *il veut* is *il voudra*, what is the conditional? _____.
10. If the future of *nous allons* is *nous irons*, what is the conditional? _____.

ANSWERS
p. 203

B. Complete the sentences with the correct future form of the given verbs.

> *Example:* Jacques et Mac (aller) *iront* voir Juliette.

1. Jeudi prochain, je (faire) _____ des courses.
2. Si tu viens, nous (pouvoir) _____ faire du ski.
3. Juliette et Charles se (fiancer) _____ le mois prochain.
4. Il y (avoir) _____ beaucoup de loisirs.
5. Vous (savoir) _____ la réponse demain.
6. Tu (aller) _____ avec nous à l'aéroport.
7. Il (faut) _____ travailler lundi prochain.
8. Nous (faire) _____ toute la vaisselle.
9. Il (garder) _____ le lit jusqu'à demain.
10. Vous (voir) _____ dès que vous (venir) _____.

ANSWERS
pp. 203–204

C. Complete the table according to the examples below.

PRESENT	IMPERFECT	FUTURE	CONDITIONAL
1. vous avez	vous aviez	vous aurez	vous auriez
2. tu achètes	_____	_____	_____
3. vous venez	_____	_____	_____
4. elle apprend	_____	_____	_____
5. tu finis	_____	_____	_____
6. elle va	_____	_____	_____
7. tu vois	_____	_____	_____
8. nous savons	_____	_____	_____
9. elle attend	_____	_____	_____
10. nous avons	_____	_____	_____

GRAMMAR III   Formation and Usage of Adverbs

A. Usage and placement of adverbs.

1. Adverbs are used to modify adjectives, verbs, and other adverbs.

   We have learned several adverbs, such as *beaucoup, bien, mal, trop, très, vite, peu, souvent, ici, bientôt, là-bas,* etc.

2. Adverbs usually are placed before adjectives and after verbs.

   > EXAMPLE: *Il va bien.*   He is well.
   >
   > *Il est très gentil*. He is very kind.

3. Adverbs of time and place are usually at the end or the beginning of a sentence.

4. The adverbs of time are: *bientôt, demain,* and *hier.*

   The adverbs of place are: *ici* and *là-bas.*

EXAMPLE: *Nous partons à Nice bientôt.*   We are leaving for Nice soon.

Ils sont heureux ici.   They are happy here.

5. Adverbs are placed after *pas* in a negative sentence.

EXAMPLE: *Il ne chante pas souvent.*   He does not sing often.

Il ne mange pas bien.   He does not eat well.

6. Adverbs are placed after the auxiliary in the *passé composé* sentences.

EXAMPLE: *Il a beaucoup parlé.*   He talked a lot.

B. Formation of adverbs.

1. Most French adverbs are formed by adding *-ment* to the adjective.

EXAMPLE: *vrai, vraiment*

aimable, aimablement

The *-ment* is often the equivalent of the English *-ly*, as in "quickly."

2. The *-ment* ending is usually added to the masculine form of the adjective. However, if the masculine form ends with a consonant, then *-ment* is added to the feminine form of the adjective. Study the following examples.

EXAMPLE: *poli* (masc.)   *poliment*

joli (masc.)   *joliment*

heureux (masc.), *heureuse* (fem.)   *heureusement*

lent (masc.), *lente* (fem.)   *lentement*

3. When the masculine form of an adjective ends in *-ent* or *-ant*, the adverb is formed by adding *-emment* to the *-ent* adjective and *-amment* to the *-ant* adjective. Study the following examples.

EXAMPLE: *différent*   *différemment* (differently)

constant   *constamment* (constantly)

4. Two adverbs do not follow any of the above rules and are the only irregular adverbs in French. They are: *brièvement* (briefly), *gentiment* (kindly). Their adjectives are *bref, brève,* (brief); *gentil, gentille* (kind).

PRACTICE YOUR ADVERBS

A. Answer the following questions.

1. How are adverbs generally formed in French? _____.

2. What adjective form is usually used to make an adverb? _____.

3. When does French require the feminine form of an adjective to make an adverb? _____.

4. Where are adverbs of time and place put in a sentence? _____.

5. Name two adverbs of place: _____ and _____.

6. Name two adverbs of time: _____ and _____.

7. Where are French adverbs placed in negative sentences? _____.

ANSWERS p. 204

B. Give the adverbial equivalent of the following adjectives.

1. gentil _____
2. heureux _____
3. actif _____
4. bref _____
5. intelligent _____
6. absolu _____
7. courant _____

8. évident _____
9. triste _____
10. certain _____
11. rapide _____
12. apparent _____
13. seul _____
14. élégant _____

ANSWERS   LESSONS 11–15

Lesson 11

Vocabulary

Practice

A. 1. J'ai deux yeux.
   2. J'ai deux oreilles.
   3. J'ai deux pieds.
   4. J'ai deux jambes.
   5. J'ai deux chevilles.
   6. J'ai deux genoux.
   7. J'ai deux épaules.
   8. J'ai deux poumons.
   9. J'ai deux sourcils.
   10. J'ai deux bras.

B. 1. Ils sont tombés malades hier.
   2. Où avez-vous mal?
   3. Est-ce que la malle était lourde?
   4. Il se sent faible.
   5. Nous pouvons nous guérir.
   6. Prends (prenez) soin de toi (de vous).
   7. Comment allez-vous? Allez-vous mieux aujourd'hui?
   8. Je me sens beaucoup mieux quand je me repose.
   9. Donne-moi ta main, je veux la voir (*or*) Donnez-moi votre main . . .
   10. J'ai été malade pendant une semaine.

Dialogue Exercises

A. 1. Charles est le frère de "Moi."
   2. Il voulait dire qu'il avait une nouvelle voisine.
   3. Les cheveux de la voisine sont blonds, frisés et longs.
   4. La sœur de Charles est en colère parce qu'elle dormait (*or*) parce que Charles l'a réveillée.
   5. Non, les cheveux de "Moi" ne sont pas blonds.
   6. "Moi" a dormi tard parce que c'était le dimanche.
   7. Le téléphone a sonné à midi et demi.
   8. "Moi" est sarcastique.
   9. Charles est du monde où les hommes n'ont pas de tact.
   10. Les dents de la voisine sont légèrement imparfaites.
   11. Non, la voisine n'a pas parlé à Charles.
   12. La voisine a montré ses dents quand elle lui a fait un grand sourire.
   13. Non, "Moi" n'est pas malade.
   14. Non, Charles n'a pas fait la connaissance de la voisine.

B. 1. Nous marchons avec les pieds.
   2. Nous regardons avec les yeux.
   3. Nous sentons avec le nez.
   4. Nous entendons avec les oreilles.
   5. Nous écrivons avec la main.
   6. Nous mangeons avec la bouche.
   7. Nous mâchons avec les dents.
   8. Nous touchons avec les doigts (*or*) avec les mains.

Grammar I

Practice

A. 1. adjectives
    2. nouns expressing numbers and amounts
    3. plus de . . . que
    4. plus que . . . and plus de . . . que
    5. moins que
    6. Il est plus sérieux qu'elle.
    7. Elle a moins de vingt dollars.
    8. Nous parlons plus sérieusement que vous.
    9. after the verb
   10. with nouns expressing numbers and amounts

B. 1. plus tard que
    2. plus vite que
    3. plus facile que
    4. plus lourdes que
    5. plus souvent que
    6. plus sociables que
    7. moins bavardes que
    8. plus long que
    9. plus d'argent que
   10. moins intelligente que

Grammar II

Practice

1. aussi . . . que, autant . . . que, and autant de . . . que.
2. with numbers and amounts
3. as many as, as much as
4. uses *le, la, les* + comparatives
5. They agree in number and gender with modifiers.
6. les meilleurs livres

7. Leurs livres sont meilleurs.

8. Ils parlent mieux.

9. Il se sent pire.

10. Il se sent aussi mal que vous.

Exercise

1. Vous avez moins de courage que nous.

2. Vous attendez moins longtemps que . . .

3. Vous êtes moins charmants que les voisins.

4. La téléphoniste est moins sérieuse que la concierge.

5. La caisse d'épargne est moins près que la banque.

6. Les parents sont moins bavards que les enfants.

Grammar III

Practice

1. ai, as, a, ons, ez, ont

2. to the infinitive

3. no

4. yes

5. dependent clause + *when*

6. ils pourront

7. ils sauront plus que nous.

8. il faudra

9. il vaudra mieux

10. il mangera aussitôt qu'il reviendra.

Exercise

1. Ma soeur sera invitée chez la voisine.

2. Nous trouverons un petit hôtel charmant.

3. Vous pourrez m'aider à préparer le dîner.

4. Juliette travaillera à la banque.

5. Nous irons à Paris après la fête de Noël.

6. Elle apprendra à jouer de la harpe.

7. Nous **saurons** écrire le chinois.

Lesson 12

Vocabulary

Practice

A.
1. un
2. une
3. une
4. une
5. un
6. une
7. un
8. une
9. une
10. un
11. un
12. un
13. un
14. une
15. un

B.
1. gros
2. calmant
3. dent
4. barbier
5. poissonnerie
6. plombage
7. balance
8. alimentation
9. (se) raser
10. maigre

C. 1. se rasera
   2. maigrira
   3. sera
   4. faudra
   5. usera
   6. avalera
   7. perdront . . . abuseront

Dialogue Exercises

A. 1. Parce qu'elle a une crise de foie.
   2. Les pilules la soulagent.
   3. Le docteur Blanchard a prescrit les pilules.
   4. C'est un calmant.
   5. Parce qu'il faut prendre les pilules trois fois par jour.
   6. "User mais pas abuser." (or) "User sans abuser."
   7. Cela ne vous fera pas mal.
   8. Un tube de pâte dentifrice, des losanges pour la gorge, et des lames de rasoir.
   9. Le prix est de soixante francs.
   10. Mme Bellan et sa fille avaient la grippe.

B. sentait . . . est allée . . . a conseillé . . . a acheté . . . a payé . . . a fait . . . avait . . . a gardé . . . est soulagée

C. 1. F   5. A
   2. G   6. C
   3. E   7. D
   4. H   8. B

Grammar I

Practice

A. 1. By dropping the -ons from the nous form of the present indicative and adding -ions.
   2. que nous formions
   3. être and avoir
   4. qu'il finisse
   5. Je veux que tu attendes ici.
   6. a dependent clause with que and an independent clause
   7. in the indicative
   8. Il est possible qu'elle parte.
   9. emotion, doubt
   10. Nous voulons que vous écoutiez.

B. 1. achetions   4. demandiez
    2. finisse   5. refusions
    3. attendes

Grammar II

Practice

A. 1. rappeler, se rappeler, épeler (to spell)
    2. changer, ranger (to put away or to put in order)
    3. payer, employer
    4. to make *c* and *g* into soft sounds
    5. nous essayions (*and*) vous essayiez
    6. Je veux que vous payiez votre facture (*or*) que tu paies ta facture.
    7. Ils veulent que vous appeliez un docteur.
    8. Elle insiste que je reste au lit (*or*) que je garde le lit.
    9. Je veux que vous commenciez à étudier le français.

B. 1. que nous voyagions
    2. que tu partages
    3. que nous épelions
    4. que vous employiez
    5. que nous achetions
    6. que nous balancions
    7. qu'ils achètent
    8. que vous changiez
    9. que tu rappelles
    10. que je paie

Grammar III

Practice

A. 1. Il faut qu'elle parle souvent.
    2. Il est bon que vous vous reposiez.
    3. Il est important que nous essayions tout.
    4. Il est naturel que vous commenciez . . .
    5. Il est certain qu'elle ne jugera personne.
    6. Il est juste que vous voyagiez . . .
    7. Il est nécessaire que nous ne répondions pas . . .
    8. Il est temps que notre réputation grandisse . . .
    9. Il vaut mieux que nous finissions . . .
    10. Il est douteux que nous payions . . .

B. 1. que vous finissiez
   2. que vous réussissiez
   3. que vous payiez
   4. que vous irez
   5. que nous sommes . . .
   6. que vous partagiez
   7. que je parte
   8. que les voisins achètent
   9. que nous commencions
  10. que tu payeras

Lesson 13

Vocabulary

Practice

A. 1. un   5. un   9. un
   2. un   6. une   10. une
   3. un   7. une   11. une
   4. une   8. un   12. une

B. 1. accélérateur   6. capot
   2. avant   7. freiner
   3. gonfler   8. assuré
   4. chauffage   9. stationner
   5. panne   10. allumer

Dialogue Exercises

A. 1. à côté de la voiture
   2. ils sont medecins, docteurs
   3. parce qu'il n'a pas trouvé son mécanicien
   4. d'apporter une boisson
   5. les phares, les freins, les indicateurs
   6. parce qu'il n'y a pas d'essence
   7. à côté du trottoir

B. 1. que tu commences   5. que tu essaies
   2. que tu te reposes   6. que tu t'arrêtes
   3. que tu partes   7. que tu gaspilles
   4. que tu gardes   8. que tu surveilles

Grammar I

Exercise

1. Il faut que Marc attende.
2. Il est douteux que Marie aille au cinéma sans son fiancé.

3. Il est douteux que Monsieur Bertrand connaisse les projets de Jacques.

4. Il faut que vous alliez chercher un mécanicien.

5. Il est nécessaire que nous ayons du courage.

Grammar II

Practice

A. 1. Indicative = fact, subjunctive = opinion

2. When the subject is the same in the two clauses.

3. Je veux chanter (or any verb).

4. Pensent-ils que nous aimions le vin blanc? (*or*) Ils ne pensent pas que nous aimions le vin blanc.

5. in the negative and interrogative forms

6. Je ne crois pas qu'il puisse changer.

7. dire

8. Vous lui dites qu'il soit sage.

B. 1. puissions

2. ont

3. soient

4. fassent

5. peut

6. vont

7. connaissent

Grammar III

Review Exercise

1. Je sais que vous savez tout.

2. Crois-tu tout savoir? (*or*) Crois-tu que tu sais tout?

3. Il est évident que vous savez tout.

4. Nous savons que vous savez tout.

5. Il est certain que vous savez tout.

6. Il est probable que vous sachiez tout.

7. Il est impossible que vous sachiez tout.

8. Je ne crois pas que vous sachiez tout.

9. Je suis sûr que vous savez tout.

10. Il est défendu que vous sachiez tout.

Lesson 14

Vocabulary

Practice

A. 1. le (masc.)   6. la (fem.)   12. l'(masc.)
   2. le (masc.)   7. le (masc.)   13. la (fem.)
   3. la (fem.)   8. le (masc.)   14. le (masc.)
   4. le (masc.)   9. la (fem.)   15. le (masc.)
   5. le (masc.)   10. l'(fem.)   16. le (masc.)
                   11. la (fem.)   17. le (masc.)

B. 1. résoudre   9. vendre
   2. imprimer   10. aimer
   3. coller   11. allumer
   4. écrire   12. compter
   5. dessiner   13. conduire
   6. brancher   14. décider
   7. sortir   15. transformer
   8. entrer

C. 1. l'achat   7. la préférence
   2. le commencement   8. l'imprimante
   3. la décision   9. la colle
   4. la suite   10. la conduite
   5. la réussite   11. la sortie
   6. l'entrée   12. l'accession

D. 1. joyeux, euse   7. poli, polie
   2. souriant(e)   8. brumeux (euse)
   3. beau, belle   9. ensoleillé(e)
   4. courtois, courtoise 10. lumineux (euse)
   5. gentil, gentille   11. journalier (ière)
   6. mensuel, mensuelle 12. grand(e)

Dialogue Exercises

A. 1. T   6. F   11. F
   2. F   7. F   12. T
   3. T   8. F   13. F
   4. F   9. F   14. F
   5. F   10. T   15. T

B. 1. Je travaille sans cesse.
   2. J'aime étudier l'informatique.
   3. Je vais enseigner la biologie.
   4. Je ne sais pas conduire.
   5. Mon ordinateur marche très bien.
   6. Il faut travailler pour vivre.
   7. Il y aura de la place pour mon ami(e).
   8. Les périphériques sont des appareils électroniques.
   9. Le travail c'est la santé; le repos c'est la conserver.
   10. La puce de l'ordinateur est une partie essentielle de l'informatique.
   11. Je viens de rentrer d'un long voyage.
   12. Je vais faire des versements mensuels.
   13. Le matériel est aussi compliqué que le logiciel.

Grammar I

Practice

   1. Il vient de vous téléphoner.
   2. Nous venons d'envoyer votre lettre.
   3. Ils viennent d'acheter une voiture.
   4. Je viens de brancher la table traçante.
   5. Elle vient de sortir.
   6. Vous venez de résoudre notre problème.

Grammar II

Practice

   1. Je vais vendre ma voiture.
   2. Il allait déjeuner avec nous.
   3. Allez-vous conduire jusqu'à New York?
   4. Allez-vous enseigner à Los Angeles?
   5. Vont-ils rester avec nous?
   6. Vous allez utiliser votre ordinateur.

Grammar III

Exercises

A. 1. Il ne fallait pas acheter du pain.
   2. Il faudra être gentil.
   3. Il faudrait suivre les règles.
   4. Il faut se reposer. (*or*) On doit se reposer.
   5. Il fallait conduire doucement.
   6. Il a fallu finir le travail.
   7. Il ne faut pas être méchant. (*or*) On ne doit pas être méchant.

8. On ne devrait pas rester debout. (*or*) Il ne faudrait pas rester debout.

9. Il ne faudra pas s'asseoir par terre.

10. On doit apprendre ses leçons. (*or*) Il faut apprendre ses leçons.

B. 1. C'est dommage.
2. Ce sera gentil.
3. Ce sera correct.
4. Ce n'est pas votre faute.
5. C'était dommage.
6. Cela (ça) aura été gentil.
7. Ce n'était pas necessaire.
8. Ce ne sera pas compliqué.
9. Cela (ça) a été un plaisir.
10. Cela n'a pas été comme d'habitude.

C. 1. Il y a beaucoup de monde (*or*) de personnes, de gens.
2. Il y a assez de soleil.
3. Il y aura un arc-en-ciel.
4. Il y a de la gentillesse.
5. Il n'y a pas assez d'ordinateurs.
6. Il y aura un contrat.
7. Il y a eu du bruit.
8. Il y aura un nouvel écran.
9. Il y avait assez d'accessoires.
10. Il y a beaucoup de Français à San Francisco.

LESSON 15

Understanding Cognates

A.   1. capacity
2. geometry
3. analogy
4. monster
5. ordinary
6. fervor
7. music
8. estuary
9. serious
10. logic
11. Australian
12. abusive
13. active
14. moderate
15. temporary
16. affirm
17. banish
18. chemist
19. offer
20. absolutely
21. dangerous
22. cultivate
23. irritate
24. multiply

Grammar I

Practice

A. 1. the infinitive
2. by adding to the infinitive the *imparfait* endings
3. with wishes and requests
4. the imperfect
5. ils finiraient, elle rendrait

B. 1. j'achèterais
2. nous examinerions
3. nous partirions
4. ils sortiraient
5. elle mangerait
6. nous admirerions
7. elle apprendrait
8. il finirait
9. tu preparerais
10. tu t'ennuyerais

C. 1. nous partirions
2. elle jouerait
3. vous sortiriez
4. il s'amuserait
5. tu attendrais
6. ils achèteraient
7. tu mangerais
8. nous finirions
9. elle admirerait
10. ils aimeraient

Grammar II

Practice

A. 1. the conditional
2. saurais
3. il pourrait
4. nous apprendrions
5. tu saurais
6. elle devrait
7. tu ferais
8. vous verriez
9. il voudrait
10. nous irions

B. 1. ferai
2. pourrons
3. fianceront
4. aura
5. saurez
6. iras
7. faudra
8. ferons
9. gardera
10. verrez, viendrez

C. 1. vous aviez, vous aurez, vous auriez
2. tu achetais, tu achèteras, tu achèterais
3. vous veniez, vous viendrez, vous viendriez
4. elle apprenait, elle apprendra, elle apprendrait
5. tu finissais, tu finiras, tu finirais
6. elle allait, elle ira, elle irait
7. tu voyais, tu verras, tu verrais

8. nous savions, nous saurons, nous saurions
9. elle attendait, elle attendra, elle attendrait
10. nous avions, nous aurons, nous aurions

Grammar III

Practice

A. 1. by adding *-ment* to the adjective
   2. the masculine form
   3. when the masculine form ends with a consonant
   4. the beginning or end of sentences
   5. ici (*and*) là-bas
   6. demain (*and*) bientôt
   7. after *pas*

B. 1. gentiment
   2. heureusement
   3. activement
   4. brièvement
   5. intelligemment
   6. absolument
   7. couramment
   8. évidemment
   9. tristement
   10. certainement
   11. rapidement
   12. apparemment
   13. seulement
   14. élégamment

REVIEW EXAM   LESSONS 11–15

PART I: VOCABULARY

A. Match the two columns (some of the articles may not be necessary).

1. _____ les poumons	A.	On sent les fleurs avec . . .
2. _____ le nez	B.	On mange et on parle avec
3. _____ les doigts	C.	On l'utilise pour tourner à droite.
4. _____ les oreilles	D.	On en a besoin, quand on a une voiture
5. _____ la langue	E.	C'est prudent de l'attacher quand on conduit
6. _____ la fièvre	F.	Il vient quand on est guéri
7. _____ la grippe	G.	Nous aide à guérir
8. _____ le rhume	H.	Quand elle arrive, on a très mal
9. _____ la toux	I.	C'est un soulagement
10. _____ l'ordonnance	J.	C'est souvent un médicament
11. _____ le remède	K.	Le docteur écrit le nom des médicaments
12. _____ le calmant	L.	On l'a quand on a mal à la gorge
13. _____ la crise	M.	Commence par un mal de tête
14. _____ le médicament	N.	C'est un rhume compliqué
15. _____ le soulagement	O.	Elle accompagne la grippe
16. _____ la ceinture	P.	Nous parlons avec la
17. _____ la matricule	Q.	Nous entendons avec les
18. _____ l'indicateur	R.	On touche avec
19. _____ la bouche	S.	On respire avec
20. _____ la gorge	T.	Il est difficile d'avaler avec un mal de . . .

B. Complete the sentences with the most appropriate word, using the proper article, and adding *de* or *d'* to verbs when needed.

1. Je ne peux pas m'arrêter si_____(compte-goutte, espoir, freins) ne marchent pas.

2. J'ai besoin d'acheter deux_____(voiture, balance, brosses) avant de sortir de la pharmacie.

3. J'ai beaucoup grossi, alors le docteur m'a conseillé de suivre_____(crise, régime, drogue).

4. Il est impossible de faire marcher le moteur sans_____(démarreur, essuie-glace, essence).

5. Le garagiste a changé mon pneu parce que j'ai eu une_____(phare, roue, crevaison).

6. Chaque fois que j'ai_____(radiologie, maladie, grippe) j'ai très mal à la tête et à la gorge.

7. En France la_____(matricule, feu rouge, vitesse) limite est de 55 miles.

8. Il est toujours prudent_____(essayer, attacher, allumer) les ceintures quand on conduit.

9. Quand on doit faire un long voyage il faut faire_____(nettoyer, ralentir, vérifier) la voiture.

10. J'ai eu une panne sèche parce que j'ai oublié de_____(dégonfler, faire le plein, faire marche arrière).

11. La voiture a capoté, alors on l'a fait _____(stationner, remorquer, reculer).

12. On préfère souvent acheter une voiture luxueuse que_____(occasion, assuré, moteur).

ANSWERS p. 210

C. **Write a related word for each of the following words. (The related word may be a verb, noun, or adjective.)**

1. tousser _____
2. soulager _____
3. le repos _____
4. calmer _____
5. grossir _____
6. la balance _____
7. l'allumette _____
8. alimenter _____
9. espérer _____
10. tard _____
11. enrhumé _____
12. ennuyer _____
13. démarreur _____
14. dépanner _____
15. freiner _____
16. la main _____
17. la volonté _____
18 l'habitude _____
19. maigrir _____
20. indiquer _____

ANSWERS p. 210

D. **Select the appropriate answer by circling the letter.**

1. L'année prochaine j'achèterai une voiture de luxe.
   a. Ma voiture est toujours en panne.
   b. Il est vrai que ma voiture ne marche pas bien.
   c. Hier j'ai fait nettoyer le pare-brise.
   d. Les freins et l'embrayage sont très importants.

2. Le docteur a prescrit un calmant pour la crise de foie.
   a. Ces crises-là sont souvent désagréables.
   b. Ce genre de crise est fréquent chez les Français.
   c. Le docteur donne de bons conseils.
   d. On trouve des hypochondriaques partout.
3. Les marques de voitures françaises sont populaires ici.
   a. Quand on veut acheter une voiture, on choisit la meilleure marque.
   b. Les Peugeot et les Renault sont partout dans cette ville.
   c. Il aime les voitures françaises.
   d. Les voitures de luxe sont souvent trop chères.
4. Il est toujours prudent de respecter la vitesse limite.
   a. Les Français conduisent aussi vite que les Américains.
   b. Quand on conduit trop vite, on peut tamponner une autre voiture.
   c. L'agent a le droit de t'arrêter si tu n'as pas la plaque d'immatriculation.
5. Le chauffeur de taxi veut mettre ta malle dans le coffre.
   a. Les chauffeurs de taxi sont souvent pressés.
   b. Les bagages prennent trop de place.
   c. Les bagages et les passagers sont séparés.
   d. Le taxi était libre quand nous sommes arrivés.
6. Crois-tu que maigrir ou grossir est plutôt psychologique?
   a. Cette question ne m'intéresse pas.
   b. La psychologie est une science intéressante.
   c. Le boucher et le boulanger sont des marchands comme l'épicier.

PART II: GRAMMAR

A. Write the appropriate future form of the verbs in parentheses.

1. Les questions_____(être) longues.
2. Le médicament la_____(soulager) demain.
3. Il_____(dire) la vérité à l'agent.
4. Il_____(faut) partir bientôt.
5. Nous_____(pouvoir) finir ce travail-là.
6. Ils_____(aller) avec nous au théâtre.
7. Dimanche prochain tu_____(savoir) la vérité.
8. Ils_____(avoir) beaucoup de plaisir à vous revoir.
9. Vous_____(voir) comme c'est facile de ne pas fumer.
10. Ils_____(arriver) à temps pour Noël.

ANSWERS
p. 211

B. Complete the following sentences with the present indicative or the present subjunctive as required.

1. Il est vrai que nos voisins_____(être) toujours absents.
2. Nous voulons que vous_____(guérir) très bientôt.
3. Il n'est pas nécessaire que tu_____(faire) ce travail-là.
4. Nous sommes certains que vous_____(aller) avec nous ce soir.
5. Le sénateur n'est pas sûr qu'il_____(pouvoir) gagner l'élection.
6. Ma fiancée veut une chambre qui_____(avoir) une grande armoire à clef.
7. Le patron a défendu que nous_____(bavarder) entre nous.
8. Il est utile que nous_____(savoir) les règles du jeu (rules of the game).
9. Je regrette que la leçon_____(être) longue.
10. Il est important qu'ils_____(avoir) assez d'argent pour le loyer.

ANSWERS
p. 211

C. Complete the sentences with the most appropriate word or expression.

1. Je ne sais rien qui _____ l'aider.
   a. soit
   b. puisse
   c. ait
   d. fasse

2. Il était _____ quand il m'a téléphoné.
   a. plus tard
   b. volontiers
   c. sans cesse
   d. en panne

3. Elle était très sophistiquée et bien habillée, elle portait _____ vert.
   a. une robe
   b. un collant
   c. un ensemble
   d. un costume

4. Avant de commencer à écrire, je dois _____ l'imprimante.
   a. imprimer
   b. brancher
   c. résoudre
   d. coller

5. Ce n'est pas nécessaire que tu _____ manier le tournevis pour faire marcher un ordinateur.
   a. ailles
   b. finisses
   c. saches
   d. réussisses

6. L'épicier m'a dit qu'il ne vend pas de lait, c'est à la crèmerie que je le _____.
   a. ferai
   b. irai
   c. sortirai
   d. trouverai

7. Quand on conduit, pour changer de la première vitesse à la quatrième, il faut employer _____.

    a. le signe   c. le volant

    b. le phare   d. l'embrayage

8. Je lui ai demandé de partir et il a dit "_____."

    a. "Je voudrais bien."   c. "Je suis fatigué."

    b. "Je n'ai pas entendu."   d. "Je suis pressé."

9. L'épicier, le boucher, et le laitier sont des _____.

    a. voisins   c. amis

    b. marchands commerçants   d. hommes

10. Il faut que je _____ quand j'arrive au feu rouge.

    a. m'arrête   c. change de vitesse

    b. freine   d. ralentisse

11. Quand j'avais la grippe je _____ beaucoup.

    a. toussais   c. m'amusais

    b. jouais   d. dansais

12. Il est illégal que vous ne _____ pas assuré.

    a. vouliez   c. passiez

    b. soyez   d. puissiez

13. Mon professeur parle cinq langues _____.

    a. terriblement   c. sérieusement

    b. couramment   d. complètement

14. Nous voudrions que vous _____ avec nous.

    a. sortiez   c. mangiez

    b. alliez   d. partiez

ANSWERS   REVIEW EXAM

LESSONS 11–15

Vocabulary

A.
1. S		11. J
2. A		12. I
3. R		13. H
4. Q		14. G
5. B		15. F
6. O		16. E
7. N		17. D
8. M		18. C
9. L		19. P
10. K		20. T

B.
1. les freins . . .
2. brosses
3. un régime
4. essence
5. une crevaison
6. la grippe
7. vitesse
8. d'attacher
9. vérifier
10. faire le plein
11. remorquer
12. qu'une d'occasion

C.
1. la toux
2. le soulagement
3. se reposer
4. un calmant
5. gros (grosse)
6. balancer
7. allumer
8. l'alimentation
9. l'espoir
10. tarder (en retard)
11. le rhume (un)
12. l'ennui (un)
13. démarrer
14. une panne (la)
15. les freins
16. manuel, manuelle
17. vouloir
18. s'habituer
19. maigre
20. l'indicateur

D.
1. a
2. b
3. b
4. b
5. c
6. a

Grammar

A.
1. seront
2. soulagera
3. dira
4. faudra
5. pourrons
6. iront
7. sauras
8. auront
9. verrez
10. arriveront

B.
1. sont
2. guérissiez
3. fasses
4. irez (*or*) allez
5. puisse
6. ait
7. bavardions
8. sachions
9. soit
10. aient

C.
1. b
2. d
3. c
4. b
5. c
6. d
7. d
8. a (*or*) c
9. b
10. a
11. a
12. b
13. b
14. c (*or*) a

Appendix A
Regular Verbs

This appendix contains examples of the conjugation rules for each of the three regular verb forms, those ending in *-er, -ir,* and *-re.* All regular verbs follow these rules.

Infinitive

parler *(to speak)*   finir *(to finish)*   attendre *(to wait)*

Present Participle

parlant *(speaking)*   finissant *(finishing)*   attendant *(waiting)*

Past Participle

parlé *(spoken)*   fini *(finished)*   attendu *(waited)*

Indicative

Present

(I speak, am speaking, do speak, will speak) je parle, tu parles, il, elle parle, nous parlons, vous parlez, ils, elles parlent

(I finish, am finishing, do finish, will finish) je finis, tu finis, il, elle finit, nous finissons, vous finissez, ils, elles finissent

(I wait, am waiting, do wait, will wait) j'attends, tu attends, il, elle attend, nous attendons, vous attendez, ils, elles attendent

Imperfect

(I was speaking, used to speak, spoke) je parlais, tu parlais, il, elle parlait, nous parlions, vous parliez, ils, elles parlaient

(I was finishing, used to finish, finished) je finissais, tu finissais, il, elle finissait, nous finissions, vous finissiez, ils, elles finissaient

(I was waiting, used to wait, waited) j'attendais, tu attendais, il, elle attendait, nous attendions, vous attendiez, ils, elles attendaient

Passé Composé

(I spoke, did peak) j'ai parlé, tu as parlé, il, elle a parlé, nous avons parlé, vous avez parlé, ils, elles ont parlé

(I finished, did finish) j'ai fini, tu as fini, il, elle a fini, nous avons fini, vous avez fini, ils, elles ont fini

(I waited, did wait) j'ai attendu, tu as attendu, il, elle a attendu, nous avons attendu, vous avez attendu, ils, elles ont attendu

Future

(I shall/will speak) je parlerai, tu parleras, il, elle parlera, nous parlerons, vous parlerez, ils, elles parleront

(I shall/will finish) je finirai, tu finiras, il, elle finira, nous finirons, vous finirez, ils, elles finiront

(I shall/will wait) j'attendrai, tu attendras, il, elle attendra, nous attendrons, vous attendrez, ils, elles attendront

Conditional

(I would speak) je parlerais, tu parlerais, il, elle parlerait, nous parlerions, vous parleriez, ils, elles parleraient

(I would finish) je finirais, tu finirais, il, elle finirait, nous finirions, vous finiriez, ils, elles finiraient

(I would wait) j'attendrais, tu attendrais, il, elle attendrait, nous attendrions, vous attendriez, ils, elles attendraient

Subjunctive

Present

(that I [may] speak) que je parle, que tu parles, qu'il, qu'elle parle, que nous parlions, que vous parliez, qu'ils, qu'elles parlent

(that I [may] finish) que je finisse, que tu finisses, qu'il, qu'elle finisse, que nous finissions, que vous finissiez, qu'ils, qu'elles finissent

(that I [may] wait) que j'attende, que tu attendes, qu'il, qu'elle attende, que nous attendions, que vous attendiez, qu'ils, qu'elles attendent

Imperative

(speak) parle, parlons, parlez

(finish) finis, finissons, finissez

(wait) attends, attendons, attendez

Appendix B
Irregular Verbs

This appendix contains a sampling of the irregular verbs and their conjugations. Most irregular verbs follow the conjugation rules exemplified by the verbs in this section.

aller   *to go*

Present Participle:	*allant,* going
Imperative:	va (tu), allons (nous), allez (vous)
Past Participle:	*allé(e),* gone
Present Indicative:	je vais, tu vas, il, elle va, nous allons, vous allez, ils, elles vont
Imperfect:	j'allais, tu allais, il, elle allait, nous allions, vous alliez, ils, elles allaient
Passé Composé:	je suis allé(e), tu es allé(e), il, elle est allé(e), nous sommes allé(e)s, vous êtes allé(e)s, ils, elles sont allé(e)s
Future:	j'irai, tu iras, il, elle ira, nous irons, vous irez, ils, elles iront
Conditional:	j'irais, tu irais, il, elle irait, nous irions, vous iriez, ils, elles iraient
Present Subjunctive:	que j'aille, que tu ailles, qu'il, elle aille, que nous allions, que vous alliez, qu'ils, elles aillent

avoir   *to have*

Present Participle:	*ayant,* having
Imperative:	aie, ayons, ayez
Past Participle:	*eu,* had
Present Indicative:	j'ai, tu as, il, elle a, nous avons, vous avez, ils, elles ont

Imperfect:	j'avais, tu avais, il, elle avait, nous avions, vous aviez, ils, elles avaient
Passé Composé:	j'ai eu, tu as eu, il, elle a eu, nous avons eu, vous avez eu, ils, elles ont eu
Future:	j'aurai, tu auras, il, elle aura, nous aurons, vous aurez, ils, elles auront
Conditional:	j'aurais, tu aurais, il, elle aurait, nous aurions, vous auriez, ils, elles auraient
Present Subjunctive:	que j'aie, que tu aies, qu'il, elle ait, que nous ayons, que vous ayez, qu'ils, elles aient

boire   *to drink*

Present Participle:	*buvant,* drinking
Imperative:	bois, buvons, buvez
Past Participle:	*bu,* drunk
Present Indicative:	je bois, tu bois, il, elle boit, nous buvons, vous buvez, ils, elles boivent
Imperfect:	je buvais, tu buvais, il, elle buvait, nous buvions, vous buviez, ils, elles buvaient
Passé Composé:	j'ai bu, tu as bu, il, elle a bu, nous avons bu, vous avez bu, ils, elles ont bu
Future:	je boirai, tu boiras, il, elle boira, nous boirons, vous boirez, ils, elles boiront
Conditional:	je boirais, tu boirais, il, elle boirait, nous boirions, vous boiriez, ils, elles boiraient
Present Subjunctive:	que je boive, que tu boives, qu'il, elle boive, que nous buvions, que vous buviez, qu'ils, elles boivent

conduire   *to drive*

Present Participle:	*conduisant,* driving
Imperative:	conduis, conduisons, conduisez
Past Participle:	*conduit,* driven
Present Indicative:	je conduis, tu conduis, il, elle conduit, nous conduisons, vous conduisez, ils, elles conduisent
Imperfect:	je conduisais, tu conduisais, il, elle conduisait, nous conduisions, vous conduisiez, ils, elles conduisaient
Passé Composé:	j'ai conduit, tu as conduit, il, elle a conduit, nous avons conduit, vous avez conduit, ils, elles ont conduit
Future:	je conduirai, tu conduiras, il, elle conduira, nous conduirons, vous conduirez, ils, elles conduiront
Conditional:	je conduirais, tu conduirais, il, elle conduirait, nous conduirions, vous conduiriez, ils, elles conduiraient
Present Subjunctive:	que je conduise, que tu conduises, qu'il, elle conduise, que nous conduisions, que vous conduisiez, qu'ils, elles conduisent

connaître *to know*

Present Participle:	*connaissant,* knowing
Imperative:	connais, connaissons, connaissez
Past Participle:	*connu,* known
Present Indicative:	je connais, tu connais, il, elle connaît, nous connaissons, vous connaissez, ils, elles connaissent
Imperfect:	je connaissais, tu connaissais, il, elle connaissait, nous connaissions, vous connaissiez, ils, elles connaissaient
Passé Composé:	j'ai connu, tu as connu, il, elle a connu, nous avons connu, vous avez connu, ils, elles ont connu
Future:	je connaîtrai, tu connaîtras, il, elle connaîtra, nous connaîtrons, vous connaîtrez, ils, elles connaîtront
Conditional:	je connaîtrais, tu connaîtrais, il, elle connaîtrait, nous connaîtrions, vous connaîtriez, ils, elles connaîtraient
Present Subjunctive:	que je connaisse, que tu connaisses, qu'il, elle connaisse, que nous connaissions, que vous connaissiez, qu'ils, elles connaissent

croire *to believe*

Present Participle:	*croyant,* believing
Imperative:	crois, croyons, croyez
Past Participle:	*cru,* believed
Present Indicative:	je crois, tu crois, il, elle croit, nous croyons, vous croyez, ils, elles croient
Imperfect:	je croyais, tu croyais, il, elle croyait, nous croyions, vous croyiez, ils, elles croyaient
Passé Composé:	j'ai cru, tu as cru, il, elle a cru, nous avons cru, vous avez cru, ils, elles ont cru
Future:	je croirai, tu croiras, il, elle croira, nous croirons, vous croirez, ils, elles croiront
Conditional:	je croirais, tu croirais, il, elle croirait, nous croirions, vous croiriez, ils, elles croiraient
Present Subjunctive:	que je croie, que tu croies, qu'il, elle croie, que nous croyions, que vous croyiez, qu'ils, elles croient

devoir *to have to, to owe*

Present Participle:	*devant,* having to, owing
Imperative:	None
Past Participle:	*dû,* had to, owed
Present Indicative:	je dois, tu dois, il, elle doit, nous devons, vous devez, ils, elles doivent
Imperfect:	je devais, tu devais, il, elle devait, nous devions, vous deviez, ils, elles devaient

Passé Composé:	j'ai dû, tu as dû, il, elle a dû, nous avons dû, vous avez dû, ils, elles ont dû
Future:	je devrai, tu devras, il, elle devra, nous devrons, vous devrez, ils, elles devront
Conditional:	je devrais, tu devrais, il, elle devrait, nous devrions, vous devriez, ils, elles devraient
Present Subjunctive:	que je doive, que tu doives, qu'il, elle doive, que nous devions, que vous deviez, qu'ils, elles doivent

dire   *to say*

Present Participle:	*disant,* saying
Imperative:	dis, disons, dites
Past Participle:	*dit,* said
Present Indicative:	je dis, tu dis, il, elle dit, nous disons, vous dites, ils, elles disent
Imperfect:	je disais, tu disais, il, elle disait, nous disions, vous disiez, ils, elles disaient
Passé Composé:	j'ai dit, tu as dit, il, elle a dit, nous avons dit, vous avez dit, ils, elles ont dit
Future:	je dirai, tu diras, il, elle dira, nous dirons, vous direz, ils, elles diront
Conditional:	je dirais, tu dirais, il, elle dirait, nous dirions, vous diriez, ils, elles diraient
Present Subjunctive:	que je dise, que tu dises, qu'il, elle dise, que nous disions, que vous disiez, qu'ils, elles disent

dormir   *to sleep*

Present Participle:	*dormant,* sleeping
Imperative:	dors, dormons, dormez
Past Participle:	*dormi,* slept
Present Indicative:	je dors, tu dors, il, elle dort, nous dormons, vous dormez, ils, elles dorment
Imperfect:	je dormais, tu dormais, il, elle dormait, nous dormions, vous dormiez, ils, elles dormaient
Passé Composé:	j'ai dormi, tu as dormi, il, elle a dormi, nous avons dormi, vous avez dormi, ils, elles ont dormi
Future:	je dormirai, tu dormiras, il, elle dormira, nous dormirons, vous dormirez, ils, elles dormiront
Conditional:	je dormirais, tu dormirais, il, elle dormirait, nous dormirions, vous dormiriez, ils, elles dormiraient
Present Subjunctive:	que je dorme, que tu dormes, qu'il, elle dorme, que nous dormions, que vous dormiez, qu'ils, elles dorment

écrire   *to write*

Present Participle:	*écrivant,* writing
Imperative:	écris, écrivons, écrivez
Past Participle:	*écrit,* written
Present Indicative:	j'écris, tu écris, il, elle écrit, nous écrivons, vous écrivez, ils, elles écrivent
Imperfect:	j'écrivais, tu écrivais, il, elle écrivait, nous écrivions, vous écriviez, ils, elles écrivaient
Passé Composé:	j'ai écrit, tu as écrit, il, elle a écrit, nous avons écrit, vous avez écrit, ils, elles ont écrit
Future:	j'écrirai, tu écriras, il, elle écrira, nous écrirons, vous écrirez, ils, elles écriront
Conditional:	j'écrirais, tu écrirais, il, elle écrirait, nous écririons, vous écririez, ils, elles écriraient
Present Subjunctive:	que j'écrive, que tu écrives, qu'il, elle écrive, que nous écrivions, que vous écriviez, qu'ils, elles écrivent

être   *to be*

Present Participle:	*étant,* being
Imperative:	sois, soyons, soyez
Past Participle:	*été,* been
Present Indicative:	je suis, tu es, il, elle est, nous sommes, vous êtes, ils, elles sont
Imperfect:	j'étais, tu étais, il, elle était, nous étions, vous étiez, ils, elles étaient
Passé Composé:	j'ai été, tu as été, il, elle a été, nous avons été, vous avez été, ils, elles ont été
Future:	je serai, tu seras, il, elle sera, nous serons, vous serez, ils, elles seront
Conditional:	je serais, tu serais, il, elle serait, nous serions, vous seriez, ils, elles seraient
Present Subjunctive:	que je sois, que tu sois, qu'il, elle soit, que nous soyons, que vous soyez, qu'ils, elles soient

faire   *to do, to make*

Present Participle:	*faisant,* doing, making
Imperative:	fais, faisons, faites
Past Participle:	*fait,* done, made
Present Indicative:	je fais, tu fais, il, elle fait, nous faisons, vous faites, ils, elles font
Imperfect:	je faisais, tu faisais, il, elle faisait, nous faisions, vous faisiez, ils, elles faisaient
Passé Composé:	j'ai fait, tu as fait, il, elle a fait, nous avons fait, vous avez fait, ils, elles ont fait
Future:	je ferai, tu feras, il, elle fera, nous ferons, vous ferez, ils, elles feront
Conditional:	je ferais, tu ferais, il, elle ferait, nous ferions, vous feriez, ils, elles feraient
Present Subjunctive:	que je fasse, que tu fasses, qu'il, elle fasse, que nous fassions, que vous fassiez, qu'ils, elles fassent

falloir *to be necessary (impersonal)*

Present Participle:	None
Imperative:	None
Past Participle:	*fallu,* was necessary
Present Indicative:	—, —, il faut, —, —, —
Imperfect:	—, —, il fallait, —, —, —
Passé Composé:	—, —, il a fallu, —, —, —
Future:	—, —, il faudra, —, —, —
Conditional:	—, —, il faudrait, —, —, —
Present Subjunctive:	—, —, qu'il faille, —, —, —

lire *to read*

Present Participle:	*lisant,* reading
Imperative:	lis, lisons, lisez
Past Participle:	*lu,* read
Present Indicative:	je lis, tu lis, il, elle lit, nous lisons, vous lisez, ils, elles lisent
Imperfect:	je lisais, tu lisais, il, elle lisait, nous lisions, vous lisiez, ils, elles lisaient
Passé Composé:	j'ai lu, tu as lu, il, elle a lu, nous avons lu, vous avez lu, ils, elles ont lu
Future:	je lirai, tu liras, il, elle lira, nous lirons, vous lirez, ils, elles liront
Conditional:	je lirais, tu lirais, il, elle lirait, nous lirions, vous liriez, ils, elles liraient
Present Subjunctive:	que je lise, que tu lises, qu'il, elle lise, que nous lisions, que vous lisiez, qu'ils, elles lisent

mettre *to put*

Present Participle:	*mettant,* putting
Imperative:	mets, mettons, mettez
Past Participle:	*mis,* put
Present Indicative:	je mets, tu mets, il, elle met, nous mettons, vous mettez, ils, elles mettent
Imperfect:	je mettais, tu mettais, il, elle mettait, nous mettions, vous mettiez, ils, elles mettaient
Passé Composé:	j'ai mis, tu as mis, il, elle a mis, nous avons mis, vous avez mis, ils, elles ont mis
Future:	je mettrai, tu mettras, il, elle mettra, nous mettrons, vous mettrez, ils, elles mettront
Conditional:	je mettrais, tu mettrais, il, elle mettrait, nous mettrions, vous mettriez, ils, elles mettraient
Present Subjunctive:	que je mette, que tu mettes, qu'il, elle mette, que nous mettions, que vous mettiez, qu'ils, elles mettent

partir   *to leave*

Present Participle:	*partant,* leaving
Imperative:	pars, partons, partez
Past Participle:	*parti(e),* left
Present Indicative:	je pars, tu pars, il, elle part, nous partons, vous partez, ils, elles partent
Imperfect:	je partais, tu partais, il, elle partait, nous partions, vous partiez, ils, elles partaient
Passé Composé:	je suis parti(e), tu es parti(e), il, elle est parti(e), nous sommes parti(e)s, vous êtes parti(e)s, ils, elles sont parti(e)s
Future:	je partirai, tu partiras, il, elle partira, nous partirons, vous partirez, ils, elles partiront
Conditional:	je partirais, tu partirais, il, elle partirait, nous partirions, vous partiriez, ils, elles partiraient
Present Subjunctive:	que je parte, que tu partes, qu'il, elle parte, que nous partions, que vous partiez, qu'ils, elles partent

pouvoir   *to be able to*

Present Participle:	*pouvant,* being able to
Imperative:	None
Past Participle:	*pu,* been able to
Present Indicative:	je peux, tu peux, il, elle peut, nous pouvous, vous pouvez, ils, elles pouvent
Imperfect:	je pouvais, tu pouvais, il, elle pouvait, nous pouvions, vous pouviez, ils, elles pouvaient
Passé Composé:	j'ai pu, tu as pu, il, elle a pu, nous avons pu, vous avez pu, ils, elles ont pu
Future:	je pourrai, tu pourras, il, elle pourra, nous pourrons, vous pourrez, ils, elles pourront
Conditional:	je pourrais, tu pourrais, il, elle pourrait, nous pourrions, vous pourriez, ils, elles pourraient
Present Subjunctive:	que je puisse, que tu puisses, qu'il, elle puisse, que nous puissions, que vous puissiez, qu'ils, elles puissent

prendre   *to take*

Present Participle:	*prenant,* taking
Imperative:	prends, prenons, prenez
Past Participle:	*pris,* taken
Present Indicative:	je prends, tu prends, il, elle prend, nous prenons, vous prenez, ils, elles prennent
Imperfect:	je prenais, tu prenais, il, elle prenait, nous prenions, vous preniez, ils, elles prenaient

Passé Composé:	j'ai pris, tu as pris, il, elle a pris, nous avons pris, vous avez pris, ils, elles ont pris
Future:	je prendrai, tu prendras, il, elle prendra, nous prendrons, vous prendrez, ils, elles prendront
Conditional:	je prendrais, tu prendrais, il, elle prendrait, nous prendrions, vous prendriez, ils, elles prendraient
Present Subjunctive:	que je prenne, que tu prennes, qu'il, elle prenne, que nous prenions, que vous preniez, qu'ils, elles prennent

recevoir   *to receive*

Present Participle:	*recevant,* receiving
Imperative:	reçois, recevons, recevez
Past Participle:	*reçu,* received
Present Indicative:	je reçois, tu reçois, il, elle reçoit, nous recevons, vous recevez, ils, elles reçoivent
Imperfect:	je recevais, tu recevais, il, elle recevait, nous recevions, vous receviez, ils, elles recevaient
Passé Composé:	j'ai reçu, tu as reçu, il, elle a reçu, nous avons reçu, vous avez reçu, qu'ils, elles ont reçu
Future:	je recevrai, tu recevras, il, elle recevra, nous recevrons, vous recevrez, ils, elles recevront
Conditional:	je recevrais, tu recevrais, il, elle recevrait, nous recevrions, vous recevriez, ils, elles recevraient
Present Subjunctive:	que je reçoive, que tu reçoives, qu'il, elle reçoive, que nous recevions, que vous receviez, qu'ils, elles reçoivent

savoir   *to know*

Present Participle:	*sachant,* knowing
Imperative:	sache, sachons, sachez
Past Participle:	*su,* known
Present Indicative:	je sais, tu sais, il, elle sait, nous savons, vous savez, ils, elles savent
Imperfect:	je savais, tu savais, il, elle savait, nous savions, vous saviez, ils, elles savaient
Passé Composé:	j'ai su, tu as su, il, elle a su, nous avons su, vous avez su, ils, elles ont su
Future:	je saurai, tu sauras, il, elle saura, nous saurons, vous saurez, ils, elles sauront
Conditional:	je saurais, tu saurais, il, elle saurait, nous saurions, vous sauriez, ils, elles sauraient
Present Subjunctive:	que je sache, que tu saches, qu'il, elle sache, que nous sachions, que vous sachiez, qu'ils, elles sachent

sentir *to smell, to feel*

Present Participle:	*sentant,* smelling, feeling
Imperative:	sens, sentons, sentez
Past Participle:	*senti,* smelled, felt
Present Indicative:	je sens, tu sens, il, elle sent, nous sentons, vous sentez, ils, elles sentent
Imperfect:	je sentais, tu sentais, il, elle sentait, nous sentions, vous sentiez, ils, elles sentaient
Passé Composé:	j'ai senti, tu as senti, il, elle a senti, nous avons senti, vous avez senti, ils, elles ont senti
Future:	je sentirai, tu sentiras, il, elle sentira, nous sentirons, vous sentirez, ils, elles sentiront
Conditional:	je sentirais, tu sentirais, il, elle sentirait, nous sentirions, vous sentiriez, ils, elles sentiraient
Present Subjunctive:	que je sente, que tu sentes, qu'il, elle sente, que nous sentions, que vous sentiez, qu'ils, elles sentent

servir *to serve*

Present Participle:	*servant,* serving
Imperative:	sers, servons, servez
Past Participle:	*servi,* served
Present Indicative:	je sers, tu sers, il, elle sert, nous servons, vous servez, ils, elles servent
Imperfect:	je servais, tu servais, il, elle servait, nous servions, vous serviez, ils, elles servaient
Passé Composé:	j'ai servi, tu as servi, il, elle a servi, nous avons servi, vous avez servi, ils, elles ont servi
Future:	je servirai, tu serviras, il, elle servira, nous servirons, vous servirez, ils, elles serviront
Conditional:	je servirais, tu servirais, il, elle servirait, nous servirions, vous serviriez, ils, elles serviraient
Present Subjunctive:	que je serve, que tu serves, qu'il, elle serve, que nous servions, que vous serviez, qu'ils, elles servent

sortir *to go out*

Present Participle:	*sortant,* going out
Imperative:	sors, sortons, sortez
Past Participle:	*sorti(e),* gone out
Present Indicative:	je sors, tu sors, il, elle sort, nous sortons, vous sortez, ils, elles sortent

Imperfect:	je sortais, tu sortais, il, elle sortait, nous sortions, vous sortiez, ils, elles sortaient
Passé Composé:	je suis sorti(e), tu es sorti(e), il, elle est sorti(e), nous sommes sorti(e)s, vous êtes sorti(e)s, ils, elles sont sorti(e)s
Future:	je sortirai, tu sortiras, il, elle sortira, nous sortirons, vous sortirez, ils, elles sortiront
Conditional:	je sortirais, tu sortirais, il, elle sortirait, nous sortirions, vous sortiriez, ils, elles sortiraient
Present Subjunctive:	que je sorte, que tu sortes, qu'il, elle sorte, que nous sortions, que vous sortiez, qu'ils, elles sortent

tenir   *to hold*

Present Participle:	*tenant,* holding
Imperative:	tiens, tenons, tenez
Past Participle:	*tenu,* held
Present Indicative:	je tiens, tu tiens, il, elle tient, nous tenons, vous tenez, ils, elles tiennent
Imperfect:	je tenais, tu tenais, il, elle tenait, nous tenions, vous teniez, il, elles tenaient
Passé Composé:	j'ai tenu, tu as tenu, il, elle a tenu, nous avons tenu, vous avez tenu, ils, elles ont tenu
Future:	je tiendrai, tu tiendras, il, elle tiendra, nous tiendrons, vous tiendrez, ils, elles tiendront
Conditional:	je tiendrais, tu tiendrais, il, elle tiendrait, nous tiendrions, vous tiendriez, ils, elles tiendraient
Present Subjunctive:	que je tienne, que tu tiennes, qu'il, elle tienne, que nous tenions, que vous teniez, qu'ils, elles tiennent

venir   *to come*

Present Participle:	*venant,* coming
Imperative:	viens, venons, venez
Past Participle:	*venu(e),* come
Present Indicative:	je viens, tu viens, il, elle vient, nous venons, vous venez, ils, elles viennent
Imperfect:	je venais, tu venais, il, elle venait, nous venions, vous veniez, il, elles venaient
Passé Composé:	je suis venu(e), tu es venu(e), il, elle est venu(e), nous sommes venu(e)s, vous êtes venu(e)s, ils, elles sont venu(e)s
Future:	je viendrai, tu viendras, il, elle viendra, nous viendrons, vous viendrez, ils, elles viendront
Conditional:	je viendrais, tu viendrais, il, elle viendrait, nous viendrions, vous viendriez, ils, elles viendraient
Present Subjunctive:	que je vienne, que tu viennes, qu'il, elle vienne, que nous venions, que vous veniez, qu'ils, elles viennent

valoir   *to be worth*

Present Participle:	*valant,* being worth
Imperative:	vaux, valons, valez
Past Participle:	*valu,* been worth
Present Indicative:	je vaux, tu vaux, il, elle vaut, nous valons, vous valez, ils, elles valent
Imperfect:	je valais, tu valais, il, elle valait, nous valions, vous valiez, ils, elles valaient
Passé Composé:	j'ai valu, tu as valu, il, elle a valu, nous avons valu, vous avez valu, ils, elles ont valu
Future:	je vaudrai, tu vaudras, il, elle vaudra, nous vaudrons, vous vaudrez, ils, elles vaudront
Conditional:	je vaudrais, tu vaudrais, il, elle vaudrait, nous vaudrions, vous vaudriez, ils, elles vaudraient
Present Subjunctive:	que je vaille, que tu vailles, qu'il, elle vaille, que nous valions, que vous valiez, qu'ils, elles vaillent

voir   *to see*

Present Participle:	*voyant,* seeing
Imperative:	vois, voyons, voyez
Past Participle:	*vu,* seen
Present Indicative:	je vois, tu vois, il, elle voit, nous voyons, vous voyez, ils, elles voient
Imperfect:	je voyais, tu voyais, il, elle voyait, nous voyions, vous voyiez, ils, elles voyaient
Passé Composé:	j'ai vu, tu as vu, il, elle a vu, nous avons vu, vous avez vu, ils, elles ont vu
Future:	je verrai, tu verras, il, elle verra, nous verrons, vous verrez, ils, elles verront
Conditional:	je verrais, tu verrais, il, elle verrait, nous verrions, vous verriez, ils, elles verraient
Present Subjunctive:	que je voie, que tu voies, qu'il, elle voie, que nous voyions, que vous voyiez, qu'ils, elles voient

vouloir   *to want*

Present Participle:	*voulant,* wanting
Imperative:	veuille, veuillons, veuillez
Past Participle:	*voulu,* wanted
Present Indicative:	je veux, tu veux, il, elle veut, nous voulons, vous voulez, ils, elles veulent
Imperfect:	je voulais, tu voulais, il, elle voulait, nous voulions, vous vouliez, ils, elles voulaient

Passé Composé: j'ai voulu, tu as voulu, il, elle a voulu, nous avons voulu, vous avez voulu, ils, elles ont voulu

Future: je voudrai, tu voudras, il, elle voudra, nous voudrons, vous voudrez, ils, elles voudront

Conditional: je voudrais, tu voudrais, il, elle voudrait, nous voudrions, vous voudriez, ils, elles voudraient

Present Subjunctive: que je veuille, que tu veuilles, qu'il, elle veuille, que nous voulions, que vous vouliez, qu'ils, elles veuillent

Appendix C
Verbs with Spelling Changes

This appendix contains a sampling of the verbs that undergo spelling changes when conjugated. These examples should help to define the patterns by which changes occur in verbs with stems that change spelling when conjugated.

acheter *to buy*

Present Participle:	*achetant,* buying
Imperative:	achète, achetons, achetez
Past Participle:	*acheté,* bought
Present Indicative:	j'achète, tu achètes, il, elle achète, nous achetons, vous achetez, ils, elles achètent
Imperfect:	j'achetais, tu achetais, il, elle achetait, nous achetions, vous achetiez, ils, elles achetaient
Passé Composé:	j'ai acheté, tu as acheté, il, elle a acheté, nous avons acheté, vous avez acheté, ils, elles ont acheté
Future:	j'achèterai, tu achèteras, il, elle achètera, nous achèterons, vous achèterez, ils, elles achèteront
Conditional:	j'achèterais, tu achèterais, il, elle achèterait, nous achèterions, vous achèteriez, ils, elles achèteraient
Present Subjunctive:	que j'achète, que tu achètes, qu'il, elle achète, que nous achetions, que vous achetiez, qu'ils, elles achètent

appeler *to call*

Present Participle:	*appelant,* calling
Imperative:	appelle, appelons, appelez
Past Participle:	*appelé,* called

Present Indicative:	j'appelle, tu appelles, il, elle appelle, nous appelons, vous appelez, ils, elles appellent
Imperfect:	j'appelais, tu appelais, il, elle appelait, nous appelions, vous appeliez, ils, elles appelaient
Passé Composé:	j'ai appelé, tu as appelé, il, elle a appelé, nous avons appelé, vous avez appelé, ils, elles ont appelé
Future:	j'appellerai, tu appelleras, il, elle appellera, nous appellerons, vous appellerez, ils, elles appelleront
Conditional:	j'appellerais, tu appellerais, il, elle appellerait, nous appellerions, vous appelleriez, ils, elles appelleraient
Present Subjunctive:	que j'appelle, que tu appelles, qu'il, elle appelle, que nous appelions, que vous appeliez, qu'ils, elles appellent

s'asseoir   *to sit down*

Present Participle:	*s'asseyant,* sitting down
Imperative:	assieds-toi, asseyons-nous, asseyez-vous
Past Participle:	*assis(e),* sat down
Present Indicative:	je m'assieds, tu t'assieds, il, elle s'assied, nous nous asseyons, vous vous asseyez, ils, elles s'asseyent
Imperfect:	je m'asseyais, tu t'asseyais, il, elle s'asseyait, nous nous asseyions, vous vous asseyiez, ils, elles s'asseyaient
Passé Composé:	je me suis assis(e), tu t'es assis(e), il, elle s'est assis(e), nous nous sommes assis(es), vous vous êtes assis(es), ils, elles se sont assis(es)
Future:	je m'assiérai, tu t'assiéras, il, elle s'assiéra, nous nous assiérons, vous vous assiérez, ils, elles s'assiéront
Conditional:	je m'assiérais, tu t'assiérais, il, elle s'assiérait, nous nous assiérions, vous vous assiériez, ils, elles s'assiéraient
Present Subjunctive:	que je m'asseye, que tu t'asseyes, qu'il, elle s'asseye, que nous nous asseyions, que vous vous asseyiez, qu'ils, elles s'asseyent

commencer   *to start*

Present Participle::	*commençant,* starting
Imperative:	commence, commençons, commencez
Past Participle:	*commencé,* started
Present Indicative:	je commence, tu commences, il, elle commence, nous commençons, vous commencez, ils, elles commencent
Imperfect:	je commençais, tu commençais, il, elle commençait, nous commencions, vous commenciez, ils, elles commençaient
Passé Composé:	j'ai commencé, tu as commencé, il, elle a commencé, nous avons commencé, vous avez commencé, ils, elles ont commencé

Future:	je commencerai, tu commenceras, il, elle comencera, nous commencerons, vous commencerez, ils, elles commenceront
Conditional:	je commencerais, tu commencerais, il, elle commencerait, nous commercerions, vous commenceriez, ils, elles commenceraient
Present Subjunctive:	que je commence, que tu commences, qu'il, elle commence, que nous commencions, que vous commenciez, qu'ils, elles commencent

envoyer   *to send*

Present Participle:	*envoyant,* sending
Imperative:	envoie, envoyons, envoyez
Past Participle:	*envoyé,* sent
Present Indicative:	j'envoie, tu envoies, il, elle envoie, nous envoyons, vous envoyez, ils, elles envoient
Imperfect:	j'envoyais, tu envoyais, il, elle envoyait, nous envoyions, vous envoyiez, ils, elles envoyaient
Passé Composé:	j'ai envoyé, tu as envoyé, il, elle a envoyé, nous avons envoyé, vous avez envoyé, ils, elles ont envoyé
Future:	j'enverrai, tu enverras, il, elle enverra, nous enverrons, vous enverrez, ils, elles enverront
Conditional:	j'enverrais, tu enverrais, il, elle enverrait, nous enverrions, vous enverriez, ils, elles enverraient
Present Subjunctive:	que j'envoie, que tu envoies, qu'il, elle envoie, que nous envoyions, que vous envoyiez, qu'ils, elles envoient

espérer   *to hope*

Present Participle:	*espérant,* hoping
Imperative:	espère, espérons, espérez
Past Participle:	*espéré,* hoped
Present Indicative:	j'espère, tu espères, il, elle espère, nous espérons, vous espérez, ils, elles espèrent
Imperfect:	j'espérais, tu espérais, il, elle espérait, nous espérions, vous espériez, ils, elles espéraient
Passé Composé:	j'ai espéré, tu as espéré, il, elle a espéré, nous avons espéré, vous avez espéré, ils, elles ont espéré
Future:	j'espérerai, tu espéreras, il, elle espérera, nous espérerons, vous espérerez, ils, elles espéreront
Conditional:	j'espérerais, tu espérerais, il, elle espérerait, nous espérerions, vous espéreriez, ils, elles espéreraient
Present Subjunctive:	que j'espère, que tu espères, qu'il, elle espère, que nous espérions, que vous espériez, qu'ils, elles espèrent

essayer   *to try*

Present Participle:	*essayant,* trying
Imperative:	essai, essayons, essayez
Past Participle:	*essayé, tried*
Present Indicative:	j'essaie, tu essaies, il, elle essaie, nous essayons, vous essayez, ils, elles essaient
Imperfect:	j'essayais, tu essayais, il, elle essayait, nous essayions, vous essayiez, ils, elles essayaient
Passé Composé:	j'ai essayé, tu as essayé, il, elle a essayé, nous avons essayé, vous avez essayé, ils, elles ont essayé
Future:	j'essaierai *or* essayerai, tu essaieras, il, elle essaiera, nous essaierons, vous essairerez, ils, elles essaieront
Conditional:	j'essaierais *or* essayerais, tu essaierais, il, elle essaierait, nous essaierions, vous essaieriez, ils, elles essaieraient
Present Subjunctive:	que j'essaie, que tu essaies, qu'il, elle essaie, que nous essayions, que vous essayiez, qu'ils, elles essaient

jeter   *to throw*

Present Participle:	*jetant,* throwing
Imperative:	jette, jetons, jetez
Past Participle:	*jeté,* thrown
Present Indicative:	je jette, tu jettes, il, elle jette, nous jetons, vous jetez, ils, elles jettent
Imperfect:	je jetais, tu jetais, il, elle jetait, nous jetions, vous jetiez, ils, elles jetaient
Passé Composé:	j'ai jeté, tu as jeté, il, elle a jeté, nous avons jeté, vous avez jeté, ils, elles ont jeté
Future:	je jetterai, tu jetteras, il, elle jettera, nous jetterons, vous jetterez, ils, elles jetteront
Conditional:	je jetterais, tu jetterais, il, elle jetterait, nous jetterions, vous jetteriez, ils, elles jetteraient
Present Subjunctive:	que je jette, que tu jettes, qu'il, elle jette, que nous jetions, que vous jetiez, qu'ils, elles jettent

lever   *to raise*

Present Participle:	*levant,* raising
Imperative:	lève, levons, levez
Past Participle:	*levé, raised*
Present Indicative:	je lève, tu lèves, il, elle lève, nous levons, vous levez, ils, elles lèvent
Imperfect:	je levais, tu levais, il, elle levait, nous levions, vous leviez, ils, elles levaient

Passé Composé:	j'ai levé, tu as levé, il, elle a levé, nous avons levé, vous avez levé, ils, elles ont levé
Future:	je lèverai, tu lèveras, il, elle lèvera, nous lèverons, vous lèverez, ils, elles lèveront
Conditional:	je lèverais, tu lèverais, il, elle lèverait, nous lèverions, vous lèveriez, ils, elles lèveraient
Present Subjunctive:	que je lève, que tu lèves, qu'il, elle lève, que nous levions, que vous leviez, qu'ils, elles lèvent

manger *to eat*

Present Participle:	*mangeant,* eating
Imperative:	mange, mangeons, mangez
Past Participle:	*mangé,* eaten
Present Indicative:	je mange, tu manges, il, elle mange, nous mangeons, vous mangez, ils, elles mangent
Imperfect:	je mangeais, tu mangeais, il, elle mangeait, nous mangions, vous mangiez, ils, elles mangeaient
Passé Composé:	j'ai mangé, tu as mangé, il, elle a mangé, nous avons mangé, vous avez mangé, ils, elles ont mangé
Future:	je mangerai, tu mangeras, il, elle mangera, nous mangerons, vous mangerez, ils, elles mangeront
Conditional:	je mangerais, tu mangerais, il, elle mangerait, nous mangerions, vous mangeriez, ils, elles mangeraient
Present Subjunctive:	que je mange, que tu manges, qu'il, elle mange, que nous mangions, que vous mangiez, qu'ils, elles mangent

payer *to pay*

Present Participle:	*payant,* paying
Imperative:	paie, payons, payez
Past Participle:	*payé,* paid
Present Indicative:	je paie, tu paies, il, elle paie, nous payons, vous payez, ils, elles paient
Imperfect:	je payais, tu payais, il, elle payait, nous payions, vous payiez, ils, elles payaient
Passé Composé:	j'ai payé, tu as payé, il, elle a payé, nous avons payé, vous avez payé, ils, elles ont payé
Future:	je payerai *or* paierai, tu payeras, il, elle payera, nous payerons, vous payerez, ils, elles payeront
Conditional:	je payerais, tu payerais, il, elle payerait, nous payerions, vous payeriez, ils, elles payeraient
Present Subjunctive:	que je paie, que tu paies, qu'il, elle paie, que nous payions, que vous payiez, qu'ils, elles paient

préférer   *to prefer*

Present Participle: *préférant,* preferring
Imperative: préfère, préférons, préférez
Past Participle: *préféré(e),* preferred
Present Indicative: je préfère, tu préféres, il, elle préfère, nous préférons, vous préférez, ils, elles préfèrent
Imperfect: je préférais, tu préférais, il, elle préférait, nous préférions, vous préfériez, ils, elles préféraient
Passé Composé: j'ai préféré, tu as préféré, il, elle a préféré, nous avons préféré, vous avez préféré, ils, elles ont préféré
Future: je préférerai, tu préféreras, il, elle préférera, nous préférerons, vous préférerez, ils, elles préféreront
Conditional: je péférerais, tu préférerais, il, elle préférerait, nous préférerions, vous préféreriez, ils, elles préféreraient
Present Subjunctive: que je préfère, que tu préfères, qu'il, elle préfère, que nous préférions, que vous préfériez, qu'ils, elles préfèrent

French-English Vocabulary

This vocabulary contains most of the words used in the first fourteen lessons. Not all cognates are listed, since Lesson 15 provides you with the necessary background to recognize them.

à at, in, with
abandonner to leave
abonnement (m.) subscription
abréviation (f.) abbreviation
abriter to shelter
absence (f.) absence, lack
absent(e) absent
absolu(e) absolute
absolument absolutely
abstrait(e) abstract
absurde absurd
abuser to abuse
à cause de because of
accéder to reach
accélérateur (m.) accelerator
accepter to accept
accès (m.) access
accompagner to accompany
accorder to agree
    d'accord agreed, o.k.
accueil (m.) welcome
accueillir to welcome, to receive
achat (m.) purchase
acheter to buy
achever to achieve, to finish
acide sour

acier (m.) steel
à côté near, beside
    à côté de next to
acteur (m.) actor
action (f.) stock
actionnaire (m.) stockholder
actrice (f.) actress
actualités newsreel
actuellement now, currently
addition (f.) bill, check, addition
à demain see you tomorrow
admirer to admire
adorer to adore
adresser to address, label
aéroport (m.) airport
affaires (f.) belongings, business
affiche (f.) poster
affiché(e) posted
afficher to post, to display
affirmer to affirm
âge (m.) age
âgé(e) old
agence (f.) agency
agenda (m.) engagement calendar
agent (m.) agent, policeman
    agent de change (m.) stockbroker

agent de voyage (m.) travel agent
agglomération (f.) urban area
agir to take action
agir (se) to be in question
   il s'agit de it is a question of, it's about
agneau (m.) lamb
agréable pleasant
agricole agricultural
agriculteur (m.) farmer
agriculture (f.) agriculture
ah bon! really?
aide (f.) help
aider to help
aie! ouch!
aigu acute, sharp
ail (m.) garlic
aile (f.) wing, fender
ailleurs elsewhere
   d'ailleurs besides
aimable nice, kind
aimer to like, to love
ainsi so, thus
   ainsi de suite and so forth
air (m.) air, looks
   avoir l'air to seem, look
   en plein air in the open
ajouter to add
à la place de in place of
à l'heure on time
aliment (m.) food
alimentaire related to food
alimentation (f.) food supply
alimenter to feed
aller to go
aller et retour round trip
allié(e) ally
allô! hello! (telephone)
allocation (f.) allowance, aid
allumer to light, to turn on
alors then, at that time
amant(e) lover
ambiance (f.) mood, atmosphere
amende (f.) fine
amener to bring
ami(e) friend, boyfriend, girlfriend
amical(e) friendly
amortir to weaken, to moderate
amour (m.) love
ampoule (f.) medicine capsule, lightbulb
amuser to amuse
amuser (se) to have fun
an (m.) year

ancêtre (m., f.) ancestor
âne (m.) donkey
animer to bring to life
animer (se) to come to life
année (f.) year
anniversaire (m.) birthday
   anniversaire de mariage (m.) wedding anniversary
annonce (f.) advertisement
   petites annonces, want ads
annoncer to announce
annuel yearly
août August
apercevoir to notice, to perceive
à peu près approximately
appareil (m.) device
   appareil photographique (m.) camera
appeler to call
appeler (se) to be called
apporter to bring
apprécier to appreciate
apprendre to learn
après after
   d'après according to
après-demain the day after tomorrow
après-midi afternoon
arbre (m.) tree
arc (m.) arch
arc-en-ciel (m.) rainbow
argent (m.) money
   argent de poche spending money
armoire (f.) wardrobe (furniture)
arracher to pull out
arrêter to stop
arrêter (se) to stop oneself
arrière (m.) back
arrivée (f.) arrival
arriver to arrive, to happen
ascenseur (m.) elevator
asseoir (se) to sit down
assez enough
assiette (f.) plate, dish
assis(e) seated
   être assis(e) to be seated
assister to attend
assuré insured
assurer to insure
assurer (se) to make sure
à temps on time
   à temps complet full time
   à mi-temps part time
à tout à l'heure see you soon
attacher to fasten, to tie

atteindre to reach
attendre to wait for
atterrir to land
atterrissage (m.) landing
attirer to attract
attraper to catch
au contraire on the contrary
augmentation increase
augmenter to increase, to raise
aujourd'hui today
au lieu de instead
au revoir goodbye
aussi also, too
   aussitôt que as soon as
automatique automatic
auto-stop hitchhiking
autour around
autre other
   l'un l'autre, les uns les autres each other, one another
autrement dit in other words
avaler to swallow
avant (m.) front
avant before
avant-hier day before yesterday
avec with
avec plaisir with pleasure
avion (m.) airplane
avoir to have
   (see Lesson 8 for expressions using avoir)
avouer to admit
avril (m.) April

bagage (m.) luggage
bague (f.) ring
baigner to bathe
baigner (se) to bathe oneself
baignoire (f.) bathtub
bain (m.) bath
   salle de bains (f.) bathroom
baisser to lower, to decrease
balance (f.) scale
balcon (m.) balcony
bande (f.) tape
banlieue (f.) suburb
banquier (m.) banker
barbe (f.) beard
   quelle barbe! how terrible!
barbier (m.) barber
bas low
   à bas down with
   en bas downstairs
bateau (m.) boat, ship

batterie (f.) battery
bavard talkative
bavardage chit-chat, gossip
bavarder to chat
beau handsome
beau-fils (m.) son-in-law
beau-frère (m.) brother-in-law
beau-père (m.) father-in-law
beaux-parents in-laws
bel(le) beautiful
belle-fille (f.) daughter-in-law
belle-mère (f.) mother-in-law
belle-sœur (f.) sister-in-law
beurre (m.) butter
bibliothèque (f.) library
bien well, fine
bien sûr of course
bientôt soon
biftek (m.) steak
bijou (m.) jewel, jewelry
bijouterie (f.) jewelry store
bilan (m.) outcome, balance sheet
billet (m.) ticket
blanc(he) white
bleu(e) blue
bloqué(e), être bloqué(e) to be stuck
bœuf (m.) beef
boire to drink
boisson (f.) drink
boîte (f.) box
   boîte de nuit nightclub
bord (m.) shore, edge
   à bord on board
   monter à bord to go on board
bouche (f.) mouth
boucher (m.) butcher
boucher to cork
boucherie (f.) butcher shop
bougie (f.) candle
bouillir to boil
boulanger (m.) baker
boulangerie (f.) bakery
bourse (f.) scholarship
   la Bourse the stock exchange
bouteille (f.) bottle
bouton (m.) button
brancher to connect (electrically)
bras (m.) arm
bricoler to putter around
brosse (f.) brush
brosser to brush
brosser (se) to brush (one's teeth, hair)

bruit (m.) noise
   faire du bruit to make noise
brûler to burn
brun(e) brown, dark
bruyant(e) noisy
bureau (m.) desk, office, den
but (m.) aim, goal

ça that
   ça ne fait rien it doesn't matter
cacher to hide
cacher (se) to hide oneself
caisse (f.) cashier's office
caissier (m.) cashier
caissière (f.) cashier
calculer to calculate
calendrier (m.) calendar
calmant (m.) sedative
camion (m.) truck
capitaine (m.) captain
capot (m.) hood
capoter to turn over (car)
car (m.) the bus (intercity)
carnet de chèques (m.) checkbook
carte (f.) card
   carte d'embarquement boarding pass
   carte grise (f.) title
   carte perforée (f.) punch card
   carte postale (f.) postcard
   carte routière (f.) road map
casse-croûte (m.) snack
casse-pieds (m.) pest
casser to break
ceci this
ceinture (f.) belt
   ceinture de sécurité (f.) safety belt
cela that
célibataire single
cendrier (m.) ashtray
ces these
chaise (f.) chair
chambre (f.) room
   chambre à coucher bedroom
champagne (m.) champagne
chance (f.) luck
chaque each
   chacun(e) each one
chat (m.) cat
chauffage (m.) heating
cher, chère dear, expensive
chercher to look for
cheval (m.) horse

cheveux (m. plural) hair
cheville (f.) ankle
chien (m.) dog
choix (m.) choice
chose (f.) thing
   quelque chose something
ci-dessous below
ci-dessus above
cil (m.) eyelash
circuit (m.) circuit
clef (f.) key
client(e) customer
cœur (m.) heart
coffre (m.) safe deposit box, car trunk
colère (f.) anger
   être en colère to be angry
colle (f.) glue
coller to glue, to stick
combien how many, how much
commander to order
commandes (f.) controls
comme as
comme-ci, comme-ça so-so
comment how
commode (f.) dresser
composer to compose, to dial
comptant (m.) cash
compte-goutte (m.) eyedropper
compter to count
conduire to drive
connaître to know
conseil (m.) advice
conseiller to advise
contravention (f.) traffic ticket
contrôleur (m.) ticket collector
corps (m.) body
cou (m.) neck
couchette (f.) bunk, berth
couleur (f.) color
couloir (m.) hallway
cour (f.) yard
courir to run
courrier électronique (m.) email
cours (m.) course
   cours de change exchange
course (f.) errand, race
   course de chevaux horse racing
court(e) short
court-circuit short circuit
cousin(e) cousin
couteau (m.) knife
coûter to cost

coûter cher to be expensive
couverture (f.) blanket
crayon (m.) pencil
crédit (m.) bank credit
   à crédit (m.) on credit
   carte de crédit credit card
créer to create
crème (f.) cream
creux (se) deep
crevaison (f.) flat tire
crevette (f.) shrimp
crise (f.) attack, crisis
critère (m.) criterion
croire to believe
cuir (m.) leather
cuire to cook

d'abord first of all
dactylo (f.) typist
danser to dance
davantage more
début (m.) beginning
débuter to begin
décevoir to disappoint
décider to decide
décoller to take off
décontracté relaxed
décorer to decorate
découvrir to discover
décrire to describe
décrocher to unhook
défendu forbidden
dégonfler to deflate
dehors out, outside
déjà already
déjeuner (m.) lunch
déjeuner to lunch
demain tomorrow
demander to ask
démarrer to start
démarreur (m.) starter
déménager to move out
dent (f.) tooth
dépanner to repair on the spot
départ (m.) departure
dépasser to exceed, to pass someone
dépêcher (se) to hurry
dépense (f.) expense
dépenser to spend
déposer to deposit
depuis since
   depuis quand since when

déranger to bother, to disturb
de rien you're welcome
descendre to go down
déshabiller (se) to undress
desirer to wish, to desire
dès que as soon as
dessin (m.) drawing, design
détacher to unfasten
détruire to destroy
devant in front of, before
devenir to become
deviner to guess
devise (f.) motto
devises (f.) foreign currency
devoir to have to, to owe
diète (f.) diet
dimanche Sunday
dinde (f.) turkey
dîner (m.) dinner
dîner to have dinner
dire to say
discuter to discuss
disponible available
doigt (m.) finger
donc therefore
donner to give
dormir to sleep
dos (m.) back
douane (f.) customs
douanier (m.) customs agent
douche (f.) shower
doute (m.) doubt
   sans doute undoubtedly
   sans aucun doute without a doubt
douter to doubt
doux (ce) soft, sweet
drap (m.) sheet
drapeau (m.) flag
drogue (f.) drug
droit(e) straight
   à droite to the right
   tout droit straight ahead
drôle funny
dur(e) hard, harsh
durant during
durer, to last

eau (f.) water
   eau minérale (f.) mineral water
échange (m.) exchange
échanger to exchange
école (f.) school

économiser to save
écouter to listen
écran (m.) screen
écrire to write
écrivain (m.) writer
édifice (m.) building
effacer to erase
égal(e) equal
égarer (se) to get lost, to wander
embarquer to board
embaucher to hire
embouteillage (m.) traffic jam
embrasser to kiss
embrayage (m.) clutch
emmenager to move in
empêcher to prevent
emprunt (m.) loan
emprunter to borrow
enchanté pleased, enchanted
encourager to encourage
endormir (se) to fall asleep
endroit (m.) place
enfant child
enfin finally
enlever to remove
ennuyer to annoy, to bore
ennuyer (se) to be bored
en plus in addition
en retard late
enseigner to teach
ensemble whole, together, entirety
ensemble (m.) lady's suit, garment
ensuite then, next
entendre to hear
entendre (se) to get along with
entre between
entrée (f.) entrance (input)
envoyer to send
épargne (f.) savings
épargner to spare, to save
　　la caisse d'epargne savings bank
épaule (f.) shoulder
épice (f.) spice
épouser to marry
époux (se) spouse
équilibrer to balance
escale (f.) calling place
　　faire escale to stop over
espérer to hope
espoir (m.) hope
essayer to try
essuie-glace (m.) windshield wiper

est (m.) east
estomac (m.) stomach
étage (m.) floor, story (in a building)
éteindre to turn off, to put out
étoile (f.) star
　　étoile de cinéma movie star
étranger foreigner
être to be
étroit(e) narrow
étude (f.) study
étudiant(e) student
étudier to study
évasion (f.) escape
évier (m.) kitchen sink
éviter to avoid
l'explorateur (m.) scanner
express (m.) express train
extraire to extract
extrait (m.) excerpt, extract

fabriquer to manufacture
fabuleux fabulous
facteur (m.) postman
facture (f.) bill
faible weak
faim (f.) hunger
　　avoir faim to be hungry
faire to do
　　faire le plein to fill the tank
　　(see Lesson 4 for expressions using faire)
faire vite to hurry
falloir to be necessary
　　(see Lesson 8 for the impersonal use of falloir)
famille (f.) family
farine (f.) flour
faute (f.) mistake
fauteuil (m.) armchair
faux (sse) false, wrong
femme (f.) woman, wife
　　femme de chambre (f.) maid
fenêtre (f.) window
fête (f.) party
fêter to celebrate
feu (m.) fire
feu rouge (m.) stoplight
février (m.) February
fiancé(e) fiancé(e)
fièvre (f.) fever
　　avoir de la fièvre to have a fever
fille (f.) daughter, girl
fils (m.) son
fin (f.) end

finir to end, to finish
fleur (f.) flower
foie (m.) liver
fonder to found
fondre to melt
fonds (m.) capital
forme (f.) shape, form
fort(e) strong
foule (f.) crowd
fouler (se) to sprain
   se fouler la cheville to sprain one's ankle
fourchette (f.) fork
fournir to supply
fourrure (f.) fur
fraise (f.) strawberry
frapper to hit, to strike
frein (m.) brake (car)
freiner to brake
fréquenter to patronize
frigo (m.) fridge
frites (plural) fries
fromage (m.) cheese
front (m.) forehead
fruits de mer (m., plural) seafood
fumer to smoke
   défense de fumer no smoking (allowed)

gagner to win, to earn
gant (m.) glove
garçon (m.) boy, waiter
garder to keep
gaspillage (m.) waste
gaspiller to waste
gâteau (m.) cake
gauche left
   à gauche to the left
genou (m.) knee
gens people
gentil(le) kind, nice
gérant(e) manager
gérer to manage
gestion (f.) management
glace (f.) ice cream
glaçon (m.) ice cube
gonfler to inflate
gorge (f.) throat
gorgée (f.) sip
   à petites gorgées, in small sips
goût (m.) taste
goûter to taste
goutte (f.) drop
grand(e) big

grand-mère (f.) grandmother
grand-père (m.) grandfather
gratuit(e) free of charge
grève (f.) strike of workmen
gros(se) fat
   le gros lot the jackpot
grossir to gain weight
guérir to heal
guichet (m.) teller window
guide d'initiation (m.) tutorial

habiller to clothe
habiller (se) to get dressed
habitant (m.) inhabitant
habiter to live in, to inhabit
haricot vert (m.) green bean
hasard (par) by chance
haut(e) high, elevated
   à haute voix out loud
haut-parleur (m.) loudspeaker
hebdomadaire (m.) weekly (journal, magazine)
hésiter to hesitate
heure (f.) hour
   Quelle heure est-il? What time is it?
   heure d'affluence (f.) rush hour
heureux (se) happy
heureusement happily
heurter to hit, to run into
hier yesterday
   avant hier day before yesterday
histoire (f.) story, history
homard (m.) lobster
homme (m.) man
   homme d'affaires (m.) businessman
honneur (m.) honor
horaire (m.) timetable, schedule
hôtesse (f.) hostess
huile (f.) oil
huître (f.) oyster
hypothèque (f.) mortgage

ici here
   par ici over here, this way
il n'y a pas de quoi you're welcome
il y a there is, there are
impôt (m.) tax
imprévu(e) unexpected
   à l'imprévu unexpectedly
imprimante (f.) printer (computer)
imprimer to print
   imprimerie (f.) printing press
incroyable incredible

indicateur (m.) signal
indiquer to indicate
informatique (f.) computer science
ingénieur (m.) engineer
inoxidable rustproof
inquiet(e) worried
inquiéter (se) to worry, to be anxious
inspecter to inspect
intérêt (m.) interest
inutile useless
investir to invest
investissement (m.) investment
invité(e) guest
inviter to invite

jamais never
jambe (f.) leg
jambon (m.) ham
janvier (m.) January
jardin (m.) garden
jauge (f.) gauge
jaune yellow
jeter to throw
jeudi (m.) Thursday
jeune young
   les jeunes gens young people
jeunesse (f.) youth
joie (f.) joy
joli(e) pretty
jouer to play
jouet (m.) toy
joueur(se) player
jour (m.) day
journal (journaux) (m.) newspaper(s)
journalier daily
journée (f.) day
juger to judge
juillet (m.) July
juin (m.) June
jusqu'à until
   jusque là up to here
juste right, just
justement exactly, as a matter of fact
justice (f.) justice
   palais (m.) de justice courthouse

kilomètre (m.) kilometer
klaxon (m.) horn
là there
   là-bas over there
laisser to leave
laisser tomber to drop

lait (m.) milk
   lait écrémé skim milk
laitue (f.) lettuce
lame (f.) blade
   lame de rasoir razor blade
langouste (f.) crayfish
langue (f.) tongue
large wide
lavabo (m.) bathroom sink
laver (se) to wash oneself
leçon (f.) lesson
lecture (f.) reading
léger (légère) light
légume (m.) vegetable
lendemain (m.) next day
lent(e) slow
lentement slowly
lèvre (f.) lip
lit (m.) bed
livre (m.) book
livrer to deliver
location (f.) rental of anything but a dwelling
logiciel (m.) software
loin de far from
loisirs (m.) activities
longtemps a long time
louer to rent
lourd(e) heavy
loyer (m.) rent (dwelling)
lumière (f.) light
lumineux (se) lighted
   le spot lumineux spotlight
lundi (m.) Monday
luxueux (se) luxurious
lycée (m.) high school

ma, mon, mes my
machiniste (m.) engineer
magasin (m.) store
   grand magasin department store
magnétophone (m.) tape recorder
mai (m.) May
maigre skinny
main (f.) hand
maintenant now
mais but
maison (f.) house
mal evil, badly
malade sick
malle (f.) trunk, suitcase
maman (f.) mom, mommy
mandat (m.) money order

manger to eat

manier to handle

manquer to miss, to lack

manteau (m.) coat, overcoat

manuel manual

marchand (m.) storekeeper, merchant

marchander to haggle over

marcher to walk, to work (machine)

mardi (m.) Tuesday

mari (m.) husband

marier (se) to get married

marque (f.) brand

mars (m.) March

marteau (m.) hammer

matelas (m.) mattress

matériel (m.) hardware (computer)

matin (m.) morning

mauvais (e) mean-spirited

méchant (e) mean

mélange (m.) mix

mensuel (le) monthly

menton (m.) chin

mer (f.) sea

mercredi (m.) Wednesday

mère (f.) mother

meuble (m.) furniture

meublé furnished

mieux better

    mieux vaut tard que jamais better late
      than never

mince slender

mode (à la) fashionable

modem (m.) modulator

moi me, I

moins less

    à moins que unless

mois (m.) month

montagne (f.) mountain

montant (m.) amount

monter to go up

montre (f.) watch

montrer to show

morceau (m.) piece

mort (f.) death

mot (m.) word

mot à la mode (m.) buzzword

moteur (m.) motor

mourir to die

moyen (m.) way, means

mûrir to ripen, to mature

musée (m.) museum

mutuellement mutually

nager to swim

nageur (se) swimmer

naissance (f.) birth

naître to be born

nappe (f.) tablecloth

narcotique (m.) narcotic

neige (f.) snow

neiger to snow

nettoyage cleaning

nettoyer to clean

neuf nine

neuf (ve) new

neveu (m.) nephew

nez (m.) nose

noir(e) black

nord (m.) north

nourrir to feed, to nourish

nourrir (se) to eat

nourriture (f.) food

nouveau (elle) new

    de nouveau again

nouvelles (f.) news

nouvelle enterprise (f.) start-up company

nu(e) naked, nude

nuageux (se) cloudy

nuit (f.) night

    il fait nuit it is dark

nuit blanche sleepless night

numéro vert (m.) toll-free number

obéir to obey

obligatoire mandatory

obtenir to obtain

    d'occasion secondhand

occupé busy

occuper to occupy, to take up space

occuper (se) to take care of

octobre (m.) October

odeur (f.) smell

œil (les yeux) (m.) eye

œuf (m.) egg

oignon (m.) onion

oiseau (m.) bird

oncle (m.) uncle

ordinateur (m.) computer

ordonnance (f.) prescription, order

ordonner to prescribe, to order

oreille (f.) ear

oreiller (m.) pillow

organiser to organise

orgueil (m.) pride

oser to dare

ou or
ou bien or
où where
oublier to forget
ouest (m.) west
ouvrir to open
ouvrir (se) to open up, to open one's mind

pain (m.) bread
paisible peaceful
paix (f.) peace
palais (m.) palace
panier (m.) basket
panne (f.) breakdown
panneau (m.) panel, board, road sign
pansement (m.) bandage
papier (m.) paper
   papier de verre sandpaper
paquet (m.) package
par by
   par avion airmail
   par exemple for example
   par jour per day
par ici over here
parapluie (m.) umbrella
parasurtenseur (m.) surge protector
pare-brise (m.) windshield
parfois sometimes
parler to speak
parmi among
part (f.) share, piece
   à part separately
partager to share
partir to leave
partout everywhere
passager (ère) passenger
passé(e) past
passe-temps (m.) pastime
passionnant exciting
pauvre poor
payer to pay for
paysage (m.) scenery
peau (f.) skin
peigne (m.) comb
peigner (se) to comb one's hair
peindre to paint
peine (f.) pain, punishment
   à peine hardly
peinture (f.) painting
pendant during, for
penser to think
penseur (se) thinker
perdre to lose, to waste

père (m.) father
perforer to pierce
   carte perforée punch card
permettre to allow
permis (m.) license
   permis de conduire driver's license
personne (f.) person
personne (m.) nobody
petit(e) small
petite-fille (f.) granddaughter
petit-fils (m.) grandson
petits pois (m.) peas
peut-être maybe
phare (m.) headlight
pied (m.) foot
   marcher à pied to walk
piéton(ne) pedestrian
pilote (m.) pilot
piscine (f.) swimming pool
piste de décollage (f.) runaway
placement (m.) investment
placer to invest
plafond (m.) ceiling
plage (f.) beach
plaindre (se) to complain
plaire to please
   s'il vous plaît please
plaisanter to joke
plaisir (m.) pleasure
plaque (f.) license plate
plat (m.) dish, plate
plâtre (m.) plaster
plein(e) full
plombage (m.) filling (tooth)
plomber to fill (tooth)
plus more
plusieurs several
plus ou moins more or less
plutôt que rather than
pneu (m.) tire
poids (m.) weight
poire (f.) pear
poisson (m.) fish
poissonnerie (f.) fish market
poitrine (f.) chest
poivre (m.) pepper
poli(e) polite
porte (f.) door
porter to carry
porteur (se) porter
poser to put
poudre (f.) powder
poulet (m.) chicken

poumon (m.) lung
pourboire (m.) tip
pour cent (m.) per cent
pourtant however
pouvoir to be able to, can
préférer to prefer
prendre to take
prendre du poids to gain weight
préparer to prepare
près near, next to
pressé(e) in a hurry
   être pressé(e) to be in a hurry
prêt(e) ready
prêter to lend
prix (m.) price
prochain(e) next
profiter to profit, to take advantage of
progrès progress
promesse (f.) promise
promettre to promise
propriétaire (m., f.) owner
puce (f.) flea, computer chip
puis then
puisque since

quai (m.) platform
quand when, while
quart (m.) quarter, fourth
que which, whom, what, that (object)
quel(le) what
quelque some, any, whatever
   quelque chose something
quelquefois sometimes
quelque part somewhere
qui who, that, which (subject)
quitter to quit, to leave
quoi what, which

raconter to tell (a story)
rail (m.) rail
ralentir to slow down
ramener to bring back
râpé(e) grated
   fromage râpé grated cheese
rasoir (m.) razor
rattacher to connect, to attach
rayon (m.) aisle
récent(e) recent
réception (f.) front desk
recevoir to receive
reconnaissant(e) grateful
reculer to back up
régime (m.) diet

reine (f.) queen
remercier to thank
remorquer to tow
remplir to fill up
recontre (f.) meeting
rencontrer to meet
rendre to give back
renseignement (m.) information
renseigner to give information
renseigner (se) to get information
rentrer to come back (home)
renverser to spill
repartir to leave again
repas (m.) meal
repos (m.) rest
reposer to put back
reposer (se) to rest
résoudre to solve
respirer to breathe
ressembler to look like
rester to stay
retard (m.) delay
   être en retard to be late
retourner to return
réunion (f.) meeting, reunion
réunir to reunite, to gather
réussir to succeed
réussite (f.) success
réveiller to wake someone
réveiller (se) to wake up
revenir to come back
rêver to dream
rez-de-chaussée (m.) ground floor
rhume (m.) cold
   être enrhumé to have a cold
rien (m.) nothing
rire to laugh
rire (m.) laughter
riz (m.) rice
robe (f.) dress
roi (m.) king
rôti (m.) roast
roue (f.) wheel
rouge red
   le feu rouge the red light
rougir to blush
route nationale (f.) highway

sa, son, ses his, hers, its
sable (m.) sand
sac (m.) purse
   sac à dos backpack
   sac de couchage sleeping bag

sain(e) healthy
salade (f.) salad
salaire (m.) salary, wages
sal(e) dirty
salle (f.) room
    salle à manger dining room
    salle de bains bathroom
    salle d'attente waiting room
salon (m.) living room
salut! hi!
samedi (m.) Saturday
sans without
    sans cesse constantly
santé (f.) health
satisfaisant(e) satisfactory
satisfait(e) satisfied
sauf (ve) safe, unhurt
sauf except
sauvage wild
savoir to know
savon (m.) soap
schéma (m.) diagram, sketch
sec (sèche) dry, harsh
    être à sec to be broke
sécher to dry
    sécher un cours to cut a class
sécurité (f.) security
sel (m.) salt
selon according to
semaine (f.) week
    la semaine prochaine next week
semblable similar
sentiment (m.) feeling, sensation
sentir to smell, to feel
sentir (se) to feel, as in je me sens bien, I feel good
septembre (m.) September
sérieux (se) serious
serviette (f.) napkin, briefcase
servir to serve
sévère strict
siège (m.) seat
simple uncomplicated
sirop (m.) syrup
sœur (f.) sister
soif (f.) thirst
    avoir soif to be thirsty
soigner to care for, to take care of
soir (m.) evening
soleil (m.) sun
sort (m.) fate
sortie (f.) exit (output)
sortie imprimante (f.) printout

sortir to go out
souci (m.) worry
soudainement suddenly
souhaiter to wish
soulagement (m.) relief
soulager to relieve
souple supple
sourcil (m.) eyebrow
sourire (m.) smile
sourire to smile
souris (f.) mouse
sous under
souvent often
station (f.) stop, station (subway)
stationner to park
stylo (m.) pen
succès (m.) success
succursale (f.) branch (of a bank)
sucre (m.) sugar
sud (m.) south
suivre to follow
superbe superb
supprimer to suppress
sur on, over
sûr(e) sure
sur-le-champ (m.) on the spot
surtout especially, mostly, above all
surveiller to watch
sympathique nice, pleasant, likable

ta, ton, tes your
tableau (m.) blackboard
taie d'oreiller (f.) pillow case
tante (f.) aunt
taper to hit
    taper à la machine to type
tapis (m.) rug
tard late
taquiner to tease
taux (m.) rate
télévision (f.) television
temps (m.) time, weather
    à temps on time
tenir to hold, to keep
    tenir à to insist, to cherish
terminer to finish, to limit
terminer (se) to end
tête (f.) head
tirer to withdraw, to pull
toilette (f.) restroom
tomber to fall
tôt early, soon

toucher to touch
   toucher un chèque to cash a check
toujours always, still
tournevis (m.) screwdriver
tousser to cough
tout(e) all
   le tout everything
   tout à fait quite
   tout de suite right away
toux (f.) cough
travailler to work
traverser to cross
trébucher (sur) to trip (over)
trésor (m.) treasure
triste sad
tromper to cheat
tromper (se) to make a mistake
trop too much
trottoir (m.) pavement
trouver to find
trouver (se) to be located, to find
   oneself

un, une one, a
uni(e) united
unir to assemble, to unite
usage (m.) usage, custom
usé(e) used
usine (f.) factory
utile useful
utiliser to use
vacances (f., plural) vacation
vaisselle (f.) dishes
   faire la vaisselle to do the dishes
valeur (f.) value
valise (f.) suitcase
valoir to be worth
   valoir la peine to be worth
     the trouble
veau (m.) veal
vedette (f.) movie star
vendeur (se) sales clerk
vendre to sell
vendredi (m.) Friday
venir to come
   venir de to have just
ventre (m.) belly, abdomen
vérifier to verify, to check
vérité (f.) truth

vers towards, about
versement (m.) payment
verser to pour
vert(e) green
vêtements (m.) clothing
viande (f.) meat
vide empty
vider to empty
vie (f.) life
visage (m.) face
vite quick
vitesse (f.) speed
vive! long live!
voir to see
voisin(e) neighbor
voisinage (m.) neighborhood
voiture (f.) car
vol (m.) flight, robbery, theft
volant (m.) steering wheel
voler to fly, to steal
voleur (se) thief, robber
volonté (f.) will
volontiers gladly, willingly
vouloir to want
   vouloir bien to be willing
   vouloir dire to mean
voyage (m.) travel, trip
   un chèque de voyage traveler's check
voyager to travel
voyageur (se) traveler
voyant(e) fortune teller
voyons! let's see!
vrai(e) true
vraiment truly
vue (f.) view, sight
   point de vue point of view

wagon (m.) wagon, coach
   wagon aux bagages (m.) baggage car
   wagon-lit (m.) sleeping car
   wagon-restaurant (m.) dining car
W.C. (m.) toilet (water closet)
week-end (m.) weekend

y there
   y compris including
yeux (m., plural) eyes

zut! darn!